The EVERGREEN EXPERT

Dr. D. G. Hessayon

All Editions & Reprints: 274,000 copies

Published by Expert Books
a division of Transworld Publishers

TRANSWORLD PUBLISHERS
61-63 Uxbridge Road, London W5 5SA
a division of the Random House Group Ltd

Distributed in the United States
by Sterling Publishing Co. Inc.,
387 Park Avenue South,
New York,
NY 10016-8810

EXPERT BOOKS

Contents

Reproduction by Spot On Digital Imaging Ltd, Gomm Road, High Wycombe, Bucks HP13 7DJ
Printed and bound by Mohn Media Mohndruck GmbH

CHAPTER 1

INTRODUCTION

It would seem to be quite a simple matter to separate plants into evergreens (types which keep their leaves in winter) and deciduous plants (types which drop their leaves in autumn or winter). A trip down the garden path in January should reveal all — the conifers are evergreens whereas the leafless oaks are obviously deciduous.

This simple example illustrates the first difficulty. There are deciduous conifers such as Larix, Ginkgo and Taxodium, and there are evergreen oaks such as the Holm Oak. So-called evergreen groups or genera often have a deciduous species or two and some basically deciduous genera have evergreen species.

Difficulty number two. Just because a plant is listed as an evergreen does not mean that you can be sure of a leafy display all winter long. Some evergreens are not fully hardy and this means that the plant as well as the leaves may be killed if the site is too cold or too exposed for the plant in question.

A third point to remember is that the overwintering foliage may not be particularly decorative. Of course the popular evergreen trees and shrubs bring a welcome touch of life and colour to the winter garden but there are numerous evergreen perennials, rock garden plants and bulbs which do little to liven the scene during the off-season.

The three points discussed above mean that you should choose carefully when looking for an evergreen for your garden. Firstly, check that the species or variety really is an evergreen — the label or catalogue should tell you. This step is especially necessary when the genus is a large and complex one — with plants like Lonicera, Berberis, Viburnum and Rhododendron there are lots of deciduous as well as evergreen species and varieties. Secondly, make sure the plant is suitable for the site where it will have to grow — do not confuse the word evergreen with winter hardy as a plant can be one without the other.

It may seem strange that this introduction should begin with words of caution rather than paragraphs of praise for this invaluable group of plants. The reason is simple — it is only by choosing wisely and avoiding the pitfalls that you can set about transforming your garden with evergreens. And you can transform your garden — not in late spring and summer, perhaps, when your beds and borders are full of leaf and flower, but without the proper use of evergreens a garden can be a sorry sight between November and March.

The use of evergreens in the average garden is often restricted to hedges of privet, yew or box and a number of trees and shrubs such as azaleas, heathers, laurels and conifers. These are the most popular ones, but you will find many others in mixed borders down any suburban street. Touches of winter colour, then, but with careful choosing and siting evergreens are capable of providing so much more. Bare patches of ground can be brought to life by using evergreen ground covers, bare rose beds can be brightened by planting some semi-evergreen varieties and the herbaceous border can be improved for winter by introducing some evergreen perennials.

Despite the name there are many colours other than green among the evergreens, and these varieties can be used to provide bright splashes when flowers are short or totally missing from the garden. Use Choisya ternata 'Sundance' or Cupressus macrocarpa 'Goldcrest' to provide a yellow highlight or plant Photinia fraseri 'Red Robin' for fiery red young foliage in spring. The many variegated-leaved evergreens have foliage which is edged or spotted with white, cream or gold — Euonymus fortunei 'Emerald 'n' Gold' can be as eye-catching as many flowering shrubs in full bloom.

With the clear advantage of providing year-round winter colour it might seem that evergreens ought to be the dominant type in the garden, but that is not so. Too many evergreens can give a static feel — with deciduous plants there is the fascination of bare branches bursting into leaf in the spring and the frequent bonus of rich hues in autumn. The usual but by no means rigid advice is to aim to have approximately the same number of evergreen and deciduous shrubs and trees.

EVERGREEN TYPES

It is convenient to separate evergreens into ten different types. The name of the type tells you one of the following features — the growth habit, the garden site where the plant is usually grown or the group to which the plant belongs. This classification has no scientific basis and is based solely on common garden usage.

CONIFERS

A conifer is a tree or shrub which bears its seeds in cones. Scots Pine is a typical conifer — an evergreen tree with narrow leaves and has cones made up of woody scales. Not all conifers, however, follow this pattern. A few (e.g Larix) lose their leaves in winter and one or two (e.g Ginkgo) have broad leaves. Cones are not always woody — some (e.g Taxus) have fleshy fruits.

CLIMBERS

A climber is a perennial which is able to attach itself to or twine around an upright structure. This climbing habit may not develop until the plant is well-established. Several shrubs, such as Pyracantha and Winter Jasmine, are not true climbers but are grown against walls and trellis-work.

TREES

A tree is a perennial plant which bears a single woody stem at ground level. The name does not indicate size — some trees are less than knee-high. The dividing line between trees and shrubs is not clear-cut — several shrubs such as Ilex and Sophora may be grown as small trees.

LEAFY SHRUBS

A shrub is a perennial plant which bears several woody stems at ground level. The leafy group are grown primarily or entirely for their foliage — flowers are either insignificant or absent. Here you will find a number of important hedging (e.g Buxus) and ground-cover plants (e.g Euonymus).

FLOWERING SHRUBS

A shrub is a perennial plant which bears several woody stems at ground level. The flowering group bear blooms which add significantly to the display provided by the plant — popular examples include Rhododendron, Erica, Berberis, Hebe, Mahonia and Lavandula. Some are grown primarily for the display of berries (e.g Pyracantha).

BORDER PERENNIALS

A border perennial is a hardy plant with non-woody stems which is large enough and showy enough to be grown in an herbaceous border. Generally the stems and leaves die down in winter, but there are a number of evergreens. Examples include Achillea and Dianthus — ground-cover types include Bergenia and Stachys.

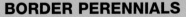

ROCK GARDEN PLANTS

A rock garden plant is a dwarf hardy perennial suitable for growing in a rockery. Some are delicate enough to require leaf protection from winter rains and others are vigorous enough to be invasive. Alpine is an alternative name although many were originally seaside rather than mountain plants. Other types found in the rock garden are dwarf conifers, dwarf shrubs, dwarf bulbs and ferns.

BULBS

A bulb (more correctly bulbous plant) is a plant which produces an underground storage organ which may be a true bulb, corm, tuber or rhizome. Most can be bought as dormant bulbs for planting and nearly all die down in winter. There are a few evergreen and semi-evergreen ones — examples in this book include Dierama and Schizostylis.

FERNS

A fern is a non-flowering plant which bears spores and not seeds. These spores are borne on leaf-like fronds which are often but not always feathery in appearance. Most are deciduous but there are evergreens such as Polypodium and Polystichum. As a general rule ferns prefer moist and shady sites.

GRASSES

Grasses have round stems bearing small flowers. The base of each narrow leaf clasps the stem. Well-known evergreen types include Arundinaria and Cortaderia, but in recent years more typically grass-like genera such as Festuca and Milium have become increasingly popular.

TREE SHAPES

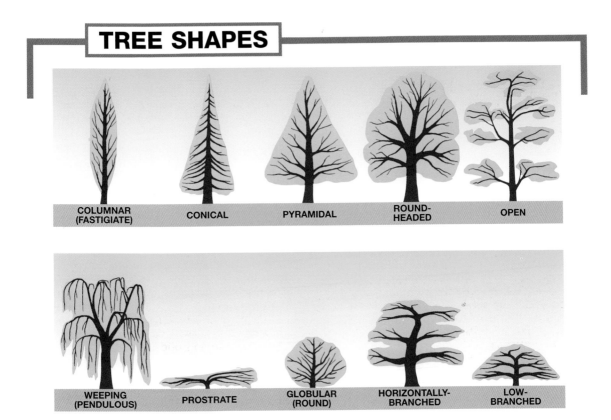

COLUMNAR (FASTIGIATE) CONICAL PYRAMIDAL ROUND-HEADED OPEN

WEEPING (PENDULOUS) PROSTRATE GLOBULAR (ROUND) HORIZONTALLY-BRANCHED LOW-BRANCHED

CHAPTER 2
EVERGREENS A-Z

This dictionary of evergreens covers over 200 genera, ranging from the mighty Sequoia rising over 100 ft into the air to the lowly Thymus which creeps along the ground. All these plants have just one feature in common — they will keep all or most of their foliage in winter if the sites are suitable for the plants' needs.

The choice of which genera to include and which to leave out is always difficult and the selection of species and varieties is even more difficult. A book of this size cannot hope to be fully comprehensive, and so it has been necessary to follow two guiding principles.

Firstly, the selected species and varieties are available from a number of nurseries in this country — see *The RHS Plant Finder* for details. The usual plan has been to give pride of place to the more popular types as these are the ones you are likely to find at your local garden centre, but in some cases you will have to order by post from a specialist supplier.

Secondly, the chosen species and varieties should be able to survive over winter in the open garden. Not all are equally hardy — shelter from icy winds may be called for and there may be an element of risk in colder parts of the country. The text will tell you if winter protection is needed, but most books (including this one) tend to be over-cautious about the tenderness of many shrubs and climbers. It is worth while being adventurous provided that the plant is not too expensive and the chosen spot is not a prime site.

With each genus the evergreen type is stated — for example conifer, climber or leafy shrub. In some cases more than one evergreen type is given for a genus. This is because it has species and/or varieties which belong to different types. Achillea (page 8) is an example. A. filipendulina grows 3-5 ft (90 cm-1.5 m) high and is a popular choice for the middle of the herbaceous border, but there are also the less common A. argentea

and A. kolbiana which are 4-6 in. (10-15 cm) dwarfs for the rockery. In the evergreen type statement the more popular one for the genus takes precedence, so the statement for Achillea on page 8 is 'Border perennial/ rock garden plant'.

Below the evergreen type statement is a line stating whether the species or varieties are evergreen and/or semi-evergreen. The meaning of 'semi-evergreen' is fairly obvious — such plants shed an appreciable number of their leaves during the winter months. The meaning of 'evergreen' is not quite so obvious — it does not indicate that leaf fall will never occur. The leaves of fully evergreen plants have a limited life. The life span of a conifer leaf may be as little as 2 years or as long as 20 years or more, but evergreen does not mean everlasting. The basic point of difference from semi-evergreens is that there is no regular annual drop of a significant number of immature leaves during the winter months.

From Abelia on the first page to Zenobia at the end of this A-Z guide there are evergreens which cover almost every type of garden plant. There are heights, shapes, colours, growth habits, cultural requirements and flowering seasons to suit nearly every need. However, mention the word 'evergreen' and for many people the types which spring to mind are conifers and leafy shrubs. With these two types a word of caution is necessary before buying — always check the estimated mature height. Sometimes the word 'dwarf' or 'slow-growing' is used and it is important to understand the difference. A dwarf has an ultimate height which is appreciably less than that of some other members of the genus or plant type. For example, Picea abies 'Nidiformis' reaches only 3 ft (1 m) when fully grown — so much smaller than the familiar Norway Spruce (P. abies). Slow-growing, on the other hand, means that the plant remains small for a number of years but there is no guarantee it will be a dwarf when it reaches its ultimate height. The well-known Monkey Puzzle Tree is an example of what can happen — for several years after planting it may hardly grow at all, but then it will start to grow rapidly and will reach a height of 70 ft (21 m) or more.

ABELIA Abelia

Abelia is often avoided because of its reputation as a tender shrub, but there are a few types which are both semi-evergreen and reasonably hardy. The outstanding feature of this plant is the duration of the flowering season — the tubular blooms first open in June and continue to appear until September or October. The reddish sepals remain after the petals have fallen and the oval leaves turn bronzy-green in winter.

VARIETIES: **A. grandiflora** is the most popular species — its arching branches bear pink-tinted white flowers and the bush may reach 8 ft (2.4 m) or more. Its most popular variety is **'Francis Mason'** — growth is less vigorous and the leaves are yellow. **A. 'Edward Goucher'** is another popular type — its ¾ in. (2 cm) long blooms are lilac-pink. Hardiest of all is **A. triflora**, but it grows too tall for small gardens.

SITE & SOIL: Any free-draining soil will do — choose a sheltered site in full sun.

PROPAGATION: Plant cuttings in a cold frame in summer.

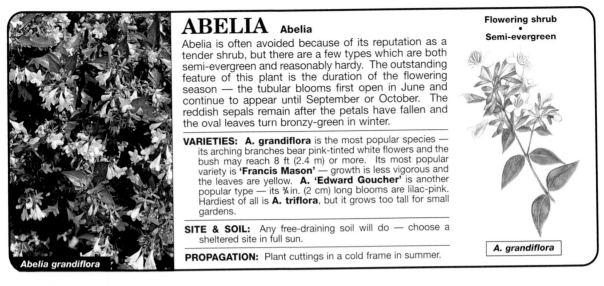
A. grandiflora

Abelia grandiflora

ABIES Silver Fir

Nearly all Silver (or True) Firs have a Christmas Tree growth habit — the trunk is straight and the radiating branches form a neat cone. Unfortunately very few of these fine specimen trees are compact enough when mature to be suitable for the average garden, and so there are two choices. You can either grow one of the dwarf or slow-growing varieties or you can plant one of the vigorous ones and remove it once it has outgrown its allotted space. The strap-like leaves of a Silver Fir are soft and leathery with a round, sucker-like base and an undersurface which is usually white or grey. The oval cones (green, brown, white or purple) are always upright and are generally borne only on the upper branches of mature trees.

VARIETIES: **A. grandis** (Giant Fir) is this country's tallest tree. Height after 10 years is 10 ft (3 m) but when fully grown it will reach 100 ft (30 m) or more. Other tall ones include **A. forrestii** (Forrest Fir) with dark purple cones, **A. alba** (Common Silver Fir) and **A. procera** (Noble Fir) with brown cones and the prickly-leaved **A. pinsapo** (Spanish Fir) which is tolerant of chalky soil. At the other end of the scale are the dwarf firs which are suitable for the average garden as they do not exceed 2-3 ft (60-90 cm) when fully grown. The most popular one is **A. balsamea 'Hudsonia'** — a rounded cone-free bush with aromatic foliage. Other dwarfs include **A. balsamea 'Nana'** and the yellow-leaved **A. nordmanniana 'Golden Spreader'**. A popular choice for the larger garden is the slow-growing Korean Fir **A. koreana** with dark green foliage and purple cones. The variety **'Silberlocke'** displays the silver reverse of its leaves.

SITE & SOIL: Most well-drained soil will do.

PROPAGATION: Buy from a reputable supplier.

Conifer
•
Evergreen

Abies balsamea 'Nana'

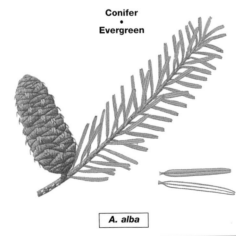
A. alba

Abies koreana

Abies nordmanniana 'Golden Spreader'

ACAENA New Zealand Burr

A. microphylla

Acaena provides a year-round colourful carpet. The stems produce a leafy pile which is only 1-3 in. (2.5-7.5 cm) high, but the spread reaches 2-3 ft (60-90 cm). Recommended uses include filling gaps between paving stones and covering the earth around spring bulbs, but it may be too invasive for a small rockery. The tiny flowers are followed by burr-like seed heads in late summer.

VARIETIES: A. microphylla is the most popular species — the silvery young leaves turn purple-bronze with age and the burrs are bright red. Varieties include **'Glauca'** (blue leaves, rust-coloured burrs) and **'Copper Carpet'** (coppery-purple leaves, red burrs, restrained growth habit). **A. 'Blue Haze'** has blue-grey leaves and dark red burrs, and the most invasive Acaena is **A. buchananii** which produces a thick mat of silvery-green foliage.

SITE & SOIL: Well-drained soil is essential — thrives in sun or light shade.

PROPAGATION: Divide clumps in autumn or spring.

Acaena microphylla

ACHILLEA Yarrow

A. filipendulina
'Coronation Gold'

The plate-like flower heads of Achillea are a familiar sight in the flower border during July and August, the flat clusters of tiny blooms being borne on firm stems above the ferny foliage. Not all types are evergreen so choose with care. The leaves of A. millefolium and its varieties ('Fire King', 'Cerise Beauty' etc) die down in winter, and so does the foliage of the white-flowered A. ptarmica ('The Pearl', 'Boule de Neige' etc).

VARIETIES: The most popular of the semi-evergreen Yarrows are the yellow varieties of **A. filipendulina** — **'Cloth of Gold'** (5 ft/1.5 m high), **'Gold Plate'** (5 ft/1.5 m high) and **'Coronation Gold'** (3 ft/90 cm). For a more compact plant with pale yellow flowers grow **A. 'Taygetea'** (2 ft/60 cm). There are several semi-evergreen dwarfs such as the white-flowered and silvery-leaved **A. argentea** (**A. clavennae**) which grows about 6 in. (15 cm) high and **A. kolbiana 'Weston'** (4 in./10 cm).

SITE & SOIL: Any well-drained soil will do — thrives best in full sun.

PROPAGATION: Divide clumps in autumn or spring.

Achillea argentea

AETHIONEMA Aethionema

A. 'Warley Rose'

During the winter months this woody perennial covers the ground with a mat of fleshy grey leaves and from May to August a forest of 1 in. (2.5 cm) high flower stalks appears. These are topped with a cluster of small 4-petalled flowers in colours ranging from the palest pink to the deepest rose. Aethionema is an easy-to-grow plant for the rockery provided the site is sunny. Alkaline soil is best, but it will grow quite happily in neutral and even slightly acid soil.

VARIETIES: Several species and varieties are available but the one most people choose is **A. 'Warley Rose'** — rosy red, height 6 in. (15 cm), spread 1 ft (30 cm). For a deeper shade of rose choose **A. 'Warley Ruber'**. For taller plants with pale pink flowers look for the 1 ft (30 cm) high **A. grandiflorum** — the dwarf is the 2 in. (5 cm) high **A. oppositifolium**.

SITE & SOIL: Any well-drained soil — full sun is necessary.

PROPAGATION: Easily raised from seed. With named varieties plant cuttings in a cold frame in early summer.

Aethionema grandiflorum

AJUGA Bugle

This is one of the best ground covers you can buy. It will spread rapidly over the soil to provide a colourful carpet under shrubs or over bulbs. Both multi-coloured and variegated forms are available, and between April and June the 6 in. (15 cm) high spikes bearing whorls of lipped flowers appear. Bugle will grow almost anywhere, but for an outstanding display it needs moist soil and partial shade.

VARIETIES: All the popular types are varieties of **A. reptans** and there is a wide range from which to make your choice. They all grow about 6 in. (15 cm) high and nearly all have blue flowers, but there is an assortment of leaf colours — **'Burgundy Glow'** (green, red, bronze and gold), **'Multicolor'** (green, bronze, red), **'Variegata'** (grey-green, white) and **'Atropurpurea'** (reddish-purple). For white flowers choose **'Alba'**. The purple-leaved **A. pyramidalis 'Metallica Crispa'** grows 1 ft (30 cm) high.

SITE & SOIL: Any reasonable soil in sun or partial shade.

PROPAGATION: Divide clumps in autumn or spring.

Ajuga reptans 'Variegata'

Border perennial
•
Evergreen

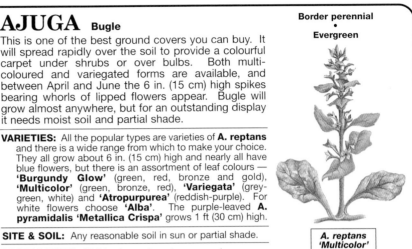
A. reptans 'Multicolor'

AKEBIA Akebia

This twining climber from Japan makes a change from the usual choices such as clematis, honeysuckle and roses. Use it to clothe walls, climb up old trees or to climb over pergolas and arches. It is a slow starter, but once established it will soon cover an area up to 20 ft (6 m) high with masses of oval leaflets and small fragrant flowers. The sausage-shaped fruits will only appear if a pair of plants are grown to ensure cross-pollination and if the season is warm and sunny.

VARIETIES: **A. quinata** is the only species which can be expected to keep part or most of its foliage in winter. These leaves are made up of 5 leaflets and in April and May pendent clusters of wine-coloured flowers appear. Tiny male blooms are at the top and the larger female cup-shaped ones are at the base of each cluster. The fleshy fruits are about 4 in. (10 cm) long. An interesting but not a showy plant.

SITE & SOIL: Prefers moist soil — good drainage is necessary. Thrives in sun or light shade.

PROPAGATION: Layer runners in May.

Climber
•
Semi-evergreen

A. quinata

Akebia quinata

A long conifer hedge need not be dull. You can produce a bright effect by planting variegated or yellow varieties alongside green ones. The result can be attractive but having too much variety can give a gaudy appearance. Make sure the plants have the same growth rate and habit — use varieties of the same genus such as Taxus (as shown) or Chamaecyparis.

Rock garden plant/ border perennial
• Evergreen

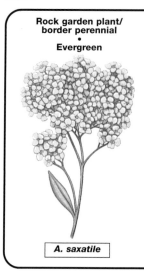

A. saxatile

ALYSSUM Alyssum

The perennial Alyssums are low-growing plants with a mat of grey leaves all year round and heads of small flowers in late spring and early summer. The usual colour is yellow, but white, buff and pink varieties are available. The place for the small varieties is in the rockery, but the vigorous ones need a site where they will not swamp other plants.

VARIETIES: By far the most popular species is **A. saxatile**, now renamed **Aurinia saxatilis**. This yellow-flowered plant (height 9 in./22.5 cm, spread 1½ ft/45 cm) is seen in rockeries everywhere. Its varieties are less common — examples are **'Flore Pleno'** (double flowers), **'Dudley Nevill'** (buff flowers) and **'Compacta'** (dwarf growth habit). The best rockery miniature is **A. montanum 'Berggold'** and for pink flowers grow **A. spinosum 'Roseum'** (1 ft/30 cm, spread 1½ ft/45 cm).

SITE & SOIL: Any well-drained soil — thrives best in full sun.

PROPAGATION: Sow seeds under glass in spring. With named varieties plant cuttings in a cold frame in early summer.

Alyssum spinosum 'Roseum'

Border perennial/ rock garden plant
• Evergreen

A. polifolia

ANDROMEDA Bog Rosemary

This uncommon dwarf shrub provides a change from rhododendrons, heathers etc in acid soil, but it does have a drawback. The colour range of the flowers is restricted to pink and white, and the leaf colour is restricted to all-green. The types range from 4 in.- 1½ ft (10-45 cm) high — all have wiry stems and leathery leaves above which the flowers are borne in late spring or early summer.

VARIETIES: The basic species is **A. polifolia**. This plant grows wild in peat bogs and you are more likely to be offered one of its more compact varieties. There are **'Compacta'** (1 ft/30 cm, pink) for bed or border and **'Alba'** (6 in./15 cm) with white flowers and compact enough for the rockery. Even smaller is **'Macrophylla'** (4 in./10 cm, white and deep pink).

SITE & SOIL: Moist, acid soil is necessary — add peat at planting time. Thrives in light shade.

PROPAGATION: Softwood cuttings in a cold frame in late summer.

Andromeda polifolia

Rock garden plant/ border perennial
• Evergreen

A. dioica

ANTENNARIA Cat's Ear

This mat-forming perennial has several uses in the garden. In the flower border its dense cover of silvery leaves forms a weed-suppressing blanket about 1½ ft (45 cm) across. In the rockery it is grown for its mass of small flower heads in May and June, and between paving stones it provides a leafy surface which can be walked on without harm. Flower colour ranges from white to crimson.

VARIETIES: You may find more than one species listed in specialist catalogues but you will find only one at the garden centre. **A. dioica** has clusters of ¼ in. (0.5 cm) flowers which are white and pink — for other colours choose one of the varieties. These include **'Minima'** (2 in./5 cm, pink), **'Nyewoods Variety'** (4 in./10 cm, deep pink), **'Aprica'** (4 in./10 cm, cream), **'Rosea'** (4 in./10 cm, pink) and **'Rubra'** (6 in./15 cm, crimson). Blooms are of the 'everlasting' type so dry for flower arranging.

SITE & SOIL: Any well-drained garden soil will do — thrives best in full sun.

PROPAGATION: Divide clumps in early autumn or spring.

Antennaria dioica 'Aprica'

ARABIS Rock Cress

Common Rock Cress grows quickly and is not fussy about soil type, and from March to June there are masses of flowers above foliage which remains grey-green all winter. It is, however, invasive and it is better to choose a more compact variety. Cut back the stems when flowering is over.

VARIETIES: The Arabis you see everywhere is the Common Rock Cress **A. albida** (height 9 in./22.5 cm). For a change from the usual white there is the pink variety **'Pink Frost'** and for double flowers you can grow **'Flore Pleno'**. Unless you have a large area of bare rock to cover it is better to choose a less rambling species. The favourite here is **A. Ferdinandi-coburgii 'Variegata'** (height 4 in./10 cm, white flowers, brightly variegated fleshy leaves). Other compact types include **A. blepharophylla** (3 in./7.5 cm, pink flowers) and **A. alpina** (6 in./15 cm, white flowers).

SITE & SOIL: Any well-drained soil in sun or light shade.

PROPAGATION: Divide clumps in autumn or plant cuttings in a cold frame in summer.

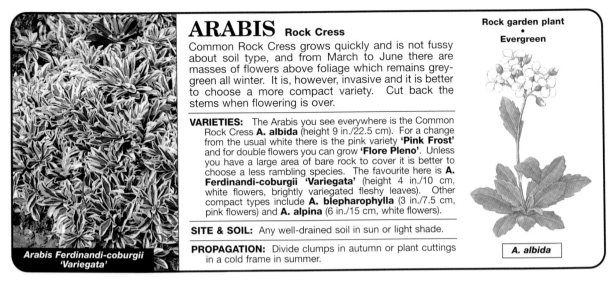

Rock garden plant
•
Evergreen

A. albida

Arabis Ferdinandi-coburgii
'Variegata'

ARAUCARIA Monkey Puzzle Tree

This Victorian favourite is easy to recognise — thick, triangular and sharply-pointed leaves are arranged spirally around each branch. It grows slowly at first, reaching only 4-5 ft (1.2-1.5 m) in the first 10 years of its life. It will then start to grow much more rapidly, putting on 1 ft (30 cm) or more each year and reaching 70 ft (21 m) under ideal conditions.

VARIETIES: The only hardy variety is **A. araucana**. It has a rather open growth habit — the tree is conical at first but it becomes round-topped with age. The branches look like thick, curved ropes and globular 6 in. (15 cm) high cones are borne on the upper branches of female trees. Male trees bear clusters of catkins which turn dark brown with age. The Monkey Puzzle Tree will grow in the shade of a house but it will quite quickly lose its lower branches and grow no more than about 30 ft (9 m) high.

SITE & SOIL: Well-drained preferably acid soil in sun or light shade with some protection against the wind.

PROPAGATION: Buy a container-grown specimen.

Araucaria araucana

Conifer
•
Evergreen

A. araucana

ARBUTUS Strawberry Tree

This shrub is a good choice for autumn and winter interest. The popular species is A. unedo, a slow-growing glossy-leaved plant which bears its clusters of pendent flowers from October to December when the ripening fruits of last year's flowers are present. These 'strawberries' are edible but insipid. Plant in pairs to ensure cross-fertilisation. Pruning is not necessary — cut back weak or unwanted branches in early spring.

VARIETIES: **A. unedo** bears white urn-shaped flowers in 3 in. (7.5 cm) long clusters and these are followed by orange or red fruits. The bush will eventually reach 10 ft (3 m) or more — for a more compact plant with pink flowers choose the variety **'Rubra'**. A. unedo may not be fully frost-hardy for its first couple of years in the garden, but it tolerates both alkaline soil and salt-laden air. **A. andrachnoides** is grown for its eye-catching red bark rather than its white flowers.

SITE & SOIL: Any reasonable garden soil will do — thrives in sun or light shade.

PROPAGATION: Difficult — buy a container-grown specimen.

Arbutus unedo

Flowering shrub
•
Evergreen

A. unedo
'Rubra'

Rock garden plant
•
Evergreen

A. montana

ARENARIA Sandwort

Sandwort is used to provide a mossy or grassy cover over stones in the rock garden. There are types for both sun and shade, and in spring or summer small star-shaped flowers appear above the prostrate leafy mat. This mat extends to about 1½ ft (45 cm) across when the plant is mature, but it can be kept in check by pruning the stem tips.

VARIETIES: **A. montana** (height 4 in./10 cm, white flowers in May and June) is one of the best species. The flowers are large for a Sandwort (¾ in./1.5 cm across) and the leaves are grass-like. It does need a sunny situation — for shade **A. balearica** is a better choice. It grows only 1 in. (2.5 cm) high and both the mossy leaves and white flowers are tiny. For pale purple blooms choose **A. purpurascens** — for yellow foliage grow **A. caespitosa 'Aurea' (Sagina subulata 'Aurea')**.

SITE & SOIL: Requires well-drained gritty soil. Sun or shade requirement depends on the species.

PROPAGATION: Divide clumps in spring.

Arenaria balearica

Rock garden plant/ border perennial
•
Evergreen

A. maritima

ARMERIA Thrift

Thrift is a popular rockery plant but it is equally at home at the front of the flower border. Each plant is a cushion of grassy leaves from which thin flower stalks grow up in spring or summer. On top of each of these stalks there is a globular head of tiny papery flowers — these flower heads are long-lasting.

VARIETIES: There are two basic species and these have numerous varieties. The more popular species is **A. maritima**, our native Thrift — height 8 in. (20 cm), spread 1 ft (30 cm), pink flowers in May-July. Some of its varieties are also pink (e.g **'Laucheana'**) but there are also deep pink (**'Vindictive'**), red (**'Bloodstone'**) and white (**'Alba'**) varieties. **A. juniperifolia (A. caespitosa)** is a more compact species — height 3 in. (7.5 cm), spread 9 in. (22.5 cm), pink flowers in April-May on very short stems. **'Bevans Variety'** is a popular cultivar.

SITE & SOIL: Any well-drained soil will do — thrives in sun.

PROPAGATION: Divide clumps in spring or root cuttings under glass in summer.

Armeria maritima 'Vindictive'

Border perennial/ leafy shrub/ rock garden plant
•
Evergreen or semi-evergreen

A. schmidtiana
'Nana'

ARTEMISIA Artemisia

This plant is grown for its leaves which are usually ferny, silvery and aromatic — the tiny flower heads have little decorative value. You can choose from a wide range of forms and sizes — there are shrubs, border perennials and rock garden plants. Most but not all varieties are evergreen or semi-evergreen and all require some pruning to keep them in check.

VARIETIES: The best known shrubby species is **A. arborescens** — a 5 ft (1.5 m) high upright bush which bears a mass of silvery filigree-like leaves. Small yellow flowers appear in summer. Its variety **'Powis Castle'** is a more compact plant. The perennial **A. absinthium 'Lambrook Silver'** (2 ft/60 cm) is one to grow in the border and there are several to choose from for the rockery — look for **A. schmidtiana 'Nana'** and **A. stelleriana 'Boughton Silver'**.

SITE & SOIL: Any well-drained garden soil will do — thrives best in full sun.

PROPAGATION: Plant cuttings in a cold frame in late spring.

Artemisia arborescens

ARUNDINARIA Bamboo

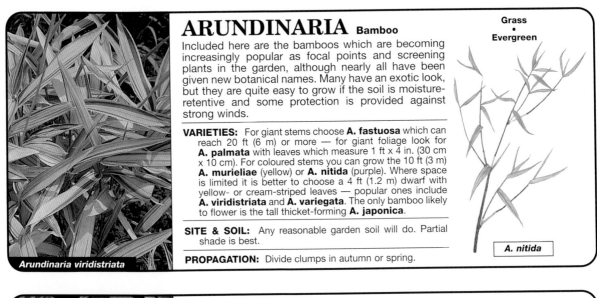

Included here are the bamboos which are becoming increasingly popular as focal points and screening plants in the garden, although nearly all have been given new botanical names. Many have an exotic look, but they are quite easy to grow if the soil is moisture-retentive and some protection is provided against strong winds.

VARIETIES: For giant stems choose **A. fastuosa** which can reach 20 ft (6 m) or more — for giant foliage look for **A. palmata** with leaves which measure 1 ft x 4 in. (30 cm x 10 cm). For coloured stems you can grow the 10 ft (3 m) **A. murieliae** (yellow) or **A. nitida** (purple). Where space is limited it is better to choose a 4 ft (1.2 m) dwarf with yellow- or cream-striped leaves — popular ones include **A. viridistriata** and **A. variegata**. The only bamboo likely to flower is the tall thicket-forming **A. japonica**.

SITE & SOIL: Any reasonable garden soil will do. Partial shade is best.

PROPAGATION: Divide clumps in autumn or spring.

Grass • Evergreen

A. nitida

Arundinaria viridistriata

ASARUM Wild Ginger

This low-growing ground cover spreads by means of underground rhizomes, but unlike nearly all other 'bulbs' it is grown for its carpet of evergreen leaves rather than its flowers. It is a useful plant for covering the soil in dense shade under trees, but it will only succeed if the ground is moist, humus-rich and lime-free. The small flowers are borne under the leaves in spring — the brown or purple petals sometimes have tail-like tips.

VARIETIES: There are two varieties which are generally available. The more popular one is **A. europaeum** — the 3 in. (7.5 cm) wide leaves are shiny and rounded, and the tiny blooms are tubular. This species grows about 4 in. (10 cm) high — for taller plants with larger kidney-shaped leaves choose **A. caudatum**. The most interesting Asarum is offered by specialist suppliers — the bronzy-green heart-shaped leaves of **A. hartwegii** have silvery green veins.

SITE & SOIL: Requires moisture-retentive soil in a shady site.

PROPAGATION: Lift and divide clumps in autumn or sow seeds in spring.

Border perennial • Evergreen

A. europaeum

Asarum caudatum

ASPLENIUM Spleenwort

Most species of this fern are not hardy — a popular example of these tender ones is the Bird's-nest Fern (A. nidus) which is sold as a house plant. There are, however, a few which are fully hardy and can be grown in a shady spot outdoors. The soil should be alkaline and moisture-retentive — add grit and peat at planting time. Under trees or between stones in the rockery are favourite sites for the spleenworts.

VARIETIES: The most popular species is **A. scolopendrium** — the Hart's-tongue Fern. The leathery strap-like fronds (leaves) are about 1½ ft (45 cm) long and are arranged in a loose shuttlecock pattern. The edges are slightly wavy — for showier fronds look for the variety **'Crispum'** which has very wavy fronds or **'Cristatum'** with its divided and crested fronds. **A. trichomanes** (Maidenhair Spleenwort) is a smaller plant and quite different — the 6 in. (15 cm) long fronds have rows of rounded 'leaflets' on thin black stalks.

SITE & SOIL: Thrives in humus-rich, gritty soil in partial shade.

PROPAGATION: Divide clumps in spring.

Fern • Evergreen

A. trichomanes

Asplenium scolopendrium

Rock garden plant
•
Evergreen

A. deltoidea

AUBRIETA Aubretia, Rock Cress

Leafy cushions of Aubrieta are to be seen in rockeries everywhere. The grey-green leaves are downy and between late March and early June they are covered with masses of 4-petalled flowers. These blooms are about ¾ in. (1.5 cm) across and a range of different colours is available. An easy and tolerant plant but it can be invasive — cut back hard after flowering.

VARIETIES: The classification of Aubrieta (and its correct spelling!) is complex — the simplest approach is to regard all the named varieties as hybrids of the basic species **A. deltoidea** — height 3-5 in. (7.5-12.5 cm), spread 2 ft (60 cm). Look for **'Aureovariegata'** (lavender flowers, gold-edged leaves), **'Bressingham Pink'** (double pink), **'Doctor Mules'** (purple) and **'Red Carpet'** (red).

SITE & SOIL: Any well-drained, non-acid soil will do — thrives best in full sun.

PROPAGATION: Divide clumps in autumn or plant cuttings in a cold frame in summer.

Aubrieta deltoidea 'Doctor Mules'

AUCUBA Aucuba

Aucuba is the usual choice when looking for an evergreen bush with large colourful leaves for a spot in partial or full shade. It is one of the few 'grow anywhere' shrubs — in starved dry soil, in polluted areas and in sun or shade. There are still three points to remember. New growth may be scorched by strong icy winds, the varieties with leaves which are heavily splashed with yellow need some sun and for berries you will need a female variety with a male one nearby. The 8 in. (20 cm) leaves are leathery and glossy. The spring flowers are insignificant but the autumn red berries on female plants can be quite showy. Cut back as required with secateurs in spring.

VARIETIES: **A. japonica** (Spotted Laurel) is the only species available. It grows about 7 ft (2.1 m) high — a rounded bush with oval, all-green leaves. A variety rather than the basic species is nearly always chosen. You can grow an all-green type with narrow leaves such as **'Lance Leaf'** (male) or **'Longifolia'** (female), but the varieties with leaves spotted and splashed with yellow are much more popular. **'Variegata'** (**'Maculata'**) and **'Gold Dust'** are examples of yellow-speckled female varieties which can be expected to produce a display of berries in September-December — male Spotted Laurels include **'Golden King'**. **'Crotonifolia'** may be labelled as either male or female at the garden centre — it is actually a female variety which rarely produces berries. As a change from the yellow-splashed types there are **'Picturata'** with yellow centred leaves and **'Sulphurea Marginata'** with yellow-edged leaves. If you want berries but can have only one plant, choose the bisexual variety **'Rozannie'**.

SITE & SOIL: Any garden soil in sun or shade.

PROPAGATION: Plant hardwood cuttings in the open in autumn.

Aucuba japonica 'Longifolia'

Leafy shrub
•
Evergreen

A. japonica 'Variegata'

A. japonica 'Crotonifolia'

Aucuba japonica 'Crotonifolia'

Aucuba japonica 'Picturata'

AZARA Azara

You will find this unusual wall shrub in numerous catalogues but not at your local garden centre. It is attractive enough to be popular — in spring or summer (depending on the species) there are clusters of small yellow flowers with showy stamens instead of petals. The problem is that Azara is a large shrub reaching 12-15 ft (4-5 m) and most species are rather tender.

VARIETIES: **A. microphylla** is the most widely available species and is the only one which can be considered hardy. In March the fragrant blooms appear on the underside of the branches — for cream-edged leaves grow the variety **'Variegata'**. **A. serrata** and **A. dentata** are not fully hardy, but their floral display in June or July is showier than A. microphylla.

SITE & SOIL: Any reasonable, well-drained soil will do — thrives in sun or light shade.

PROPAGATION: Plant cuttings in a cold frame in summer.

A. dentata

Azara microphylla

BERBERIDOPSIS Coral Plant

This twining climber is even rarer than Azara described above, although like Azara it is not short of visual appeal. The lax woody stems will climb for about 10 ft (3 m) up old trees or around supports to provide an eye-catching display of red blooms in August-September above the oval leathery foliage. Apply a mulch around the base of the plant before the onset of winter.

VARIETIES: **B. corallina** is the only species and is available from specialist tree and shrub nurseries. The 4 in. (10 cm) long leaves are dark green and are spiny along the edges, and the ½ in. (1 cm) round flowers are borne on long stalks. Attractive and unusual, but very fussy. The soil has to be damp and peaty in a location which is shady, protected from strong winds and relatively frost-free.

SITE & SOIL: Well-drained, acid and humus-rich soil is necessary — thrives in partial shade.

PROPAGATION: Layer stems or plant cuttings in a cold frame in summer.

B. corallina

Berberidopsis corallina

For people who love Rhododendrons but have soil which is alkaline the answer is to grow a specimen in a pot filled with ericaceous compost. A well-chosen container and an attractive variety can provide year-round foliage and bright spring flowers — shown here is R. yakushimanum 'Heinje's Select' in a balcony garden.

BERBERIS Barberry

There are several reasons why Berberis is one of our most popular evergreen flowering shrubs. First of all, it is an easy plant to grow and can be planted in heavy soil, against shady walls or on exposed sites. Next, it does not need regular pruning — all you have to do is cut back any unwanted branches immediately after flowering. In addition it is not prone to insect attack nor disease, and there is no tiresome staking to worry about. Above all there is the year-round colourful display. The small glossy leaves on the spiny stems sometimes have attractive autumn colours — in April and May the clusters of yellow or orange flowers appear and are followed by berries in late summer. Check the label before buying — not all species of Berberis are evergreen.

VARIETIES: You will find a wide choice at your garden centre — you can buy varieties for the rock garden and shrub border or for hedging, screening, ground cover or for use as specimen shrubs. The most popular species is **B. darwinii** which grows 8 ft (2.4 m) high with miniature holly leaves, golden flowers and blue-black berries. Other tall-growing types include **B. linearifolia 'Orange King'** (8 ft/2.4 m, orange flowers, blue-black berries) and **B. julianae** (10 ft/3 m, suitable for screening, red-tinged yellow flowers, black berries, red-tinged foliage in autumn). Where space is restricted choose one of the 3 ft (1 m) compact varieties described below. **B. stenophylla** (10 ft/3 m, suitable for hedging, double yellow flowers, blue-black berries) has several dwarf varieties, including **'Claret Cascade'** (bronzy-green young foliage), **'Coccinea'** (red-tinged yellow flowers) and **'Irwinii'** (orange flowers). **B. verruculosa** and **B. candidula** bear their flowers singly rather than in clusters — B. candidula is wide-spreading and is used for ground cover.

SITE & SOIL: Any reasonable soil will do — thrives in sun or partial shade.

PROPAGATION: Layer branches or plant cuttings in a cold frame in summer.

Berberis darwinii

Flowering shrub
•
Evergreen

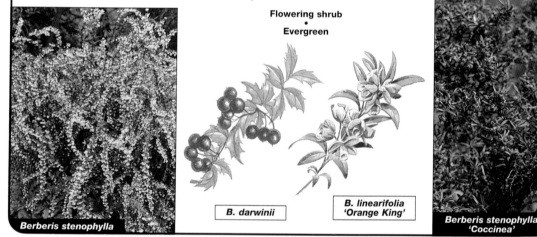

B. darwinii

B. linearifolia 'Orange King'

Berberis stenophylla

Berberis stenophylla 'Coccinea'

Border perennial
•
Semi-evergreen

BERGENIA Elephant's Ears

Look no further if you are seeking a ground cover with large bold leaves and a showy display of flowers in spring. It is not fussy about soil type or shade and is fully hardy. Plant it in the open or under trees and large shrubs where it will spread rapidly to produce a carpet of 4-10 in. (10-25 cm) leaves which may turn red in autumn. The bell-shaped flowers are borne on hyacinth-like spikes.

VARIETIES: The basic species is **B. cordifolia**. It grows about 1½ ft (45 cm) high and the drooping sprays of dark pink flowers appear in April-May. **'Purpurea'** (purple flowers, red-tinged leaves in winter) is a popular variety. Many hybrids are available — look for **'Bressingham White'** (white flowers, late), **'Silverlight'** (rose red flowers), **'Evening Glow'** (red flowers, maroon leaves in winter) and **'Sunningdale'** (lilac flowers, coppery leaves in winter).

SITE & SOIL: Any well-drained garden soil will do — thrives in sun or partial shade.

PROPAGATION: Divide clumps in autumn.

B. cordifolia

Bergenia cordifolia 'Purpurea'

BLECHNUM Hard Fern

Another evergreen fern, but unlike the one on page 13 Blechnum needs lime-free and not alkaline soil. The 'leaflets' are arranged in herringbone fashion on the fronds and there are two species which are hardy enough to be grown outdoors without the need for any form of frost protection. The place for these ferns is in a shady border, under trees or in a rockery which gets some shade during the day.

VARIETIES: The tall outdoor Blechnum is **B. spicant** (Hard Fern) — the fronds grow about 1½ ft (45 cm) high and the creeping rhizomes spread to give a plant about 2 ft (60 cm) wide. Where space is limited the Dwarf Hard Fern (**B. penna-marina**) is a better choice. The dark green finely-divided fronds grow no more than 6 in. (15 cm) high, and the spread is 1 ft (30 cm). The outdoor Blechnums which require some form of frost protection in winter are **B. tabulare, B. nudum** and **B. discolor**.

SITE & SOIL: An acid, moist soil in partial or full shade.

PROPAGATION: Divide clumps in spring.

Blechnum spicant

B. spicant

BUDDLEIA Buddleia

Buddleia is often thought of as a deciduous shrub as by far the most popular species is the Butterfly Bush (B. davidii) which loses its leaves in winter and bears its tiny flowers in cone-like clusters in summer. There are, however, a few evergreen and semi-evergreen species which can be grown in the garden.

VARIETIES: The only evergreen or semi-evergreen Buddleia you are likely to find at the garden centre is the Orange Ball Tree (**B. globosa**). It is an upright but rather straggly bush which can grow 10 ft (3 m) tall with a spread of about 10 ft (3 m). In May or June the 1½ in. (4 cm) wide flower heads appear — round yellow balls made up of tiny flowers. You will find the other evergreen garden Buddleias in specialist catalogues — look for **B. auriculata** (10 ft/3 m high with creamy-white ball-like flower heads) and **B. salviifolia** (10 ft/3 m high with lilac flower clusters). Cut out one-third of the old wood after flowering.

SITE & SOIL: Well-drained soil in a sunny situation.

PROPAGATION: Plant cuttings in the open in spring.

Buddleia globosa

B. globosa

BUPLEURUM Shrubby Hare's Ear

There is just one shrubby evergreen Bupleurum for growing outdoors and it may not be available at your local garden centre. Send off for a specimen from a shrub nursery if you like to grow unusual plants, but it is not worth bothering with for most situations. The foliage is quite attractive but the round heads of tiny greenish-yellow flowers are not showy. Pruning is not necessary — cut back unwanted or damaged shoots in spring.

VARIETIES: The bush for garden use is **B. fruticosum**. It grows about 5 ft (1.5 m) high and the spreading branches bear oval leathery leaves. The tiny starry flowers are borne in dome-shaped 4 in. (10 cm) wide heads from midsummer to early autumn and the brown seed heads which follow remain on the plant over winter. Bupleurum is reasonably hardy in most areas but a newly-planted specimen may not survive a cold winter on an exposed site.

SITE & SOIL: Light, well-drained soil in sun or light shade.

PROPAGATION: Plant cuttings in a cold frame in summer.

Bupleurum fruticosum

B. fruticosum

Leafy shrub
•
Evergreen

B. sempervirens
'Aureovariegata'

BUXUS Box

Box is a popular choice for hedging, including dwarf hedging around beds and parterres. The stems bearing small and glossy leaves can be clipped regularly which means that this plant is an excellent choice for formal screening and topiary. It stands up well to wind, alkaline soil and some shade.

VARIETIES: There are two basic species. **B. sempervirens** (Common Box) is the most popular one, with oval leaves measuring 1 in. (2.5 cm) or more in length. It will grow up to 10 ft (3 m) if left untrimmed, but there are numerous more compact and colourful varieties. Look for **'Aureovariegata'** (yellow-blotched leaves) and **'Latifolia Maculata'** (all-yellow young leaves). **'Suffruticosa'** is the variety to choose for dwarf hedging. **B. microphylla** (Small-leaved Box) has leaves which are $\frac{3}{4}$ in. (2 cm) or less in length. **'Compacta'** is a 1 ft (30 cm) dwarf variety — **'Curly Locks'** has twisted stems.

SITE & SOIL: Any reasonable soil in sun or partial shade.

PROPAGATION: Plant cuttings in a cold frame in summer.

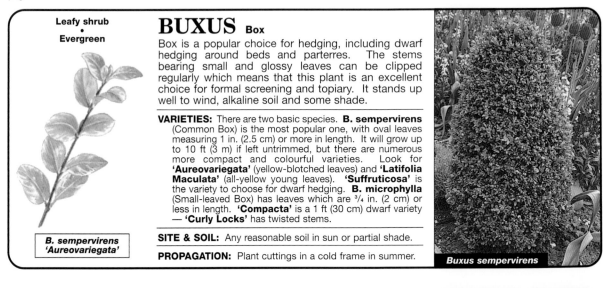

Buxus sempervirens

Flowering shrub
•
Evergreen

C. citrinus
'Splendens'

CALLISTEMON Bottle Brush

Callistemon and many other rather tender shrubs are often regarded as too frost-sensitive for the average garden, but there is at least one hardy species of this Australian shrub and a few others appear to be hardier than most text books claim. The basic features of this plant are long narrow leaves and a flower head which looks like a bottle brush.

VARIETIES: **C. subulatus** is a hardy species which grows about 5 ft (1.5 m) high — the arching branches bear 2 in. (5 cm) long red 'bottle brushes' in June-August. **C. sieberi** (3 ft/90 cm, yellow flowers) and **C. linearis** (8 ft/2.4 m, red flowers) may need some frost protection. The most popular variety is **C. citrinus 'Splendens'** — a 7 ft (2.1 m) shrub with leaves which emit a lemon aroma when crushed and with bright red 'bottle brushes' in summer. Given the shelter of a south-facing wall it will survive most winters without protection.

SITE & SOIL: Lime-free soil, some shelter and full sun.

PROPAGATION: Plant cuttings in a cold frame in summer.

Callistemon sieberi

Flowering shrub
•
Evergreen

C. vulgaris
'H. E. Beale'

CALLUNA Heather, Ling

The popular heathers grown in the garden are varieties of either Calluna or Erica, and it is easy to confuse the two. There are, however, a number of differences. There are no midwinter– or spring-flowering varieties of Calluna and none of them can tolerate lime. With most Callunas the showy part of the flower is the calyx and not the petals and variously-coloured foliage (red, golden, grey, bronze etc) is much more common than with Ericas. Flowers appear in the August-October period — trim the plants in March.

VARIETIES: There is one species (**C. vulgaris**) and a multitude of varieties. Listed below are a few popular ones. **'Beoley Gold'** ($1\frac{1}{2}$ ft /45 cm, white, golden foliage), **'Blazeaway'** ($1\frac{1}{2}$ ft /45 cm, lilac, red foliage in winter), **'County Wicklow'** (8 in./20 cm, silvery-pink, grey foliage), **'Golden Carpet'** (4 in./10 cm, purple, variegated golden foliage) and **'H. E. Beale'** ($1\frac{1}{2}$ ft /45 cm, double pink).

SITE & SOIL: Well-drained, acid soil — full sun is preferred.

PROPAGATION: Layer shoots or plant cuttings in summer.

Calluna vulgaris
'County Wicklow'

CALOCEDRUS Incense Cedar

Conifer
•
Evergreen

The Incense Cedar grown in parks and gardens is one of the slimmest and most elegant of all our large trees. Tiny, scale-like leaves with outward-spreading tips clasp the stems and these leaves when crushed emit an incense-like aroma. Brown 1 in.(2.5 cm)-long cones appear at the tips of drooping shoots. You may find the Incense Cedar listed as Libocedrus.

VARIETIES: **C. decurrens** is the only fully hardy species and the only one you are likely to find. When mature it may reach 60 ft (18 m), but it is a slow-growing tree and after 10 years it will only have reached about 6 ft (1.8 m). Its shape is broadly conical at first, but it becomes column-like with age and remains clothed with leafy branches down to ground level. Choose the variety **'Aureovariegata'** for gold-splashed leaves and an even slower growth habit.

SITE & SOIL: Any free-draining garden soil will do. Thrives in sun or partial shade.

PROPAGATION: Buy from a reputable supplier.

C. decurrens

Calocedrus decurrens

CAMELLIA Camellia

It is doubtful if any garden shrub can offer a wider range of desirable features than the Camellia. Its glossy oval leaves are present all year round and the showy blooms are available in a wide range of colours and sizes from 2-5 in. (5-12.5 cm) across. The cup or bowl-shaped flowers are sometimes single, but the semi-double and double varieties are more popular. Apart from the beauty of these blooms there is the time when they appear — you can pick types to give a display from early December to mid May. Camellias are hardy and very attractive, but they are not for every situation. Non-alkaline soil is essential, and avoid sites which are open and exposed to the early morning sun.

VARIETIES: Most Camellias are varieties of **C. japonica**, growing up to 6 ft (1.8 m) high and blooming between February and late April. Popular varieties include **'Adolphe Audusson'** (5 in./12.5 cm blooms, semi-double, red), **'Alba Simplex'** (5 in./12.5 cm, single, white), **'Elegans'** (5 in./12.5 cm, anemone-shaped, peach-pink), **'Jupiter'** (3 in./7.5 cm, semi-double, white-blotched red) and **'Lady Clare'** (4 in./10 cm, semi-double, deep pink). Streaked blooms include **'Contessa Lavinia Maggi'** (4 in./10 cm, double, rose-striped white). The hybrids of **C. williamsii** offer a number of advantages — they are hardier, taller, freer-flowering, with a longer flowering season and with the virtue of the dead blooms dropping off naturally. Look for the very popular **'Donation'** (4 in./10 cm, semi-double, pink), **'Anticipation'** (4 in./10 cm, paeony-shaped, deep pink) and **'J. C. Williams'** (3 in./7.5 cm, single, pale pink). Popular hybrids include **C. 'Leonard Messel'** (4 in./10 cm, semi-double, pink) and **C. 'Cornish Snow'** (3 in./7.5 cm, single, white).

SITE & SOIL: Requires acid or neutral soil — prefers light shade.

PROPAGATION: Layer shoots in autumn or plant cuttings in a cold frame in summer.

Camellia japonica 'Contessa Lavinia Maggi'

Flowering shrub
•
Evergreen

C. japonica 'Adolphe Audusson'

C. japonica 'Alba Simplex'

C. williamsii 'J. C. Williams'

C. 'Leonard Messel'

Camellia williamsii 'Donation'

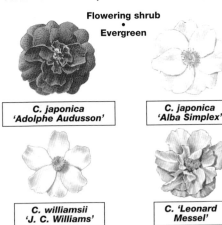

Camellia japonica 'Jupiter'

**Border perennial/
rock garden plant**
•
**Evergreen or
semi-evergreen**

C. persicifolia

CAMPANULA Bellflower

Campanulas have been favourite flower border and rockery garden plants for generations. The starry or bell-shaped blooms in blue, lavender or white appear in large numbers between June and August. The popular ones are easy to grow provided the soil is not acid. Some of the rockery ones can be invasive.

VARIETIES: The popular border evergreen is **C. persicifolia** which keeps its basal rosette of leaves throughout the winter. Cup-shaped flowers are borne on 2 ft (60 cm) stems — varieties include **'Telham Beauty'** (light blue) and **'Alba'** (white). **C. latiloba** is quite similar but the lavender-blue flowers are stalkless. For the rock garden there is **C. portenschlagiana (C. muralis)** which forms leafy 4 in. (10 cm) high mounds and masses of purple flowers all summer long. The semi-evergreen **C. poscharskyana** grows about 10 in. (25 cm) high.

SITE & SOIL: Well-drained soil in sun or light shade.

PROPAGATION: Sow seeds under glass or divide clumps in spring. Plant cuttings in a cold frame in late spring.

Campanula portenschlagiana

Grass
•
**Evergreen or
semi-evergreen**

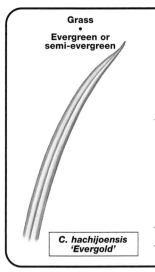

C. hachijoensis
'Evergold'

CAREX Sedge

Carex is not a true grass, but it is an excellent choice where an ornamental grass-like effect is required. It is usually grown for its arching foliage which may be golden, bronze or variegated as well as all-green. The tiny green or brown flowers usually add little to the display, but a few species such as C. pendula have showy flower heads.

VARIETIES: The tallest species you will find is the Weeping Sedge (**C. pendula**) — the all-green leaves are 3 ft (90 cm) long and the stems bearing drooping seed heads grow about 4 ft (1.2 m) high. The yellow-leaved **C. elata 'Aurea'** is another large Carex with clumps of 1½ ft (45 cm) long leaves — both these plants need moist or wet soil. For a more compact plant you can grow **C. hachijoensis 'Evergold'** with 10 in. (25 cm) long yellow-striped leaves or the even smaller **C. ornithopoda 'Variegata'**. **C. buchananii** has bronze-coloured foliage.

SITE & SOIL: Any garden soil in sun or light shade.

PROPAGATION: Divide clumps in spring.

Carex elata 'Aurea'

Flowering shrub
•
Evergreen

C. californica

CARPENTERIA Tree Anemone

You will not find this shrub in any of the best seller lists or popular selections, and you may not find it at your local garden centre. It is regarded as rather tender, but do not let this put you off if you have a south-facing wall which is reasonably protected from the wind. The foliage is attractive and the flowers in June and July are large and fragrant.

VARIETIES: **C. californica** is the only species. It grows to produce a rounded bush measuring about 6 x 6 ft (1.8 x 1.8 m) which is clothed with lance-shaped leaves — shiny green above and woolly white below. In midsummer clusters of pure white flowers appear, each one bearing a central boss of showy golden stamens. Look for the variety **'Ladham's Variety'** — it is freer-flowering than the species and the blooms measure 3 in. (7.5 cm) across.

SITE & SOIL: Any free-draining garden soil will do — full sun and some shelter from the wind are necessary.

PROPAGATION: Layer shoots or plant cuttings in a cold frame in summer.

Carpenteria californica

CASSINIA Cassinia

Flowering shrub
•
Evergreen

The two heather-like plants on this page are unusual. Neither one is really special so search for them only if you have an acid soil and like to grow rarities. Cassinia can be used to add height to a heather bed as it grows over 3 ft (90 cm) high — the foliage is yellow, green or grey and in summer flat heads of tiny white flowers appear. Cut back straggly shoots in March.

VARIETIES: **C. fulvida** (Golden Heather) is the species which is most likely to be listed. It has a dull golden appearance as the sticky stems are yellow and so are the undersides of the small leaves. In July and August the flower heads appear at the top of upright stems, each 3 in. (7.5 cm) head bearing numerous small daisy-like blooms. **C. vauvilliersii** grows about 6 ft (1.8 m) high and has dark green leaves — this can look rather dull so it is better to grow the variety **'Albida'** (Silver Heather) with silvery shoots and leaves which are mealy white below.

SITE & SOIL: Well-drained, acid soil in full sun.

PROPAGATION: Plant cuttings in a cold frame in summer.

C. vauvilliersii

Cassinia fulvida

CASSIOPE Cassiope

Flowering shrub
•
Evergreen

Unlike Calluna and Erica this heather-like plant has scale-like leaves which clasp the stem to give a whipcord effect. Not a spectacular evergreen but it makes a useful addition to a peat bed or rockery provided the site is moist, acidic and not too shady. In late spring white bell-like flowers appear along the stems.

VARIETIES: **C. mertensiana** is one of the more popular species — it grows about 8 in. (20 cm) high and the 1/4 in. (0.5 cm) wide creamy white bells have red or green sepals. Look for the varieties **'Muirhead'** and **'Randle Cooke'**. **C. lycopodioides** is an easy one to grow — a prostrate plant growing only 3 in. (7.5 cm) high but with a spread of 1 1/2 ft (45 cm) or more. Another one is the erect hybrid **C. 'Edinburgh'** which grows about 10 in. (25 cm) high — the same height as **C. tetragona** with its red-topped bells.

SITE & SOIL: Humus-rich, acid soil is essential — thrives in sun or light shade.

PROPAGATION: Plant cuttings in a cold frame in summer.

C. 'Edinburgh'

Cassiope mertensiana 'Muirhead'

Geometric topiary is an ancient art but still very popular. The trimming of evergreens to form spheres, cones, cylinders etc began in early Rome and was a feature of monastery gardens in mediaeval Europe. Today the most popular shapes are the topiary ball on top of a short standard tree and the topiary cone — illustrated here is a more ambitious scheme. The most popular material is Box, but Juniper, Yew and Privet are also widely used.

CEANOTHUS Californian Lilac

Most but not all varieties of Ceanothus are evergreens and unfortunately they are less hardy than the ones which lose their leaves in winter. Try to give them a site in full sun with some protection against the wind — Ceanothus is well worth the effort of careful choice and siting because few blue-flowered plants can match the impressive display of a Ceanothus in full bloom. The basic features are small, dark green and glossy leaves with tight thimble-like clusters of tiny flowers in blue or more rarely white. Many are upright and will grow to 10 ft (3 m) or more but there are also dwarf-growing ones, so there are many places for Ceanothus in the garden.

VARIETIES: Nearly all of the evergreen species and varieties bloom in the May-June period and should be lightly trimmed after flowering. The smaller ones form 3 ft (90 cm) mounds — examples include **C. divergens** (purple-blue) and **C. thrysiflorus 'Repens'** (mid blue). Larger 5 ft (1.5 m) mounds are produced by **C. 'Blue Mound'** (dark blue), **C. 'Pin Cushion'** (light blue), **C. dentatus** (dark blue) and **C. 'Skylark'** (dark blue). Tall ones (10-15 ft/3-4.5 m) to grow in the border or against a wall include the arching **C. 'Cascade'** (pale blue) and the hardy ones **C. impressus 'Puget Blue'** (dark blue) and **C. thrysiflorus** (mid blue). Tallest of all is the rather tender **C. arboreus 'Trewithen Blue'** (20 x 20 ft/6 x 6 m, mid blue) and for something different you can grow the white-flowered **C. americanus**. Two popular varieties do not bloom in late spring — for July-September flowers grow **C. 'Autumnal Blue'** (8 ft/2.4 m, pale blue) or **C. 'Burkwoodii'** (6 ft/1.8 m, mid blue) and lightly trim the shrub in April. **C. 'A. T. Johnson'** (8 ft/2.4 m, mid blue) flowers in both late spring and late autumn.

SITE & SOIL: Choose a well-drained site in full sun.

PROPAGATION: Plant cuttings in a cold frame in summer.

Ceanothus 'Blue Mound'

Flowering shrub
•
Evergreen

Ceanothus impressus 'Puget Blue'

C. 'Burkwoodii'

Ceanothus arboreus 'Trewithen Blue'

Conifers can provide a wide range of colours in winter. Included in this two-year-old bed are yellow (Chamaecyparis pisifera 'Filifera Aurea'), yellow and green (Taxus baccata 'Standishii'), steely blue (Picea pungens and Chamaecyparis lawsoniana 'Pembury Blue'), blue-green (Juniperus chinensis 'Pyramidalis'), copper (Thuja occidentalis 'Rheingold') and dark red (Cryptomeria japonica 'Elegans') as well as many shades of green.

CEDRUS Cedar

The basic species of cedar are stately trees which can reach 80 ft (24 m) or more when fully grown. They are an impressive sight in parkland but quite out of place in the ordinary garden. This does not mean that cedars are not right for you — there are dwarfs which grow no more than 2-3 ft (60-90 cm) high and there are slow-growing weeping types. The rule is to check the height before you buy. With most species and varieties the tree is roughly conical at first but it may become flat-topped when mature. The young branches have spirally-arranged needle-like leaves — on older branches these needles are arranged in tufts on short shoots. On mature trees the barrel-shaped female cones appear and remain on the tree for 2 years before they ripen.

Cedrus libani

VARIETIES: Pride of place goes to **C. libani**, the magnificent Cedar of Lebanon which is a common sight in parks and country estates. It starts off slowly reaching only 6 ft (1.8 m) in 10 years, but in time its wide-spreading horizontal branches and great height rule it out as a garden conifer. There are, however, several much smaller varieties, such as the prostrate **'Sargentii'** and the squat **'Nana'** which grows only 5 ft (1.5 m) high. **C. atlantica** is the Atlas Cedar which has ascending branches — it is too big for the garden and its varieties **'Glauca'** and **'Glauca Pendula'** are preferred with their blue-green leaves and blue-tinged cones. **'Aurea'** is a yellow-leaved variety. The third species is **C. deodora**, which differs from the other two basic species by having descending (drooping) branches. A graceful tree which will reach 10 ft (3 m) in 10 years and 80 ft (24 m) in time — choose instead the much less robust variety **'Aurea'** or the spreading dwarf **'Golden Horizon'** which bears yellow leaves on a sunny site.

SITE & SOIL: Any well-drained garden soil will do — prefers full sun.

PROPAGATION: Buy a container-grown plant from a reputable supplier.

Conifer
•
Evergreen

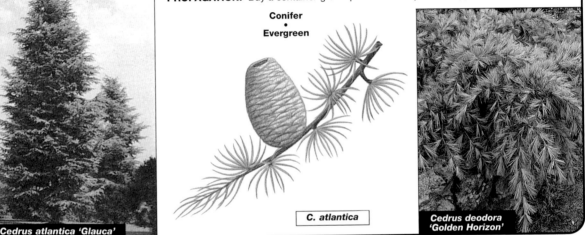

C. atlantica

Cedrus atlantica 'Glauca'

Cedrus deodora 'Golden Horizon'

CEPHALOTAXUS Plum Yew

At any garden centre you will find numerous varieties of the conifer on the next page, but you will be lucky to find a single specimen of this one. This scarcity is surprising. Cephalotaxus is a neat shrub which can be hard pruned to provide a hedge or screen. Other advantages include the ability to flourish in shade and to grow in alkaline soil.

VARIETIES: The plants listed in the catalogues are types of **C. harringtonia**. The variety **'Drupacea'** rarely grows higher than 10 ft (3 m) and looks like a yew with unusually long (1½ in./4 cm) leaves. The fruits, however, are quite different — this plant bears 1 in. (2.5 cm) long olive-like fruits which take 2 years to ripen. **'Fastigiata'** is the variety you are most likely to find. This differs from the one above in the colour and arrangement of its leaves (near black leaves arranged spirally around the stem) and its growth habit (upright rather than bushy).

SITE & SOIL: Any well-drained soil will do in partial shade.

PROPAGATION: Buy from a reputable supplier.

Conifer
•
Evergreen

C. harringtonia 'Drupacea'

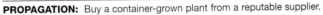

Cephalotaxus harringtonia 'Fastigiata'

CERASTIUM Snow-in-summer

Some of the evergreens in this book are rare and much admired — Cerastium is the opposite. It suffers from over-exposure as it seems to be in every front-garden rockery, and it is almost universally condemned as a rampant invader. It is true that in a small rock garden the silvery-leaved sheet is too invasive, but there is little to beat Cerastium if you want to quickly cover a large bank of dry and poor soil.

VARIETIES: The only Cerastium you are likely to find is **C. tomentosum**. It grows about 4 in. (10 cm) high but rapidly spreads to 2 ft (60 cm) or more. Between May and July loose clusters of white flowers with notched petals appear above the woolly lance-shaped leaves. The variety **'Columnae'** grows only 1-2 in. (2.5-5 cm) high but it is just as invasive. The only Cerastium which doesn't spread everywhere is **C. alpinum 'Lanatum'**. This one is grown for its furry grey leaves and not for its flowers.

SITE & SOIL: Any well-drained soil — thrives best in full sun.

PROPAGATION: Sow seeds or divide clumps in spring.

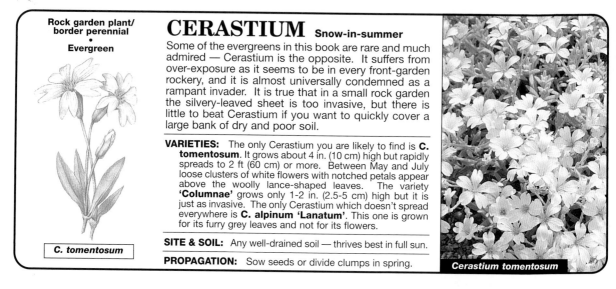

C. tomentosum

Cerastium tomentosum

CHAMAECYPARIS False Cypress

Whatever growth habit or size you require there is a Chamaecyparis variety to match your needs. There are dwarfs for the rockery, compact bushes for the mixed border and tall trees to grow as specimen plants or high screens. The problem is that they are all fairly compact at the garden centre, so it is essential to check the anticipated ultimate height. You will have no difficulty in finding specimens — even a modest garden centre will offer several varieties and you will find scores listed in the catalogues of specialist nurseries. Chamaecyparis was formerly grouped with Cupressus, but the two have been divided although the old name is sometimes used. Both Chamaecyparis and Cupressus have tiny, scale-like leaves grouped in fours around the stem, but with Chamaecyparis species and varieties the branches are flat sprays whereas Cupressus has branchlets which grow all round the stem. Another difference is the size of the cones — Chamaecyparis cones measure about ½ in. (1.5 cm) across and the Cupressus ones are 1-1½ in. (2.5-4 cm) in diameter. Chamaecyparis is also hardier and easier to transplant, but do not regard it as a grow-anywhere plant. Chamaecyparis does not like poorly-drained, exposed sites and some varieties can fail in such situations. But for nearly all sites Chamaecyparis is an excellent choice if you take a little extra care at planting time, and it is our most popular evergreen tree. Prune hedges between May and September — take care not to cut into old wood.

SITE & SOIL: Thrives best in well-drained soil in full sun.

PROPAGATION: Buy from a reputable supplier. Root cuttings in summer or sow seeds in the spring if you have patience.

*Chamaecyparis lawsoniana
'Elwoodii'*

*Chamaecyparis lawsoniana
'Elwood's Gold'*

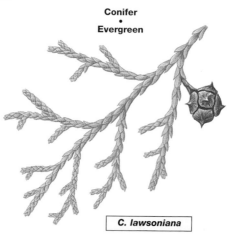

C. lawsoniana

*Chamaecyparis lawsoniana
'Fletcheri'*

CHAMAECYPARIS continued

VARIETIES: C. lawsoniana is the most popular species and **'Elwoodii'** is the most popular variety — you will see this dense, conical bush in tubs, rockeries and borders everywhere. It is a slow-growing plant, reaching about 5 ft (1.5 m) in 10 years and 15 ft (4.5 m) when fully grown. The grey-green foliage turns steely blue in winter, but there are several sports which have different colours. Examples include **'Elwood's Gold'** (very popular, slower growing, green branchlets tipped with gold) and **'Elwood's White'** (green/white variegated leaves). **'Fletcheri'** is similar in shape to 'Elwoodii' but it grows more rapidly and is more suitable for hedging than for the rock garden. The variety **'Allumii'** forms a narrower cone than the varieties described above — it is a popular blue-grey Chamaecyparis used for specimen planting in lawns or for hedging. Even narrower is **'Columnaris'** — one of the best of all column-shaped conifers. The foliage is blue-grey and the eventual height is 25 ft (7.5 m). There are three popular golden Lawson varieties in the medium height range — **'Lane'**, **'Lutea'** and **'Stewartii'**. The dwarfs reach about 1 ft (30 cm) in 10 years and ultimately grow to 3 ft (90 cm) — look for **'Minima Aurea'** (yellow leaves), **'Minima Glauca'** (green foliage) and **'Pygmaea Argentea'** (silvery-tipped blue-green foliage). The species **C. nootkatensis** is usually represented by the variety **'Pendula'** — one of the most pendulous of all the tall conifers if the leading shoot is trained vertically after planting. It reaches about 8 ft (2.4 m) after 10 years. **C. obtusa** has produced many varieties of which **'Nana Gracilis'** is the most popular. Shell-shaped sprays of branchlets radiate from the centre of the compact bush. The most popular variety of **C. pisifera** is **'Boulevard'** — a neat slow-growing cone of silvery-blue feathery foliage which may reach 10 ft (3 m) when mature.

Chamaecyparis lawsoniana
'Lutea'

Chamaecyparis lawsoniana
'Stewartii'

Chamaecyparis lawsoniana
'Minima Aurea'

Chamaecyparis lawsoniana
'Minima Glauca'

Chamaecyparis lawsoniana
'Pygmaea Argentea'

Chamaecyparis nootkatensis
'Pendula'

Chamaecyparis pisifera
'Boulevard'

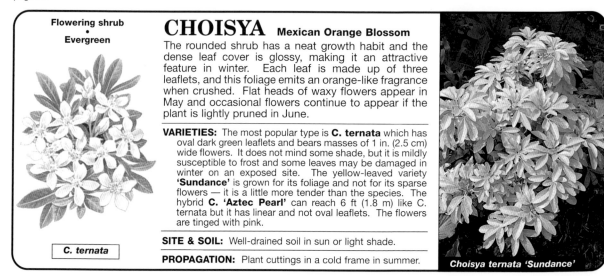

Flowering shrub
•
Evergreen

CHOISYA Mexican Orange Blossom

The rounded shrub has a neat growth habit and the dense leaf cover is glossy, making it an attractive feature in winter. Each leaf is made up of three leaflets, and this foliage emits an orange-like fragrance when crushed. Flat heads of waxy flowers appear in May and occasional flowers continue to appear if the plant is lightly pruned in June.

VARIETIES: The most popular type is **C. ternata** which has oval dark green leaflets and bears masses of 1 in. (2.5 cm) wide flowers. It does not mind some shade, but it is mildly susceptible to frost and some leaves may be damaged in winter on an exposed site. The yellow-leaved variety **'Sundance'** is grown for its foliage and not for its sparse flowers — it is a little more tender than the species. The hybrid **C. 'Aztec Pearl'** can reach 6 ft (1.8 m) like C. ternata but it has linear and not oval leaflets. The flowers are tinged with pink.

SITE & SOIL: Well-drained soil in sun or light shade.

PROPAGATION: Plant cuttings in a cold frame in summer.

C. ternata

Choisya ternata 'Sundance'

CISTUS Rock Rose

Cistus forms a rounded evergreen bush which is an excellent choice for a container, mixed border, sunny bank or against a wall. The flowers look like single roses with petals which are often blotched with red or purple at the base. These blooms are short-lived — the papery petals open in the morning and drop before nightfall, but new buds appear regularly and the shrub is constantly in bloom from early June to mid August. Cistus thrives in a number of difficult situations — infertile sands, seaside gardens, chalky soils etc, but they do not thrive in clay or shade and can be harmed by frosts.

VARIETIES: There are three groups — the short Cistus varieties which grow to 3 ft (90 cm) or less, the tall Cistus varieties which grow over 3 ft (90 cm) and the Halimium/Halimiocistus varieties. An example of the short group is **C. corbariensis (C. hybridus)** — one of the hardiest species with red buds and small white flowers. Other examples include **C. 'Silver Pink'** (3 in./7.5 cm wide silvery-pink flowers), **C. skanbergii** (pale pink flowers, grey-green leaves), **C. pulverulentus 'Sunset'** (deep pink flowers until late September) and **C. dansereaui 'Decumbens'** (white flowers with maroon-blotched centres). The tall group varieties tend to be less hardy than the short ones. Popular types include **C. cyprius** (6 ft/1.8 m, white flowers with maroon-blotched centres), **C. ladanifer** (6 ft/1.8 m, white flowers with red-blotched centres) and **C. purpureus** (4 ft/1.2 m, deep pink flowers with maroon-blotched centres). The hardiest tall Cistus is **C. laurifolius** (5 ft/1.5 m, white flowers). The final group is represented by the yellow **Halimium lasianthum** (3 ft/90 cm) and its cream-coloured hybrid **Halimiocistus wintonensis 'Merrist Wood Cream'** (3 ft/90 cm).

SITE & SOIL: Well-drained soil in full sun is essential. Protect from cold winds.

PROPAGATION: Sow seeds in spring or plant cuttings in a cold frame in summer.

Cistus pulverulentus 'Sunset'

Flowering shrub
•
Evergreen

C. 'Silver Pink'

C. cyprius

C. purpureus

C. laurifolius

Cistus ladanifer

Halimium lasianthum

CLEMATIS Virgin's Bower

Clematis is our most popular climbing plant and you will see the Large-flowered Hybrids in bloom everywhere between May and October. Unfortunately these showy types are not evergreen — for varieties which keep their leaves in winter you will have to pick from the Species group which bloom in spring, have small flowers and are usually easier to grow. Carefully follow the instructions on the label.

VARIETIES: There are two species which can be properly classed as evergreen. **C. armandii** has large glossy leaves and bears waxy white 2 in. (5 cm) flowers in April. **C. cirrhosa 'Balearica'** is quite different — the leaves are bronzy and fern-like, the cream-coloured flowers are speckled with brown and they open in late winter. The variety **'Freckles'** has flowers which are flecked and streaked with red. A few varieties are semi-evergreen — included here are **C. ternifolia** and **C. florida**.

SITE & SOIL: Well-drained, fertile soil in sun or partial shade.

PROPAGATION: Plant cuttings in a propagator in summer.

Clematis ternifolia

C. armandii

CONVOLVULUS Shrubby Bindweed

Shrubby Bindweed is a useful front-of-the-border plant or it can be used in a large rockery to provide year-round interest. The leaves are silvery-grey and the flowers appear throughout the summer months. Although it is closely related to the climbing weed of the garden it requires neither staking nor pruning, but it is a rather tender plant. The best place is against a south-facing wall.

VARIETIES: **C. cneorum** is the evergreen Convolvulus you will find at the garden centre. The 2 ft (60 cm) bush is densely clothed with 1 in. (2.5 cm) long leaves which are covered with silky hairs. These hairs give the plant an overall silvery appearance and against this background the pink buds begin to open in May into trumpet-shaped flowers. These 1½ in. (4 cm) wide blooms are white and flushed with pink on the reverse. Flowering continues until August — cut back straggly branches in spring.

SITE & SOIL: Well-drained sandy soil in full sun.

PROPAGATION: Plant cuttings in a cold frame in summer.

Convolvulus cneorum

C. cneorum

CORDYLINE Cabbage Palm

Cordyline is usually bought as a rosette of arching leaves — it becomes a short tree with a stout 3 ft (90 cm) trunk after 10 years. Grow it in a large pot or in a sunny border to give a tropical touch if your garden is in a reasonably mild locality. For it to become a permanent feature it needs well-drained soil, protection from the wind and some form of winter insulation.

VARIETIES: **C. australis** is the only species you are likely to find. The leaves grow 1-3 ft (30-90 cm) long and in June heads of small white flowers may appear. The leaves are pale green — for more interesting colours choose a variety such as **'Sundance'** (striped red and green), **'Torbay Dazzler'** (striped cream and green), **'Purpurea'** (purple) and **'Albertii'** (red, pink, cream and green). Cut off dead lower leaves in spring to heighten the palm-like effect.

SITE & SOIL: Well-drained soil away from a frost pocket is essential — thrives in full sun or partial shade.

PROPAGATION: Plant rooted suckers in spring.

Cordyline australis 'Torbay Dazzler'

C. australis

Flowering shrub • Evergreen

C. valentina

CORONILLA Coronilla

This unusual shrub is worth growing if you can give it the protection of a sunny wall. Its virtue is that its clusters of fragrant pea-like flowers start to appear in early May and then continue to open at intervals until the first frosts of autumn. It will grow in most soils, including chalky ones, but it is not completely hardy. Cut out a few old stems in early spring.

VARIETIES: Not all species of Coronilla are evergreen — the hardiest one (C. emerus) loses its leaves in winter. **C. valentina** is more widely available and is evergreen — the slender bush bears grey-green leaves made up of 4-6 pairs of leaflets and its 1/2 in. (1.5 cm) long flowers are bright yellow. It grows about 5 ft (1.5 m) high but its variety **'Glauca'** has leaves with only 2 or 3 pairs of leaflets and it reaches about 3 ft (90 cm). **'Glauca Citrina'** has pale yellow flowers and **'Glauca Variegata'** bears cream-splashed leaves.

SITE & SOIL: Well-drained soil in full sun.

PROPAGATION: Plant cuttings in a cold frame in summer.

Coronilla valentina 'Glauca Variegata'

Grass • Evergreen

C. selloana

CORTADERIA Pampas Grass

Cortaderia is the most spectacular decorative grass. The silvery silky plumes of Pampas Grass are about 1 1/2 ft (45 cm) long and their tips are up to 10 ft (3 m) above the ground. Plant in April in a spot where the plant will be a focal point — in the lawn or against dark evergreen foliage are favourite sites. In late autumn cut off the flowering stems and in early spring cut away the dead leaves.

VARIETIES: **C. selloana** (C. argentea) is the species sold at your garden centre — the narrow arching leaves are about 6 ft (1.8 m) long. The largest plumes are produced by the variety **'Sunningdale Silver'** — the flower heads are more spreading than those of the other types such as **'Pumila'** (4 ft/1.2 m dwarf), **'Gold Band'** (yellow-striped green foliage) and **'Rendatleri'** (silvery-purple plumes). The late summer display is best after a hot and sunny season.

SITE & SOIL: Well-drained soil in sun or partial shade.

PROPAGATION: Clumps can be divided in April but it is better to buy new plants.

Cortaderia selloana 'Gold Band'

Fanciful topiary shares a long history with geometric topiary (see page 21) but it is far less popular. The idea of pruning an evergreen into a sculptured form does not appeal to everyone, and the skill involved and work required generally put off even the most ardent enthusiast. Animals are the most popular theme and peacocks the most popular type, but dotted around the country you will find chairs, cars, umbrellas etc.

COTONEASTER   Cotoneaster

Cotoneaster is one of the most important berrying shrubs and is widely used for ground cover, clothing walls and as a specimen shrub. At first glance it can be confused with Pyracantha, but its leaves are smooth-edged and they are borne on thornless branches. In May or June the pink buds open into small white flowers — and this decorative floral show is followed by the display of red, yellow or orange berries in autumn and early winter. Cotoneaster is a good choice for difficult situations — it will grow in sandy, clayey and chalky soils and thrives in sun or shade. Birds do not find the berries particularly attractive and pruning is not necessary apart from the removal of unwanted and damaged branches in spring.

VARIETIES: There are many species in all sorts of shapes and sizes but only some of them are evergreen — the old favourite C. horizontalis loses its leaves in winter. Among the evergreens there are several prostrate types such as **C. 'Coral Beauty'** (orange berries), **C. dammeri** (red berries) and **C. salicifolius 'Repens'** (red berries). There are two other excellent prostrate types (**C. 'Gnom'** and **C. 'Skegholm'**) which unfortunately produce few berries. These Cotoneasters are used for ground cover or for growing at the front of the border, as are the low-growing bushes such as **C. conspicuus 'Decorus'** and **C. microphyllus**. The favourite rock garden species is the dwarf mound-forming **C. congestus**. At the other end of the scale are the tall species — look for **C. lacteus** (10 ft/3 m) and **C. salicifolius** (15 ft/4.5 m, arching). Among the tall semi-evergreen types are **C. simonsii**, **C. 'Cornubia'**, **C. franchetii** and **C. 'Rothschildianus'**.

SITE & SOIL: Any garden soil in full sun or partial shade.

PROPAGATION: Plant cuttings in a cold frame in summer.

Cotoneaster dammeri

Cotoneaster microphyllus

Flowering shrub
•
Evergreen or semi-evergreen

C. conspicuus 'Decorus'

Cotoneaster salicifolius

CRINODENDRON   Lantern Tree

You will not find this one in a list of popular shrubs although its description and photograph in the catalogues make it sound more desirable than many long-standing favourites. The 1 in. (2.5 cm) long fleshy-petalled flowers hang down from the branches on long stalks, but despite its charms it is not widely grown. The reason is its fussy requirements — the soil must be well-drained, acid and moist, and the site must be mild and sheltered.

VARIETIES: **C. hookerianum** is an upright bush with 2 in. (5 cm) long dark green lance-shaped leaves. It grows to 8 ft (2.4 m) or more and in May and June the red flowers hang down like lanterns. Their development is unusual — the buds appear in winter, swell in spring and open fully in early summer. **C. patagua** is less hardy and has a different flowering habit. The blooms are white and bell-shaped, and they do not open until late summer.

SITE & SOIL: Moist, lime-free soil in light shade.

PROPAGATION: Plant cuttings in a cold frame in summer.

Flowering shrub
•
Evergreen

Crinodendron hookerianum

C. hookerianum

Conifer
•
Evergreen

C. japonica

CRYPTOMERIA Japanese Cedar

Cryptomeria japonica grows to 150 ft (45 m) in its natural habitat in China and Japan, and so this broadly conical tree has no place in the garden. There are, however, several varieties which are slow-growing and make a valuable addition to the shrub border or rockery. An interesting feature is the seasonal change of colour — the green leaves change to reddish-bronze or reddish-purple in winter.

VARIETIES: C. japonica has long and feathery needle-like leaves at the juvenile stage — adult leaves are short and awl-shaped. The scales on the 1 in. (2.5 cm) round cones have curved hooks. The variety **'Elegans'** keeps the juvenile foliage all its life and reaches a maximum height of 30 ft (9 m). For a more compact bush choose the dwarf variety **'Nana'** which does not exceed 6 ft (1.8 m) when fully grown. The rock garden variety is **'Vilmoriniana'** which grows to only 1 ft (30 cm) after 10 years.

SITE & SOIL: Grows best in lime-free, moist soil in full sun.

PROPAGATION: Buy from a reputable supplier.

Cryptomeria japonica 'Elegans'

Conifer
•
Evergreen

C. lanceolata

CUNNINGHAMIA Chinese Fir

If you like to grow trees which your neighbour will have not seen before then Chinese Fir is a good choice. You will have to search to find a supplier and you will have to find it a suitable site — it needs acid soil, sun and protection from cold winds. When young the tree is conical and the branches are densely clothed with bright green and lustrous leaves which give the tree a 'Monkey Puzzle' appearance.

VARIETIES: C. lanceolata makes an attractive specimen tree when young. As noted above it is clothed with attractive foliage — these 2 in. (5 cm) long, lance-shaped leaves are arranged spirally around the branches. The 1½ in. (4 cm) round cones have sharply-pointed scales. Cunninghamia is not a good long-term choice — once established it soon becomes a gaunt tree with dead leaves and bare branches which do not fall.

SITE & SOIL: Requires acid soil in full sun — protection from strong winds is necessary.

PROPAGATION: Buy from a reputable supplier.

Cunninghamia lanceolata

Conifer
•
Evergreen

C. leylandii

CUPRESSOCYPARIS Leyland Cypress

In 1888 a chance cross occurred between Cupressus macrocarpa and Chamaecyparis nootkatensis on the estate of Mr. Leyland — Cupressocyparis leylandii was born. It got off to a slow start commercially but is now the most widely-used conifer for hedging. It has replaced the Lawson Cypress (page 24) for this purpose as it grows more rapidly (3 ft/90 cm a year) and withstands hard pruning.

VARIETIES: C. leylandii is a columnar tree that can reach 70 ft (21 m) — its flattened branchlets bear tiny, scale-like leaves grouped in fours and the round cones are pea-sized. When grown as a hedge it needs a minimum height of 8 ft (2.4 m) but always buy as small plants (maximum height 3 ft/90 cm) as taller specimens establish very slowly. Prune hedges about three times between late spring and early autumn. Varieties include the golden-yellow **'Castlewellan'** and **'Robinson's Gold'**.

SITE & SOIL: Well-drained soil in sun or partial shade.

PROPAGATION: Plant cuttings in a cold frame in summer.

Cupressocyparis leylandii 'Castlewellan'

CUPRESSUS Cypress

Branches of Cupressus and the much more popular Chamaecyparis look quite similar — both have tiny scale-like leaves grouped in fours around the branched stems. The two basic differences are the arrangement of the branchlets (on Cupressus they grow in all directions unlike the flattened sprays of Chamaecyparis) and the size of the cones (on Cupressus they are large, leathery and knobbly). There is a stout tap root so always choose a small specimen which has been container-grown and not lifted from open ground. Do not prune and stake securely for the first couple of years. The branches of Italian Cypress varieties may be damaged in a severe winter.

VARIETIES: The Italian Cypress (**C. sempervirens**) is a much-loved feature of the Mediterranean landscape — dark green columns standing out against the sky. In the garden it will reach about 8 ft (2.4 m) in 10 years — varieties include **'Stricta'**, **'Totem Pole'** and **'Swane's Gold'**. The Arizona Cypress (**C. arizonica**) grows at about the same rate — the shape is roughly conical, the leaves are blue-grey and the bark is purple. The varieties on offer include **'Pyramidalis'**, **'Conica'** and **'Blue Ice'**. The Monterey Cypress (**C. macrocarpa**) was a popular Victorian tree, but it has been replaced by the much more reliable Cupressocyparis leylandii. It loses its lower branches with age and cannot tolerate hard pruning and so is not a good choice. Its variety **'Goldcrest'** is a good choice and is the most popular Cypress. It is hardier and more compact than its parent, reaching no more than 25 ft (7.5 m) when mature. It is a narrow conical tree with golden-yellow foliage.

SITE & SOIL: Any well-drained garden soil will do — thrives best in full sun.

PROPAGATION: Buy from a reputable supplier.

Cupressus sempervirens

Cupressus arizonica

Conifer
•
Evergreen

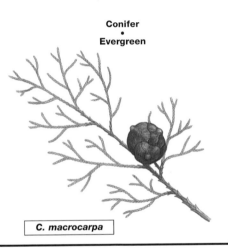

C. macrocarpa

Cupressus macrocarpa 'Goldcrest'

CYTISUS Broom

Nearly all types of Cytisus have green reed-like branches, tiny leaves and a mass of pea-like flowers in early summer. Many varieties lose all these leaves in winter but there is little change in the appearance of the bush, and the branches make it look like an evergreen. Most books class all varieties as deciduous, but some are semi-evergreen.

VARIETIES: The most popular types of Cytisus are hybrids of the Common Broom (C. scoparius) and they are not evergreens. For plants which are semi-evergreen you will have to turn to the tall-growing species. **C. albus (C. multiflorus)** grows about 10 ft (3 m) high and has white flowers — **C. 'Porlock'** reaches the same height and bears 1 in. (2.5 cm) long leaves and fragrant yellow flowers. **C. nigricans** is a late summer yellow-flowered species — for something different grow **C. battandieri** for its cones of yellow flowers.

SITE & SOIL: Sandy soil in full sun.

PROPAGATION: Plant cuttings in a cold frame in summer.

Flowering shrub
•
Semi-evergreen

C. albus

Cytisus nigricans

Flowering shrub
•
Evergreen

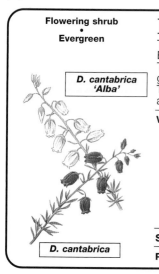

D. cantabrica
'Alba'

D. cantabrica

DABOECIA Irish Heath

The heaths and heathers are nearly always varieties of Erica and Calluna — the Irish Heath is not often seen. This is hard to understand as it is no more difficult to grow than Calluna and its bell-like flowers are larger. The flowering stems (1½ ft/45 cm) are tall for a heath and the flowers are not tightly clustered.

VARIETIES: The usual species is **D. cantabrica** (St. Daboec's Heath). The dark green leaves are silvery underneath and the ½ in. (1.5 cm) long pale purple flowers are borne from June until October. The species is rarely grown — the ones on offer are varieties such as **'Alba'** (white flowers), **'Praegerae'** (deep pink), **'Waley's Red'** (deep red), **'Bicolor'** (white and purple) and **'Atropurpurea'** (deep purple). The only other species is **D. scotica** which grows about 1 ft (30 cm) high — look for the varieties **'Jack Drake'** (deep red) and **'William Buchanan'** (deep purple).

SITE & SOIL: Well-drained, acid soil in sun or light shade.

PROPAGATION: Plant cuttings in a cold frame in summer.

Daboecia cantabrica 'Bicolor'

Leafy shrub
•
Evergreen

D. racemosa

DANAE Alexandrian Laurel

You will find Danae in some catalogues but not at your garden centre, as it seems to have little to offer most gardeners. It is a plain-looking shrub with all-green leaves and a display of small greenish-yellow flowers in early summer. Despite its lack of a showy floral display it has an important role to play in a specific situation. It will thrive and steadily spread by means of its creeping rootstock in the dense shade under trees where little else will grow.

VARIETIES: D. racemosa (**Ruscus racemosus**) has arching stems which bear 4 in. (10 cm) long leaves which are lance-shaped and glossy. As with Butcher's Broom these leaves are really flattened stems and cut branches provide excellent material for flower arranging — the orange berries which appear in autumn are an added feature for indoor decoration in winter. The shrub grows about 3 ft (90 cm) tall — cut back old and/or unwanted shoots in spring.

SITE & SOIL: Moist soil in partial or deep shade.

PROPAGATION: Plant rooted suckers in autumn.

Danae racemosa

Flowering shrub
•
Evergreen or
semi-evergreen

D. burkwoodii

DAPHNE Daphne

The most popular Daphne (D. mezereum) lights up the February or March border with its purple flowers, but unfortunately it is deciduous. The evergreen and semi-evergreen species are not as easy to grow, but most are attractive and well worth the effort. Like all Daphnes they have 4-lobed tubular flowers which are fragrant. Remove unwanted branches in spring.

VARIETIES: The most popular evergreen Daphne is **D. odora 'Aureomarginata'**. It is a rounded bush 4 ft (1.2 m) high and 5 ft (1.5 m) wide. The lance-shaped leaves have pale green and yellow markings and the February-March flowers are reddish-purple. **D. tangutica** is also widely available — it is more compact, the leaves are dull and the pink-flushed white flowers open in May. **D. cneorum** is a 1 ft (30 cm) pink-flowered dwarf and **D. 'Somerset'** is a semi-evergreen with mauve flowers in May. **D. burkwoodii** is a pink-flowered semi-evergreen.

SITE & SOIL: Humus-rich soil in sun or partial shade.

PROPAGATION: Plant cuttings in a cold frame in summer.

Daphne odora 'Aureomarginata'

DESFONTAINIA Desfontainia

This rounded shrub from the Far East may look similar to holly but its requirements are quite different. It has none of the vigour or hardiness of the Christmas favourite and it is certainly not a grow-anywhere plant. For Desfontainia to flourish it needs a reasonably mild area of the country with a partially shaded wall to protect it from strong winter winds. It will take several years before it is fully established.

VARIETIES: You will find **D. spinosa** in some but not all garden centres — buy a large specimen if you can as it grows very slowly for the first 10 years of its life but reaches about 6 ft (1.8 m) when fully mature. The first flowers appear in July — 1½ in. (4 cm) red trumpets with yellow mouths. This floral display will continue until October if the soil is kept moist. The flowers of the variety **'Harold Comber'** are larger and all-red.

SITE & SOIL: Well-drained, neutral or acid soil is necessary — thrives best in partial shade.

PROPAGATION: Plant cuttings in a cold frame in summer.

D. spinosa

Desfontainia spinosa

DIANTHUS Carnation

The hardy evergreen and semi-evergreen carnations are classified into several groups. Showiest of all are the Border Carnations — 1½ -2 ft (45-60 cm) high with large flowers in July or August. The petals are smooth edged (unlike the Florist Carnation) and there are selfs (one colour), fancies (2 or more colours) and picotees (pale colour with a darker edge). Pinks grow about 1 ft (30 cm) tall and have more delicate stems, narrower leaves and smaller flowers. A typical carnation is quite different to a typical pink, but the dividing line is not a clear one. The Rockery Pink forms either a neat cushion or spreading carpet of grassy leaves and is studded in summer with sweet-smelling flowers.

VARIETIES: *Border Carnations* are not as popular as pinks, but the list of varieties which are available is very large. Examples include **'Catherine Glover'** (red/yellow), **'Fiery Cross'** (red), **'Sandra Neal'** (gold/pink), **'Golden Cross'** (yellow) and **'Forest Treasure'** (white/purple) — all bear 5 or more double flowers on stout stems. There are 2 types of Border Pinks. *Old-fashioned Pinks* are slow-growing and produce a single flush of flowers in June. In the catalogues you will find **'Mrs. Sinkins'** (white), **'Musgrave's Pink'** (pink), **'Inchmery'** (lavender-pink) etc — but *Modern Pinks* are a better choice. They are faster growing and bloom in autumn as well as in June and July. Popular ones include **'Doris'** (salmon-pink), **'Laced Monarch'** (pink/red) and **'Gran's Favourite'** (white/mauve). Finally there are the low-growing *Rockery Pinks* — look for the Maiden Pink (**D. deltoides**) with June-September flowers and the Cheddar Pink (**D. gratianopolitanus**) which flowers in May-July. Both grow about 6 in. (15 cm) high — for a smaller plant with larger flowers choose the Alpine Pink (**D. alpinus**).

SITE & SOIL: Any well-drained, non-acid soil will do — choose a sunny spot.

PROPAGATION: Sow seeds under glass in April or plant cuttings in a cold frame in July.

Dianthus plumarius 'Mrs. Sinkins'

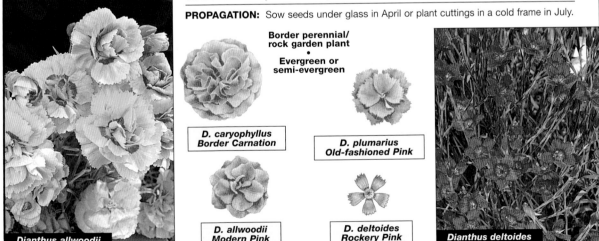

D. caryophyllus
Border Carnation

D. plumarius
Old-fashioned Pink

D. allwoodii
Modern Pink

D. deltoides
Rockery Pink

Dianthus allwoodii
'Doris'

Dianthus deltoides
'Flashing Light'

DIERAMA Wand Flower

D. pulcherrimum

You will find this plant in many catalogues but not in many gardens — it can be raised by planting the corms 3 in. (7.5 cm) deep in late autumn but it is more usual to buy it as a pot-grown specimen. Most of the long grassy leaves remain green over winter and in late summer tubular or bell-shaped blooms appear on wiry arching stems. These tassels of 2 in. (5 cm) long blooms wave in the breeze — hence the common name.

VARIETIES: The usual species is **D. pulcherrimum** — the stems bearing the blooms are about 4-5 ft (1.2-1.5 m) high, but these stalks are bowed down by the weight of the blooms. Pink or purplish-red are the usual colours, but there are white (**'Album'**) and violet (**'Blackbird'**) varieties. **D. pendulum** has a similar growth habit but the flowers are open bells. Grow **D. dracomontanum** where space is limited — spread is only 1 ft (30 cm) and the flower stalks are about 2 ft (60 cm) high.

SITE & SOIL: Well-drained soil and full sun are necessary.

PROPAGATION: Plant corms in spring.

Dierama pendulum

DIGITALIS Perennial Foxglove

Border perennial
•
Evergreen

D. grandiflora

Foxgloves are not usually thought of as evergreen perennials. The usual ones are varieties or hybrids of D. purpurea and these are grown as biennials, dying down in winter and producing tall spikes of spotted bell-like flowers in early summer. In addition to these short-lived deciduous types there are two evergreen perennials which have the same growth habit as their more popular relatives.

VARIETIES: D. grandiflora is the yellow Foxglove. Its flower stems grow about 2 ft (60 cm) high, rising above oval glossy leaves and bearing spikes of 2 in. (5 cm) long pale yellow flowers which are marked with brown. **D. mertonensis** is a hybrid of D. grandiflora (from which it inherits its glossy leaves and evergreen nature) and D. purpurea from which it derives its spotted pink flowers which appear in late spring. Both these species are an excellent choice for growing in damp soil under trees.

SITE & SOIL: Humus-rich soil in partial shade.

PROPAGATION: Sow seeds in a cold frame in late spring.

Digitalis mertonensis

DRYAS Mountain Avens

Rock garden plant/
border perennial
•
Evergreen

D. octopetala

An attractive creeping plant for clothing rocks, covering bare ground or edging the front of the border. The woody stems bear oak-like shiny leaves which are green above and silvery below. In late spring or early summer the large 8-petalled flowers appear on short stalks and these are followed by decorative fluffy seed heads. A good choice for sun-drenched starved soil.

VARIETIES: The most popular species is **D. octopetala** — a wild flower found in rocky regions in Britain and other N. European countries. Its matted stems spread to about 2 ft (60 cm) and the 4 in. (10 cm) high stems bear golden-centred 1½ in. (4 cm) blooms in May and June. The American **D. drummondii** has drooping bell-shaped flowers which are all-yellow. **D. suendermannii** is a hybrid of these two species — the cup-shaped flowers are cream-coloured. All three are fully hardy and easy to grow.

SITE & SOIL: Well-drained soil and full sun are necessary.

PROPAGATION: Plant stem cuttings in a cold frame in summer.

Dryas octopetala

ELAEAGNUS Oleaster

Leafy shrub
•
Evergreen

This shrub is grown for its year-round display of oval leaves — the showy variegated types provide bright winter colour in the mixed or shrub border and the plain-leaved ones are often grown as hedging material in seaside areas. All types are popular for flower arranging as the leaves last for a long time indoors.

VARIETIES: The usual choice is **E. pungens** and the variety at the garden centre is nearly always **'Maculata'**. The 4 in. (10 cm) long green leaves have a large central yellow blotch, but there are others such as **'Frederici'** and **'Quicksilver'** in the catalogues. Remove branches bearing all-green leaves. **E. ebbingei** produces a fast-growing screen. The leathery leaves are silvery below and the white flowers which appear in autumn are followed by orange berries. **'Gilt Edge'** and **'Limelight'** have yellow-splashed leaves.

SITE & SOIL: Any reasonable garden soil will do — plant in full sun or partial shade.

PROPAGATION: Remove rooted suckers from the parent bush or plant cuttings in a cold frame in summer.

Elaeagnus ebbingei
'Gilt Edge'

E. pungens
'Maculata'

EMBOTHRIUM Chilean Fire Bush

Flowering shrub
•
Evergreen

The 1½ in. (4 cm) long flowers are borne on this upright bush in late spring or early summer. These blooms grow in dense clusters and may be numerous enough to make the plant appear to be on fire. Each flower is a narrow tube with a prominent style — with maturity the flower tube splits into 4 coiled strips.

VARIETIES: A single species is available. **E. coccineum** is a branching slender bush which grows to 15 ft (4.5 m). The lance-shaped leaves are 4 in. (10 cm) long and the flowers are scarlet. You will find it in some tree and shrub catalogues but in very few garden centres. The variety **'Longifolium'** is hardier than the species and **'Lanceolatum Norquinco'** has bright red flowers and narrow leaves. All Embothriums are happiest in woodland situations.

SITE & SOIL: Requires well-drained, acid soil which is rich in humus. Some wind protection is essential and so is light shade.

PROPAGATION: Remove rooted suckers and plant in autumn.

Embothrium coccineum
'Longifolium'

E. coccineum

EPIMEDIUM Bishop's Hat

Border perennial
•
Evergreen

Epimedium is used to provide ground cover under trees and large shrubs — the thin flower stalks bear loose clusters of ½-1 in. (1-2.5 cm) wide flowers in late spring or early summer. The compound leaves are borne on wiry stalks — the leathery leaflets are heart-shaped and about 2-3 in. (5-7.5 cm) long. One of the charms of this plant is the way the leaflets change colour as the season progresses, pink-veined in spring and overall bronze in autumn.

VARIETIES: **E. perralchicum 'Frohnleiten'** (1½ ft/45 cm, yellow flowers) is a typical evergreen Epimedium — other yellow varieties include **E. pinnatum colchicum** and **E. perralderianum**. For mauve flowers you should grow **E. acuminatum** — if you want a larger plant with 2 ft (60 cm) flower stalks there is **E. warleyense** with small yellow flowers surrounded by pale red sepals.

SITE & SOIL: Any reasonable garden soil in partial shade.

PROPAGATION: Divide clumps in autumn or spring.

Epimedium perralchicum
'Frohnleiten'

E. warleyense

ERICA   Heather

Growing heathers is one of the basic ways of providing winter colour in the garden, and the two popular types are Erica and Calluna. They look quite similar on the bench at the garden centre — the leaves are tiny, the stems are wiry and the clustered blooms are urn-shaped. There are, however, important differences — Erica is a more versatile plant in a number of ways. Unlike Calluna there is no standard flowering period for Erica — by choosing carefully you can have a bed in bloom all year round. Erica colours range from pure white to near black and there are lime-tolerant as well as lime-hating species. Plant firmly and mulch around the plants in spring.

Erica carnea 'Myretoun Ruby'

VARIETIES: Choose from one of the four species in the *Lime-tolerant Group* if your soil is neutral or alkaline. **E. carnea** varieties dominate this group — the characteristics of these Winter Heathers are height 6-9 in. (15-22.5 cm), spread 1½ ft (45 cm), flowering period January-April. Some are mainly grown for their coloured foliage — examples include **'Foxhollow'** (golden leaves, pink flowers), **'Vivellii'** (bronzy leaves, red flowers) and **'Ann Sparkes'** (golden leaves, red flowers). Many other varieties (e.g **'Springwood White'**, **'Pink Spangles'** and **'Myretoun Ruby'**) are widely available. **E. darleyensis** (November-April) is a 2 ft (60 cm) high lime-tolerant species — the others in this group are varieties of **E. mediterranea** (3 ft/90 cm, March-May flowers) or **E. terminalis** (4 ft/1.2 m, July-September flowers). The *Lime-hating Group* is dominated by **E. cinerea** varieties — height 9 in.-1 ft (22.5-30 cm), flowering period July-September. Other lime-haters include **E. tetralix** (June-October), **E. ciliaris** (July-October), **E. vagans** (July-October) and the 6 ft/1.8 m Tree Heath **E. arborea** (April).

SITE & SOIL: Well-drained soil is necessary — thrives best in full sun.

PROPAGATION: Layer shoots or plant cuttings in a cold frame in summer.

Erica tetralix

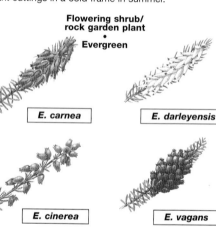

Flowering shrub/
rock garden plant
•
Evergreen

E. carnea

E. darleyensis

E. cinerea

E. vagans

Erica arborea

Border perennial
•
Evergreen

E. variifolium

ERYNGIUM   Sea Holly

The popular varieties of Sea Holly provide long-lasting flower heads for the herbaceous border and excellent material for drying for the flower arranger. The basal rosette of leaves is often white-veined and the branching stems usually have a bluish tinge. On the top of these stems each thimble-like flower head is made up of tiny stalkless blue flowers and has a spiny ruff at its base.

VARIETIES: Not all Eryngiums are evergreen so check before buying. Where space is limited **E. variifolium** is a good choice — the rosette of leaves below the 1½ ft (45 cm) stems bears conspicuous white veins and the pale blue flower heads have a white ruff — the flowering period is July-September. **E. planum** is larger (3 ft/90 cm) but for a giant grow **E. pandanifolium** which has 4 ft (1.2 m) long spiny sword-like leaves and 8 ft (2.4 m) high stems.

SITE & SOIL: Any well-drained garden soil will do — thrives best in full sun.

PROPAGATION: Divide clumps in spring.

Eryngium planum

ERYSIMUM Perennial Wallflower

Wallflowers are seen everywhere in spring but their perennial cousins are much less common. This is surprising as some varieties have a much more attractive growth habit than the biennial Wallflower and at least one (Bowles Mauve) will remain in flower for most of the year if the growing conditions are right.

VARIETIES: The Erysimum you are most likely to find is **E. 'Bowles Mauve'**. This vigorous shrubby plant has narrow grey-green leaves and the heads of mauve flowers are borne from late winter to late summer on 3 ft (90 cm) stalks. There are other sizes and colours. For a mixture of mauve and yellow flowers choose **E. 'Wenlock Beauty'** or **E. 'Plant World Gold'**. For yellow flowers there are **E. 'Harpur Crewe'** (1 ft/30 cm) and **E. 'Moonlight'** (10 in./25 cm). **E. 'Orange Flame'** is a 6 in. (15 cm) dwarf with tangerine flowers.

SITE & SOIL: Any well-drained, neutral or alkaline soil will do — thrives best in full sun.

PROPAGATION: Plant cuttings in a cold frame in late spring.

Erysimum 'Bowles Mauve'

Border perennial/ rock garden plant
•
Evergreen

E. 'Orange Flame'

ESCALLONIA Escallonia

The popular Escallonias bear arching stems clothed with shiny leaves and in June and July a mass of bell-shaped flowers. They are not fussy about soil type and will flourish in light shade, dry conditions and salt-laden air. But not all are completely hardy — some of the types with larger-than-average leaves lose some of their foliage on exposed sites in winter.

VARIETIES: The most popular variety is **E. 'Apple Blossom'** — a slow-growing bush which eventually reaches 6 ft x 6 ft (1.8 m x 1.8 m) and bears white and pink flowers. **E. 'Donard Seedling'** (8 ft/2.4 m, pink buds, white flowers) is a hardier variety and **E. 'C. F. Ball'** (8 ft/2.4 m, red flowers) is more vigorous. The white-flowered **E. 'Iveyi'** blooms in autumn and needs the protection of a south-facing wall. For hedging grow **E. macrantha** or **E. rubra 'Red Spire'** — both are tall-growing red-flowered Escallonias.

SITE & SOIL: Any garden soil in sun or light shade.

PROPAGATION: Plant cuttings in a cold frame in summer.

Escallonia 'Donard Seedling'

Flowering shrub
•
Evergreen or semi-evergreen

E. 'Apple Blossom'

EUCALYPTUS Gum Tree

You are likely to find only one at the garden centre. This is the Cider Gum (E. gunnii) which can be treated in two ways. You can prune it each year to maintain it as a shrub with waxy blue juvenile foliage or you can grow it as a tree with grey-green adult foliage.

VARIETIES: **E. gunnii** grows very quickly — the juvenile oval leaves are replaced by lance-shaped ones as the plant matures and when fully grown it becomes a graceful 50 ft (15 m) high tree. The leaves can be damaged by severe frost — the Snow Gum (**E. niphophila**) is hardier and the branches are covered with a waxy white bloom. The Mountain Gum (**E. dalrympleana**) has bronze juvenile foliage which is replaced by grey-green leaves. The Spinning Gum (**E. perriniana**) has juvenile foliage which spins in the breeze.

SITE & SOIL: A well-drained, non-chalky soil is necessary — thrives best in full sun.

PROPAGATION: Buy a pot-grown plant or sow seeds under glass in spring.

Eucalyptus gunnii

Tree
•
Evergreen

E. gunnii

Flowering shrub
•
Evergreen

E. nymansensis
'Nymansay'

EUCRYPHIA Eucryphia

You would think that the appearance of this shrub would make it a popular choice for the larger garden. The evergreen variety which you are most likely to find at the garden centre has glossy dark green leaves and bears masses of 3 in. (7.5 cm) wide white flowers in late summer. Despite its charm this plant is not often grown. It needs a lot of space, shelter from cold winds and well-drained moist soil — it is not easy to grow.

VARIETIES: **E. nymansensis 'Nymansay'** is the variety described above — the cone-shaped shrub reaches about 10 ft (3 m) in 10 years and the flowers which appear in August and September have a prominent central boss of yellow stamens. You will find the slender shrub **E. milliganii** in numerous catalogues — its 2 in. (5 cm) wide white blooms appear in July. **E. intermedia 'Rostrevor'** is a good choice where space is more limited.

SITE & SOIL: Deep, lime-free soil and light shade are necessary.

PROPAGATION: Plant cuttings in a cold frame in summer.

Eucryphia nymansensis
'Nymansay'

EUONYMUS Euonymus

The evergreen varieties of Euonymus are perhaps the best of all ground covers for providing winter colour around shrubs and under trees. They will grow in all sorts of soils in both sun and partial shade and although leaf growth is dense they do not become rampant invaders. All-green plants are available but it is more usual to choose a variegated type with leaves splashed or edged with gold or silver. Ground cover is not the only use for evergreen Euonymus. Some varieties can be used as climbers, clinging to the wall like Ivy — tall-growing types can be used as specimen shrubs or for hedging. You will find a choice of varieties at any garden centre — no problems, but they are a breeding ground for blackfly.

VARIETIES: There are lots of varieties but only two species from which to make your choice. **E. fortunei** (**E. radicans**) is the usual one — the varieties are low-growing shrubs which are ideal for ground cover. The oval leaves are usually about 1 in. (2.5 cm) long and small poisonous berries may be produced. Popular examples include **'Emerald 'n' Gold'** (colourful mounds of gold-edged green leaves, bronzy-green in winter), **'Blondy'** (yellow-hearted leaves) and **'Emerald Gaiety'** (green leaves with a prominent silver edge). For a climber reaching up to 10 ft (3 m) against a wall choose the white-edged **'Silver Queen'**. **E. japonicus** is the less usual species — grow it as a bush or hedge. It has all-green leaves and is remarkably tolerant of poor conditions, but a coloured variety is usually chosen. Popular ones are **'Aureopictus'** (yellow-hearted), **'Ovatus Aureus'** (yellow-edged) and **'Microphyllus Albovariegatus'** (white-edged).

SITE & SOIL: Any garden soil will do in sun or partial shade. Heavily variegated varieties prefer full sun.

PROPAGATION: Plant cuttings in a cold frame or layer shoots in summer.

Euonymus fortunei
'Emerald 'n' Gold'

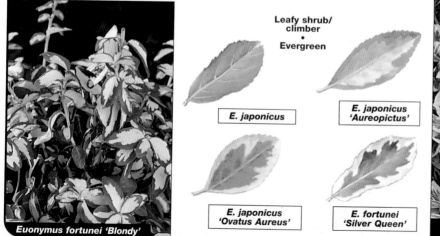

Leafy shrub/ climber
•
Evergreen

E. japonicus

E. japonicus
'Aureopictus'

E. japonicus
'Ovatus Aureus'

E. fortunei
'Silver Queen'

Euonymus fortunei 'Blondy'

Euonymus japonicus
'Microphyllus Albovariegatus'

Euphorbia amygdaloides 'Robbiae'

EUPHORBIA Spurge

The Euphorbias make up a vast genus of plants with about 2000 varieties and a host of uses. One (E. marginata) is grown as a bedding plant, and some others such as the well-known Poinsettia and the Crown of Thorns are grown as house plants. Here we are concerned with the garden perennial varieties. Some of these perennials are herbaceous, but there are a number of useful evergreens which should be more widely grown. As noted below they have a role to play in both the border and rock garden, and the blooms are sometimes used as cut flowers. The actual flowers are insignificant — the display comes from the petal-like white or yellow bracts which surround each tiny bloom. The Spurges flourish in poor soil and thrive in both sun and shade, but they require a word of caution. All parts are poisonous and the milky sap can cause severe skin irritation.

VARIETIES: **E. amygdaloides** (Wood Spurge) is a typical border Euphorbia and its popular variety **'Robbiae'** (Mrs. Robb's Bonnet) is an excellent ground cover plant. The dark and shiny leaves are closely set in tight-fitting rosettes — these spread by means of underground rhizomes and the plant can be invasive. In April and May showy yellowish-green flower heads appear on 2 ft (60 cm) stalks. **'Purpurea'** has purplish-red leaves. For something taller choose **E. characias 'Wulfenii'** which has narrow grey-green leaves and 4 ft (1.2 m) high flower stems. **E. myrsinites** is a semi-prostrate species for the rockery and the Honey Spurge (**E. mellifera**) is a large shrub which bears pea-like fruit in autumn.

SITE & SOIL: Any well-drained soil will do — thrives in sun or partial shade.

PROPAGATION: Plant cuttings in a cold frame in spring or divide clumps in autumn or spring.

Border perennial/ rock garden plant
•
Evergreen

E. myrsinites

Euphorbia amygdaloides 'Purpurea'

Euphorbia characias 'Wulfenii'

Lawson Cypress, Leyland Cypress and Juniper tower above and around the gardener, but he planted them as small specimens from a garden centre only 8 years before. In this estate setting their height is desirable, but in a small plot the result would have been disastrous. The message is clear — always check the expected ultimate height before buying a conifer.

Flowering shrub
•
Evergreen

F. imbricata
'Violacea'

F. imbricata

FABIANA Fabiana

At first glance Fabiana looks like a tall heather, especially the Tree Heath (Erica arborea). The wiry stems are clothed with overlapping tiny leaves and in May and June a profusion of small flowers cover these leafy stems. On closer inspection Fabiana is clearly not a heather — it is a member of the potato family and each bloom is a long open-mouthed tube and not an urn- or bell-shaped structure.

VARIETIES: You will find the single species **F. imbricata** in many catalogues and some garden centres. The flower-covered shoots in early summer look like white plumes and in about 10 years the spreading shrub will reach about 6 ft (1.8 m). Where space is limited the mound-forming variety **'Prostrata'** is a better choice. For a change of colour pick **'Violacea'** for mauve blooms. Pruning is not necessary.

SITE & SOIL: Well-drained, non-chalky soil is required. Choose a sheltered sunny site.

PROPAGATION: Plant cuttings in a propagator in summer.

Fabiana imbricata

Flowering shrub
•
Evergreen

F. japonica

FATSIA Fatsia

There are numerous shrubs which will provide a strong architectural effect but very few are suitable for a sunless spot. Fatsia is the one to choose — there are large glossy leaves all year round and candelabra-like flower heads in autumn. Fatsia is better known as a house plant, but do not buy your plant from the indoor gardening section of your garden centre — greenhouse-grown plants need a long hardening-off period.

VARIETIES: F. japonica is known as the Castor Oil Plant, Aralia and Fig-leaf Palm. Its flowers are silvery-green in bud and creamy-white when open, but it is grown for its 1 ft (30 cm) leaves rather than its blooms. These leaves have 7-8 finger-like lobes and the plant reaches 10 ft x 10 ft (3 m x 3 m) when fully grown. The foliage is dark green — for white-edged leaves you can grow the variety **'Variegata'** provided your garden is relatively frost-free.

SITE & SOIL: Any reasonable garden soil will do. A shady sheltered site is necessary.

PROPAGATION: Plant cuttings in a cold frame in summer.

Fatsia japonica 'Variegata'

Grass
•
Evergreen

F. glauca

FESTUCA Fescue

Some fescue species are used as turf grasses where a fine quality lawn is required. The species described here are ornamental grasses grown for their display of attractive blue leaves — the large varieties are planted among the flowers and shrubs in the border and the compact types are used to provide a contrast in shape and colour among the alpines in the rock garden.

VARIETIES: The most popular species is the Blue Fescue (**F. glauca**). The blue-grey fine foliage is crowded into dense tufts which grow about 6 in. (15 cm) high and in summer 1 ft (30 cm) tall flower spikes appear. There are several varieties — **'Seeigel'** has hair-like leaves, **'Harz'** has purple-tipped foliage and **'Blau Fuchs'** has pure blue leaves. **F. amethystina** is larger than F. glauca and its leaves are grey-blue — **F. valesiaca 'Silbersee'** is a silver-blue dwarf for the rockery.

SITE & SOIL: Well-drained soil which is not too fertile nor too moist is required. Thrives best in full sun.

PROPAGATION: Divide clumps in spring.

Festuca glauca

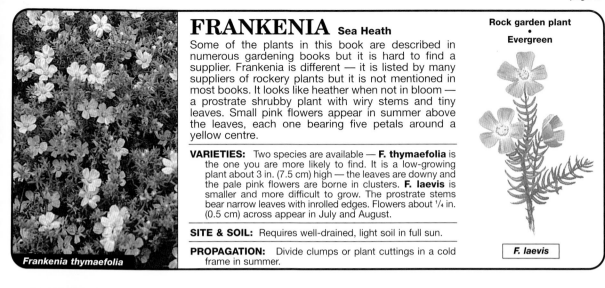

Frankenia thymaefolia

FRANKENIA Sea Heath

Rock garden plant
•
Evergreen

Some of the plants in this book are described in numerous gardening books but it is hard to find a supplier. Frankenia is different — it is listed by many suppliers of rockery plants but it is not mentioned in most books. It looks like heather when not in bloom — a prostrate shrubby plant with wiry stems and tiny leaves. Small pink flowers appear in summer above the leaves, each one bearing five petals around a yellow centre.

VARIETIES: Two species are available — **F. thymaefolia** is the one you are more likely to find. It is a low-growing plant about 3 in. (7.5 cm) high — the leaves are downy and the pale pink flowers are borne in clusters. **F. laevis** is smaller and more difficult to grow. The prostrate stems bear narrow leaves with inrolled edges. Flowers about ¼ in. (0.5 cm) across appear in July and August.

SITE & SOIL: Requires well-drained, light soil in full sun.

PROPAGATION: Divide clumps or plant cuttings in a cold frame in summer.

F. laevis

FREMONTODENDRON Flannel Flower

Flowering shrub
•
Evergreen or semi-evergreen

It is a shame that such a splendid wall shrub should be so rarely seen. From late summer to mid autumn there is a showy display of large yellow blooms and all round the year the stems are clothed with leathery lobed leaves. The undersides of these leaves have a brown felty coating which can irritate the skin. The reason for the lack of popularity is its reputation as a tender plant, but once established it is quite hardy.

VARIETIES: **F. californicum** grows about 12 ft (3.6 m) high in time — the lobed leaves are about 3 in. (7.5 cm) long and the saucer-shaped blooms measure 2½ in.(6 cm) across. In addition to this species you may find two of its hybrids in the catalogues. **F. 'California Glory'** is equally vigorous with flowers which are flushed red on the outside and **F. 'Pacific Sunset'** with blooms which are at first deep orange. **F. mexicanum** blooms are star-shaped.

SITE & SOIL: Any well-drained soil will do — thrives best in full sun. Provide protection against cold winds.

PROPAGATION: Plant cuttings in a propagator in spring.

F. californicum

Fremontodendron californicum

GARRYA Silk Tassel Bush

Flowering shrub
•
Evergreen

For most of the year Garrya is a fairly ordinary evergreen bush. It has an upright growth habit and is densely clothed with oval leathery leaves which are glossy green above and woolly grey below. In January and February the plant comes into its own when it is festooned with long and slender catkins. It will flourish in poor soil, coastal areas and shade.

VARIETIES: **G. elliptica** reaches about 12 ft (3.6 m) when fully grown and the leaves are about 3 in. (7.5 cm) long. The tassel-like catkins are up to 8 in. (20 cm) long — grey-green at first and then dull cream. Look for the variety **'James Roof'** rather than the species — the tassels of this male plant are thicker and longer. For something more unusual than the ordinary Silk Tassel Bush there is **G. issaquahensis 'Pat Ballard'** (purplish tassels) and **G. fremontii** (twisted leaves).

SITE & SOIL: Any free-draining soil in sun or shade will do — plant against a wall in cold areas.

PROPAGATION: Plant cuttings in a cold frame in summer.

G. elliptica

Garrya elliptica 'James Roof'

GAULTHERIA Wintergreen

Gaultheria procumbens

Gaultheria is a lime-hating plant and its most common use is to act as ground cover under rhododendrons, camellias etc. But there is at least one tall variety which becomes a medium-sized bush when mature and several which are small enough for a peaty rock garden. It is grown for its Lily of the Valley-like blooms in late spring or summer and its showy berries (white, pink, red, blue or purple) in autumn and winter.

VARIETIES: For a dense thicket choose **G. shallon** (5 ft/ 1.5 m high, dark purple berries) but a more popular choice is the Checkerberry **G. procumbens**. The spreading branches bear glossy dark leaves and the white urn-shaped flowers appear in July to be followed by red berries in autumn. It grows about 6 in. (15 cm) high — for taller 1 ft (30 cm) plants choose the white-berrying varieties **G. cuneata** and **G. miqueliana**.

SITE & SOIL: Requires lime-free soil in partial shade.

PROPAGATION: Layer shoots or plant rooted suckers in spring.

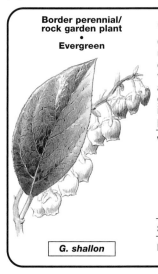

G. shallon

GENISTA Broom

Flowering shrub
•
Evergreen or
semi-evergreen

To the purist and plantsperson Genista is certainly not an evergreen — it loses most or all of its tiny leaves in winter. To the ordinary gardener, however, many varieties are 'evergreen' as the green reed-like branches of the popular species change very little in appearance during the leafless phase. All have yellow or cream blooms and they may be spiny or thornless.

VARIETIES: **G. lydia** is a ground cover species which grows about 2 ft (60 cm) high with a spread of 3 ft (90 cm). Yellow pea-like flowers appear in May and June and as with most other Genistas cover the stems and tiny leaves in the right conditions. **G. hispanica** (1 ft/30 cm) has spiny stems and **G. sagitallis** has flattened 'evergreen' stems and cones of flowers. **G. pilosa 'Vancouver Gold'** is a thornless carpeter and **G. aetnensis** is a 12 ft (3.6 m) giant which blooms in July and August.

SITE & SOIL: Requires well-drained soil in full sun — do not feed.

PROPAGATION: Plant cuttings in a cold frame in summer.

G. lydia

Genista hispanica

A colourful bed at Windsor Great Park made up entirely of varieties of Erica carnea — 'Springwood White', 'Myretoun Ruby' etc. The effect when all the plants are in bloom in spring is stunning, but for the ordinary garden bed it is better to extend the display period by including coloured-foliage varieties such as the golden-leaved 'Foxhollow', and also to include summer-flowering species such as Erica vagans and Erica tetralix.

Geranium endressii 'Wargrave Pink'

GERANIUM Crane's Bill

The border geranium should not be confused with the bedding and house plant 'geraniums' with their large heads and showy blooms which are really species and varieties of Pelargonium. The plants described here are hardy perennials which form mounds of deeply divided or lobed leaves. This foliage may be green, red, grey or bronze coloured and their most popular use is as ground cover around shrubs and trees. The blooms are usually saucer-shaped and there are varieties in white, pink, blue and red. Some have prominently-veined petals. Many types lose their leaves in winter but there are numerous varieties which cover the ground with foliage all year round and some are effective weed suppressors. Keep watch for slugs in spring.

VARIETIES: **G. endressii** and **G. oxonianum** are popular evergreen species — their varieties grow about 1½ ft (45 cm) high and the plants are in flower from May to September. Examples to look for are **'Wargrave Pink'** (salmon-pink), **'Winscombe'** (dark-veined pink), **'A. T. Johnson'** (silvery pink), **'Claridge Druce'** (dark-veined pink) and **'Rose Clair'** (pale-veined purplish-red). **G. macrorrhizum** is another popular evergreen and is a good choice for shady situations — the two most important varieties are **'Variegatum'** (cream-splashed grey-green leaves, mauve flowers) and **'Ingwersen's Variety'** (pale green leaves, pink flowers). Other evergreens include **G. sanguineum** (cup-shaped deep pink flowers), **G. cinereum 'Ballerina'** (dark-veined, dark-eyed pink flowers), **G. asphodeloides** (white, pink or mauve star-shaped flowers), **G. dalmaticum** (dwarf, pink flowers) and **G. palmatum** (dark-centred, mauve flowers).

SITE & SOIL: Any well-drained soil will do — thrives in sun or light shade.

PROPAGATION: Sow seeds of species outdoors or divide clumps in spring.

Border perennial
•
Evergreen or
semi-evergreen

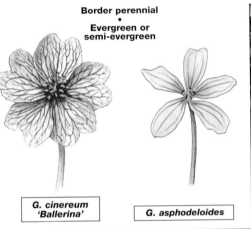

G. cinereum 'Ballerina'

G. asphodeloides

Geranium macrorrhizum

Geranium sanguineum

GREVILLEA Spider Flower

For nearly everyone who grows this exotic shrub from Australia it is a conservatory plant to be set out in summer once the danger of frost has passed, but not all species are frost-tender. The ones described below can withstand several degrees of frost and are certainly worth considering if you have a protected south-facing border in a mild area.

VARIETIES: Each flower head is made up of numerous tubular blooms with curled-back lobes and prominent styles. **G. juniperina** grows about 6 ft (1.8 m) high and bears narrow bright green leaves — the variety **'Sulphurea'** produces pale yellow flower heads in May and June. For pink and cream flowers in midsummer choose **G. rosmarinifolia** and for a spring-flowering shorter variety with red and cream blooms pick **G. alpina 'Olympic Flame'**.

SITE & SOIL: Well-drained, non-alkaline soil with full sun and shelter are necessary.

PROPAGATION: Plant cuttings in a cold frame in summer.

Flowering shrub
•
Evergreen or
semi-evergreen

Grevillea alpina 'Olympic Flame'

G. juniperina 'Sulphurea'

Leafy shrub
•
Evergreen

*G. littoralis
'Dixon's Cream'*

GRISELINIA Griselinia

Griselinia is a work-horse of a plant rather than a showpiece. It is used to provide a vigorous and upright shrub densely clothed with attractive leathery leaves especially in situations where there are not too many alternatives. Coastal areas are an example — you will find Griselinia hedges in many seaside towns as it is not harmed by salt-laden air. Another use is to provide greenery in chalky soil under trees.

VARIETIES: **G. littoralis** is the only species you are likely to find. It will grow to 10 ft (3 m) or more in time but it can be kept in check by pruning each year. Griselinia is not completely frost hardy and as a result some leaves may be damaged when the temperature falls to 23°F (-5°C) on an exposed site. The variegated types are even more tender. Look for **'Dixon's Cream'** (cream-hearted green) and **'Variegata'** (cream-edged green).

SITE & SOIL: Any well-drained soil will do — thrives in sun or partial shade.

PROPAGATION: Plant cuttings in a cold frame in summer.

Griselinia littoralis 'Variegata'

HEBE Shrubby Veronica

These popular evergreens are available in a range of shapes and sizes at the garden centre and it is convenient to divide them into three groups. First of all there are the Whipcord Hebes with scale-like leaves which hug the stem, and then there are the ones with oval leaves. These leafy varieties are either Low-growing Hebes which reach 1½ ft (45 cm) or less or Tall-growing Hebes which exceed 1½ ft (45 cm). The typical Hebe is a 2 ft (60 cm) compact bush with dense foliage and spikes of white or blue flowers. Some but not all are hardy — the larger the leaf, the more tender the variety is likely to be. Tenderness apart, Hebes are easy to grow even in smoky or salt-laden air and many will flower all summer and autumn long.

VARIETIES: The favourite *Whipcord Hebe* is **H. ochracea 'James Stirling'** (1½ ft/ 45 cm, erect golden stems, green in summer). Others include **H. armstrongii** (3 ft/90 cm, yellowish-green) and **H. cupressoides** (4 ft/1.2 m, grey-green). One of the best of the *Low-growing Hebes* is **H. pinguifolia 'Pagei'** (1 ft x 3 ft/30 cm x 90 cm) — an excellent ground cover with greyish-blue leaves and white flowers in May-August. Other low-growing ones include **H. albicans** (grey-green leaves, white flowers) and **H. 'Red Edge'** which is similar apart from the red-edged leaves. **H. rakaiensis** is excellent in shade and **H. 'Carl Teschner'** is attractive but rather tender. There are many *Tall-growing Hebes* — popular ones include **H. 'Autumn Glory'** (violet-blue flowers June-November), **H. 'Great Orme'** (pink flowers July-October), **H. 'Mrs. Winder'** (purple leaves, blue flowers June-September) and the 6 ft (1.8 m) **H. salicifolia** (lavender-tinted white flowers July-September).

SITE & SOIL: Any reasonable garden soil will do — thrives best in full sun.

PROPAGATION: Plant cuttings in a cold frame in summer.

Hebe cupressoides

Hebe 'Carl Teschner'

Hebe albicans

Flowering shrub/
rock garden plant
•
Evergreen

*H. pinguifolia
'Pagei'*

H. armstrongii

H. 'Autumn Glory'

H. 'Great Orme'

HEDERA Ivy

Ivy is often inherited when buying a house — ordinary all-green climbers clinging to old walls or clothing old trees. But if you choose the right variety and prune it properly it is a reliable and attractive climber which will grow anywhere. Despite popular belief neither trees nor sound brickwork is damaged by Ivy, but you should keep it in check by pruning so that it does not become too heavy for the supporting structure. Brightly variegated types are available, and these make excellent ground cover to provide colour and interest below leafless shrubs in winter. The leaves are often deeply lobed but these become smooth-edged and oval when the plant is mature.

VARIETIES: Common Ivy (**H. helix**) is known to everyone. The species has 3- or 5-lobed triangular leaves with a dark green glossy surface — for garden use it is better to choose one of the many interesting variations. For eye-catching leaf shape there are **'Ivalace'** and **'Green Ripple'** and for a change from all-green there are **'Buttercup'** (all-yellow), **'Goldheart'** and **'Goldchild'** (green/yellow), **'Glacier'** and **'Little Diamond'** (green/grey), **'Sagittifolia Variegata'** (grey/cream) and **'Atropurpurea'** (purple in winter). Some Ivy varieties are dwarfs suited to the rockery — for quick cover of a large area of wall choose the vigorous Irish Ivy (**H. hibernica**). For ground cover a good choice is the Persian Ivy (**H. colchica**) which has the largest leaves of all. It is dark green — for yellow-edged leaves pick the variety **'Dentata Variegata'**. **H. canariensis 'Variegata'** is rather similar with large, yellow-splashed leaves, but it has red stems and is not fully hardy.

SITE & SOIL: Any garden soil will do. Thrives in shade, but the variegated types need some sunshine.

PROPAGATION: Remove and plant rooted runners.

Hedera helix 'Buttercup'

Hedera helix 'Glacier'

Climber
•
Evergreen

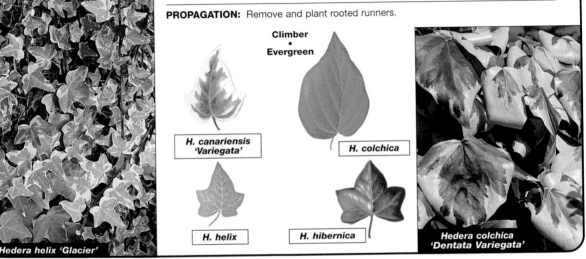

H. canariensis 'Variegata'

H. colchica

H. helix

H. hibernica

Hedera colchica 'Dentata Variegata'

HELIANTHEMUM Sun Rose

This lowly sub-shrub really comes into its own in full sun and sandy soil. The papery blooms form a sheet of colour and this lasts for about 8 weeks between May and July. Each bloom lasts for only a day or two but new ones appear constantly during the flowering period. White, yellow, orange, pink and red varieties are available to liven up containers, rockeries, border edges and dry banks.

VARIETIES: The named varieties at the garden centre are all hybrids of **H. nummularium** and **H. apenninum**. There are a few 4 in. x 1 ft (10 cm x 30 cm) dwarfs such as **'Amy Baring'**, but most grow about 8 in. (20 cm) high with a spread of 2 ft (60 cm). The Wisley Series (**'Wisley White'**, **'Wisley Pink'** and **'Wisley Primrose'**) have grey leaves, **'Jubilee'** and **'Mrs. C. W. Earle'** have double flowers and the Ben Series (**'Ben Hope'**, **'Ben Nevis'** etc) are the hardiest. For vivid orange flowers pick **H. 'Fire Dragon'**.

SITE & SOIL: Light and well-drained soil in full sun.

PROPAGATION: Plant cuttings in a cold frame in summer.

Rock garden plant/ border perennial
•
Evergreen

H. 'Fire Dragon'

Helianthemum 'Wisley Pink'

HELICHRYSUM — Shrubby Helichrysum

Flowering shrub • Evergreen

H. splendidum

There are several shrubby species of Helichrysum which are evergreen and hardy enough to be grown in the garden. Both the leaves and flowers are distinctive. The leaves are woolly or densely hairy and sometimes aromatic. The flowers are button-like and are borne in clusters — these heads are nearly always yellow and are of the 'everlasting' type and can be cut and dried for flower arranging. Trim back the stems in April.

VARIETIES: The favourite species is the Curry Plant which you will find labelled as **H. serotinum** or **H. italicum 'Serotinum'**. It is a 1½ ft (45 cm) high shrub with grey needle-like leaves which smell strongly of curry but are not suitable for cooking — the flower heads appear in June-August. Other species include **H. splendidum** (3 ft/90 cm), **H. 'Schwefel Licht'** (1½ ft/45 cm), **H. italicum** (2 ft/60 cm) and the white-flowered dwarf **H. milfordiae**.

SITE & SOIL: Requires light and well-drained soil — full sun is necessary.

PROPAGATION: Plant cuttings in a cold frame in summer.

Helichrysum serotinum

HELLEBORUS — Hellebore

Border perennial • Evergreen or semi-evergreen

H. niger

H. orientalis

The situation with deciduous Hellebores is straightforward — they lose their leaves in winter. The remaining species keep some or all of their leaves in winter and these are replaced by new foliage in spring. Some books describe this as 'overwintering' rather than 'evergreen' foliage — in this book they are classed as evergreens. These deeply-lobed leaves provide good ground cover and the large saucer-shaped flowers appear in winter or spring.

VARIETIES: The Christmas Rose (**H. niger**) grows about 1 ft (30 cm) high. In January-March nodding white or pink-tinged flowers appear above the leaves — the variety **'Potter's Wheel'** has 5 in. (12.5 cm) wide blooms. The Lentern Rose (**H. orientalis**) flowers in February-April — the blooms range from white to purple and are often spotted. Other colours include purple-edged yellow (**H. foetidus**) and apple green (**H. argutifolius**).

SITE & SOIL: Any well-drained soil in partial shade.

PROPAGATION: Divide clumps after flowering.

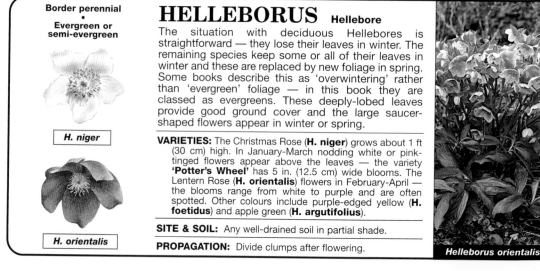

Helleborus orientalis

HEUCHERA — Coral Flower

Border perennial • Evergreen or semi-evergreen

H. sanguinea

Heuchera, Tellima and Tiarella are a group of mound-forming plants which are used as ground cover. The general leaf form is oval or heart-shaped, lobed, hairy and veined — the small flowers are borne on upright stalks. You may confuse these plants at the all-leaf stage but not when in flower — Heuchera blooms are small bells borne in panicles (see glossary).

VARIETIES: The flowers are borne on 1½-2½ ft (45-75 cm) stalks between May and June and these plants are grown for their decorative flowers and/or leaves. There is a wide range — look for **H. sanguinea** (pink flowers, pale green/dark green leaves), **H. micrantha 'Palace Purple'** (white flowers, purple leaves), **H. 'Pewter Moon'** (pink flowers, grey-marbled leaves), **H. 'Red Spangles'** (red flowers, pale green/dark green leaves), **H. 'Rachel'** (pink flowers, pale green/dark green leaves) and **H. 'Greenfinch'** (green flowers, green leaves).

SITE & SOIL: Any well-drained soil in sun or light shade.

PROPAGATION: Divide clumps in autumn or spring.

Heuchera 'Pewter Moon'

HOLCUS   Creeping Soft Grass

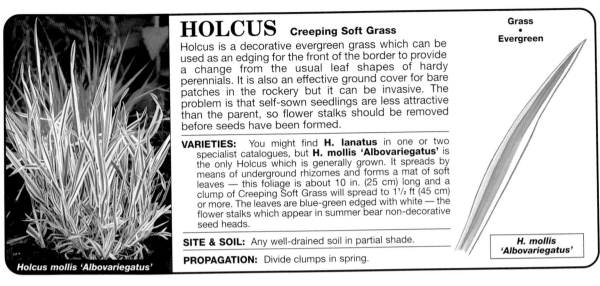

Holcus is a decorative evergreen grass which can be used as an edging for the front of the border to provide a change from the usual leaf shapes of hardy perennials. It is also an effective ground cover for bare patches in the rockery but it can be invasive. The problem is that self-sown seedlings are less attractive than the parent, so flower stalks should be removed before seeds have been formed.

VARIETIES: You might find **H. lanatus** in one or two specialist catalogues, but **H. mollis 'Albovariegatus'** is the only Holcus which is generally grown. It spreads by means of underground rhizomes and forms a mat of soft leaves — this foliage is about 10 in. (25 cm) long and a clump of Creeping Soft Grass will spread to 1½ ft (45 cm) or more. The leaves are blue-green edged with white — the flower stalks which appear in summer bear non-decorative seed heads.

SITE & SOIL: Any well-drained soil in partial shade.

PROPAGATION: Divide clumps in spring.

Grass
•
Evergreen

H. mollis 'Albovariegatus'

Holcus mollis 'Albovariegatus'

HYPERICUM   St. John's Wort

The common feature of the Hypericums is the form of the flower — a flat yellow disc with a central boss of stamens. Some produce a showy display of red or black fruits and one is grown for its colourful leaves. The heights of the various types range from small rockery species to 6 ft (1.8 m) vigorous shrubs for the back of the border. Sensitivity to frost also varies — the popular ones are fully hardy but a few species require a sheltered spot in the garden. The usual choice is Rose of Sharon which is an undemanding low-growing shrub which will thrive almost anywhere in sun or shade. The only problem is that it spreads quickly and can be invasive — cut it back to almost ground level in March. The tall varieties should have the top third of their stems removed in spring.

VARIETIES: Some but not all are evergreen or semi-evergreen — nearly all of the rockery types which grow to 1 ft (30 cm) or less lose their leaves in winter. Rose of Sharon is **H. calycinum** which reaches a height of about 1½ ft (45 cm). The oval leaves are 2-4 in. (5-10 cm) long and the shrub is in flower from late June to mid October. There are several alternatives to Rose of Sharon if you want a 1½ -3 ft (45-90 cm) shrub which is less invasive. Look for **H. moserianum 'Tricolor'** with small flowers and leaves which are a blend of green, cream and pink, **H. 'Sungold'** with 2½ in. (6.5 cm) wide flowers and red fruits, and **H. aegypticum** which has star-shaped blooms. The tall Hypericums are perhaps best of all with **H. 'Hidcote'** as the star. Others in the 3-6 ft (90 cm-1.8 m) range include **H. inodorum 'Elstead'** (small starry flowers, red fruits), **H. patulum 'Henryi'** (red-tinged green fruits) and the rather tender **H. 'Rowallane'** (3 in./7.5 cm flowers). Evergreen dwarfs include **H. coris** and **H. balearicum**.

SITE & SOIL: Any non-waterlogged soil will do — thrives in sun or partial shade.

PROPAGATION: Plant cuttings in a cold frame in summer.

Hypericum calycinum

Hypericum moserianum 'Tricolor'

Flowering shrub
•
Evergreen or semi-evergreen

H. inodorum 'Elstead'

H. calycinum

H. moserianum 'Tricolor'

H. 'Hidcote'

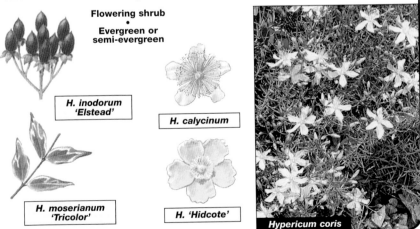
Hypericum coris

**Rock garden plant/
border perennial**
•
Evergreen

I. sempervirens

IBERIS   Perennial Candytuft

Perennial Candytuft is an old favourite in the rock garden and at the front of the mixed border. Each plant forms a mound of narrow leaves which is covered with a mass of white flower heads between mid April and June. Each bloom in the flower head has the four-petalled arrangement of the cabbage family, but there are two long petals and two short ones.

VARIETIES: The species you will find on sale at the garden centre is **I. sempervirens** — a vigorous sub-shrub which grows 10 in. (25 cm) high and spreads to 2 ft (60 cm). It is preferable to grow a variety rather than the species and **'Snowflake'** is the best. Where space is a problem grow one of the dwarfs such as **'Pygmaea'** (3 in./7.5 cm) or **'Little Gem'** (4 in./10 cm). **I. saxatilis** is an unusual 6 in. (15 cm) dwarf species — the leaves are fleshy and the white flowers are tinged with purple.

SITE & SOIL: Any well-drained soil will do — thrives best in full sun.

PROPAGATION: Plant cuttings in a cold frame in summer.

*Iberis sempervirens
'Snowflake'*

ILEX   Holly

Holly is usually thought of as a tree, shrub or hedge with all-green prickly leaves and red berries at Christmas. Of course such plants are a common sight but these days there are many more unusual and more decorative varieties for your garden. First of all there are the variegated ones with gold- or silver-splashed green foliage to brighten up the winter border. Then there are both smooth-edged and fiercely-prickly varieties as well as types with yellow, orange or black berries. Finally there is the Box-leaved Holly with small oval leaves. With all this variety holly is well worth considering if you want a bright but slow-growing hedge or shrub for a difficult situation such as shade or chalky soil. Trim hedges in spring and shrubs in summer.

VARIETIES: A basic point to remember before choosing a variety of holly is that nearly all types are male or female, which means that more than one variety must be planted to ensure berry production. The most popular species is the Common Holly (**I. aquifolium**) which is an erect shrub with 2-4 in. (5-10 cm) long leaves. For a green and gold effect choose the badly-named male variety **'Golden Queen'** — others include **'Golden Milkboy'** (male) and **'Golden van Tol'** (female). Strongly-spined varieties include **'Madame Briot'** (female) and **'Ferox Argentea'** (male) and for a white edged or splashed holly there is **'Argentea Marginata'** (female) or **'Silver van Tol'** (female). **'Bacciflava'** has yellow berries. **I. altaclerensis** is best known for its variegated female variety **'Golden King'** and the Box-leaved Holly (**I. crenata**) is best known for its low-growing yellow-leaved variety **'Golden Gem'**. If you have room for only one holly then grow a self-fertile one such as **I. aquifolium 'Pyramidalis'** or **'J. C. van Tol'**.

SITE & SOIL: Any reasonable garden soil will do — thrives in full sun or partial shade.

PROPAGATION: Layer branches in summer or plant cuttings in a cold frame in autumn.

*Ilex aquifolium
'Golden Queen'*

**Tree/
flowering shrub**
•
Evergreen

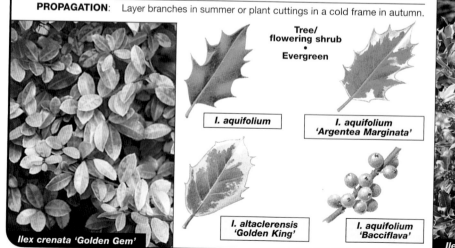

I. aquifolium

*I. aquifolium
'Argentea Marginata'*

*I. altaclerensis
'Golden King'*

*I. aquifolium
'Bacciflava'*

Ilex crenata 'Golden Gem'

Ilex aquifolium 'Pyramidalis'

IRIS Iris

Iris germanica 'Jane Phillips'

Irises are a vast group of plants ranging from bold-flowering species with 4 ft (1.2 m) stems to tiny alpines, but nearly all have the same flower form — three inner petals ('standards') generally standing erect and three outer petals ('falls') generally hanging downwards. Detailed classification is highly complex but in simple terms there are just two basic groups — the Bulb group and the Rhizome group. The Bulb group are small plants which lose their leaves in winter and have no place in this book. The Rhizome group spread by means of thickened horizontal stems and here you will find some evergreens. Try not to disturb the clumps — lifting and division should not take place until at least four years after planting.

VARIETIES: The Bearded Irises with fleshy hairs at the base of the falls are the most popular members of the Rhizome group, but out of the thousands of named types you will have to pick a variety of **I. pallida** or **I. germanica** if you want evergreen leaves. With the Beardless Irises the choice is larger — these moisture-loving plants have long and narrow leaves, and the flowers are usually bicoloured. Species which belong here include **I. innominata**, the winter-flowering **I. stylosa (I. unguicularis)** and **I. foetidissima** which is grown for its decorative orange seeds. The Crested species are a section of the Beardless Irises with a ridge rather than a beard on the falls. The evergreen here is **I. japonica** which is only moderately hardy, so grow its hardier offspring **'Ledger's Variety'**. The Water species of the Beardless Irises grow in ponds and are evergreen — included here are the yellow-flowered **I. pseudacorus** and the blue-flowered **I. laevigata**.

SITE & SOIL: Most evergreen Irises thrive best in moist soil and full sun.

PROPAGATION: Divide rhizomes in late summer every four years.

Border perennial
•
Evergreen

Iris innominata

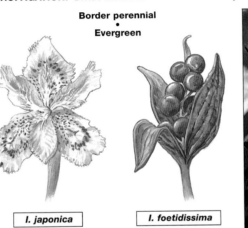

I. japonica

I. foetidissima

Iris laevigata 'Midnight'

ITEA Sweetspire

Itea ilicifolia

Two species of Sweetspire are available from tree and shrub nurseries and from some larger garden centres, but only one of these shrubs is evergreen. The Virginia Sweetspire (I. virginica) has foliage which turns red in autumn and then falls in winter, so only I. ilicifolia is dealt with here. This evergreen grows as a spreading bush with arching stems — you can plant it in the border but it is much better against a wall.

VARIETIES: The Holly-leaf Sweetspire (**I. ilicifolia**) can be grown as an open bush and kept to about 5 ft (1.5 m) high with a spread of about 3 ft (90 cm), or it can be allowed to climb in the shelter of a wall and reach 9 ft (2.7 m) or more. The holly-like leaves are dark green above and silvery below and in August and September the flowers appear. These ¼ in. (0.5 cm) greenish-white blooms are borne on pendent tassels.

SITE & SOIL: Well-drained, fertile soil with some shelter is necessary — thrives in sun or light shade.

PROPAGATION: Plant cuttings in a cold frame in summer.

Flowering shrub/ climber
•
Evergreen

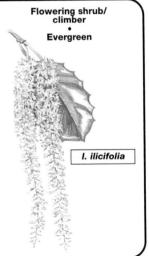

I. ilicifolia

Climber/ flowering shrub • Evergreen

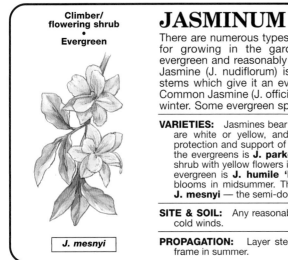

J. mesnyi

JASMINUM Jasmine

There are numerous types of Jasmine which are sold for growing in the garden, but only a few are evergreen and reasonably hardy. The popular Winter Jasmine (J. nudiflorum) is hardy but it is the green stems which give it an evergreen look in winter. The Common Jasmine (J. officinale) also loses its leaves in winter. Some evergreen species are quite tender.

VARIETIES: Jasmines bear trumpet-shaped flowers which are white or yellow, and the stems usually need the protection and support of a wall. Perhaps the hardiest of the evergreens is **J. parkeri**, a domed 1 ft (30 cm) high shrub with yellow flowers in early summer. Another bushy evergreen is **J. humile 'Revolutum'** which has yellow blooms in midsummer. The most reliable tall climber is **J. mesnyi** — the semi-double flowers appear in spring.

SITE & SOIL: Any reasonable soil in a site protected from cold winds.

PROPAGATION: Layer stems or plant cuttings in a cold frame in summer.

Jasminum humile 'Revolutum'

JUNIPERUS Juniper

The Junipers are now supreme when it comes to dwarf and ground-covering types. The value of the low-growing Junipers has long been realised in the U.S but it is only in quite recent times that they have become really popular in Britain. These tiny-leaved conifers have two great virtues — their ease of cultivation and their attractive growth habit. First, ease of cultivation. They are extremely hardy and are not troubled by cold winds on exposed sites, nor is inhospitable soil type a problem — chalky soil, acid land and gravelly ground are all quite suitable for Junipers. They can also withstand drought much better than most conifers, but prefer a dry sunny spot to a dry shady one. These plants respond well to pruning — cut back hedges and trim prostrate forms in midsummer to increase bushiness. The other virtue apart from their easy-to-please nature is the attractiveness of both shape and leaf form. A range of spreading mats in green, grey, blue, gold and bronze is available — in addition there are upright types varying from cones, broad columns and mounds to narrow pencils and neat pyramids. An interesting feature is that there are two types of leaves. As shown in the illustration below the juvenile ones are small ($1/4$-$1/2$ in./0.5-1 cm long), narrow and awl-like — the adult leaves are tiny, scale-like and overlapping on the shoot. With some Junipers the juvenile leaves are quickly replaced by adult ones, but with other species the juvenile foliage is dominant even on a mature tree. The cones are pea-sized with fused and fleshy scales.

Juniperus squamata 'Meyeri'

SITE & SOIL: Any reasonable soil in sun or light shade will do.

PROPAGATION: Buy from a reputable supplier. Plant cuttings outdoors in autumn.

Conifer • Evergreen

Juniperus media 'Pfitzeriana Aurea'

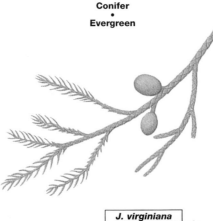

J. virginiana

Juniperus horizontalis 'Hughes'

JUNIPERUS continued

VARIETIES: **J. squamata** is typical of the low-growing Junipers. **'Blue Carpet'** is a low-growing blue variety — it spreads to about 5 ft (1.5 m) in time. For something smaller choose **'Blue Star'** with a 3 ft (90 cm) spread. **'Meyeri'** has blue foliage and nodding branches like the others, but it is a spreading bush reaching a height of 4 ft (1.2 m) or more in ten years. **J. media** has both spreading and shrubby varieties like J. squamata. **'Pfitzeriana'** is the best-known one with its strong branches rising at an angle of 45° and with gracefully drooping tips. It spreads widely, as does the golden version **'Pfitzeriana Aurea'**. For a more compact variety choose **'Old Gold'**. The Creeping Juniper (**J. horizontalis**) has ground-hugging branches with whipcord-like ends. Popular varieties include **'Glauca'** (steely blue), **'Hughes'** (grey-green) and **'Bar Harbor'** (grey-blue). **J. procumbens 'Nana'** is another ground-hugging Juniper — it differs from the ones above by having branch ends which turn upwards. The varieties of **J. communis** come in various shapes and sizes. **'Compressa'** forms a miniature, column-like tree for the rockery. **'Hibernica'** (Irish Juniper) is a narrow column reaching 15 ft (4.5 m) when mature and the wide-spreading ones for ground cover include **'Depressa Aurea'** (gold), **'Repanda'** (green) and **'Hornibrookii'** (green). The Spanish Juniper (**J. sabina 'Tamariscifolia'**) is an old favourite — the horizontal branches bearing feathery foliage build up as a series of layers. The varieties of **J. chinensis** are either upright trees or spreading bushes — **'Pyramidalis'** is a slow-growing conical tree which, like other J. chinensis types, has foliage which is almost entirely juvenile. Other tree types include **'Aurea'**, **'Obelisk'** and **'Stricta'** — for a spreading shrub grow **'Japonica'** or **'Kaizuka'**. Finally there is **J. virginiana** with the popular **'Skyrocket'** variety (narrow columnar tree) and **'Grey Owl'** (silver-grey spreading bush.)

Juniperus communis
'Compressa'

Juniperus communis
'Hibernica'

Juniperus communis
'Depressa Aurea'

Juniperus sabina
'Tamariscifolia'

Juniperus chinensis
'Aurea'

Juniperus chinensis
'Stricta'

Juniperus virginiana
'Skyrocket'

Flowering shrub
•
Evergreen

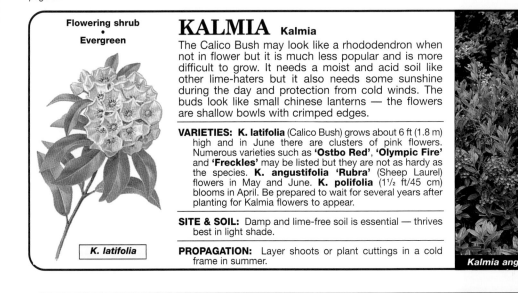

K. latifolia

KALMIA Kalmia

The Calico Bush may look like a rhododendron when not in flower but it is much less popular and is more difficult to grow. It needs a moist and acid soil like other lime-haters but it also needs some sunshine during the day and protection from cold winds. The buds look like small chinese lanterns — the flowers are shallow bowls with crimped edges.

VARIETIES: **K. latifolia** (Calico Bush) grows about 6 ft (1.8 m) high and in June there are clusters of pink flowers. Numerous varieties such as **'Ostbo Red'**, **'Olympic Fire'** and **'Freckles'** may be listed but they are not as hardy as the species. **K. angustifolia 'Rubra'** (Sheep Laurel) flowers in May and June. **K. polifolia** (1½ ft/45 cm) blooms in April. Be prepared to wait for several years after planting for Kalmia flowers to appear.

SITE & SOIL: Damp and lime-free soil is essential — thrives best in light shade.

PROPAGATION: Layer shoots or plant cuttings in a cold frame in summer.

Kalmia angustifolia 'Rubra'

Border perennial
•
Evergreen

K. 'Atlanta'

KNIPHOFIA Red Hot Poker

Kniphofia is an old favourite in the herbaceous border and one which everyone can recognise — a clump of grass-like foliage and spikes of long tubular flowers. Some but not all have the traditional 'red hot poker' appearance — a flower head which is red at the top and yellow at the base. Other colours include white, yellow, orange, red and even pale green. In winter cover the crowns with peat or straw.

VARIETIES: Choose with care as not all varieties are evergreen — the evergreen ones have broader and longer leaves than the deciduous types. The popular Kniphofias are hybrids, growing 3-5 ft (90 cm-1.5 m) high and flowering in July-September. Examples of evergreens include **'Atlanta'** (red/pale yellow), **'Percy's Pride'** (yellow) and **'Bees' Sunset'** (orange). Several of the species are evergreen — look for **K. caulescens** (orange/yellow), **K. uvaria** (orange/yellow) and **K. northiae** (yellow).

SITE & SOIL: Any well-drained soil will do — thrives best in full sun.

PROPAGATION: Divide mature clumps in spring.

Kniphofia uvaria

Border perennial/ rock garden plant
•
Evergreen or semi-evergreen

L. maculatum 'Beacon Silver'

LAMIUM Dead Nettle

An excellent ground cover if you have an area in partial or full shade. A few varieties are compact enough for the rockery but the rest are invasive. Lipped flowers in white, pink, mauve or yellow appear in late spring or early summer, but Lamium is grown mainly for its foliage. The nettle-like leaves are usually prominently striped or splashed with silver.

VARIETIES: **L. maculatum** (height 8 in.-1 ft/20-30 cm, spread up to 3 ft/90 cm) is the most popular species. One of the varieties and not the species is usually chosen and the brightest and perhaps the best carpeter is **'Beacon Silver'** with green-margined silver leaves. Others include the similarly-coloured **'White Nancy'** and the pink-flowered, yellow-leaved **'Aureum'**. **L. orvala** is compact enough for the rockery — the yellow-flowered **L. galeobdolon** is non-invasive.

SITE & SOIL: Any well-drained soil will do — thrives best in partial shade.

PROPAGATION: Divide clumps in autumn or spring.

Lamium maculatum

LAPAGERIA   Chilean Bellflower

This S. American climber is best known as a conservatory plant but you can try it outdoors if you live in a relatively frost-free part of the country and like a challenge. The blooms are certainly worth it — 3-4 in. (7.5-10 cm) long pendent bells with waxy petals hang down from the twining stems from midsummer to autumn. The shelter of a wall is essential and so is soil which is lime-free. Pruning is not necessary.

VARIETIES: **L. rosea** is the only species you will find in the catalogues. It is a tall climber, capable of growing 10 ft (3 m) or more in a warm and sheltered spot. The plant will need some shade during the day and a mulch of peat or straw in winter. The oblong leaves are leathery and the blooms are pink or red. They appear in clusters of two or three — for a change of colour there are the varieties **'Albiflora'** (white) and **'Nash Court'** (red-blotched pink).

SITE & SOIL: Well-drained, non-alkaline soil in partial shade is essential. Provide wind protection.

PROPAGATION: Layer plants in autumn.

L. rosea

Lapageria rosea

LAURUS   Bay Laurel

Do not confuse this plant which has leaves used for flavouring with the much more popular laurel (Prunus lusitanica) which is widely used for hedging and has poisonous foliage. The trouble with the Bay Laurel is its susceptibility to frost damage — plant it in a sheltered spot. The popular place for Laurus is in the herb garden or neatly trimmed in a container.

VARIETIES: **L. nobilis** will grow into a pyramid-shaped tree 20 ft (6 m) or more high if left unpruned, but it is much more usual to keep the plant in check by trimming in summer. The oval leaves with wavy edges are glossy and aromatic, and in spring yellow flowers appear and these are followed by black berries on female plants. Remove any frost-damaged stems and leaves in late spring. For golden foliage grow the variety **'Aurea'**.

SITE & SOIL: Any reasonable garden soil in a sheltered site will do — thrives in sun or partial shade.

PROPAGATION: Layer shoots or plant cuttings in a cold frame in summer.

L. nobilis

Laurus nobilis

Rose trees and climbers look gaunt and bare in winter, so evergreens are often planted nearby to add a touch of life and colour during the dead season. Lavender is a popular choice — the pastel shades of the flowers blend well with most rose colours and their small size means that in summer they do not compete for attention with the rose blooms. Remember that white-flowered lavender is available — see page 54.

LAVANDULA Lavender

The traditional lavender which has graced the British garden with its appearance and fragrance for centuries has bushy stems and grey-green leaves with pale purple or blue flowers from July to September. It is an accommodating plant which will grow in many situations, but it prefers light land which is not acid — in badly-drained soil it may die in a wet winter. This old favourite is used in many ways. Tall varieties are used in the shrub border and the dwarfs are useful in the rockery — many varieties make excellent hedges or edging around beds and borders and the dried leaves and flowers are basic materials for pot-pourri. One of the drawbacks is that the plants can soon become leggy, so pruning is necessary. Remove flower stalks when blooms have faded, and in April trim back the plants but do not cut into old wood.

VARIETIES: It is usual but not strictly correct for garden centres to group all Old English Lavenders together as **L. spica**, **L. angustifolia** or **L. officinalis**. The pale blue or pale purple flowers are borne on dense spikes on 2-3 ft (60-90 cm) stems. There are several popular varieties which differ in both height and colour — look for **'Hidcote'** (1½ ft/45 cm, silvery leaves, purple flowers), **'Alba'** (4 ft/1.2 m, white flowers), **'Nana Alba'** (1 ft/30 cm, white flowers), **'Munstead'** (1½ ft/45 cm, green leaves, lavender-blue flowers) and **'Rosea'** (1½ ft/45 cm, green leaves, pink flowers). The variety **'Vera'** (Dutch Lavender) has broad silvery leaves and blue flowers. **L. stoechas 'Papillon'** (French Lavender) has downy leaves and showy purple bracts above the purple flowers — **L. viridis** has green bracts and white flowers.

SITE & SOIL: Any well-drained garden soil will do — thrives best in full sun.

PROPAGATION: Plant cuttings in a cold frame in summer.

Lavandula spica 'Alba'

Flowering shrub
•
Evergreen

L. spica
'Hidcote'

Lavandula spica 'Munstead'

Lavandula stoechas

Flowering shrub
•
Semi-evergreen

LAVATERA Tree Mallow

It is not surprising that Lavatera has increased in popularity. A small plant bought from a garden centre in spring soon becomes a large bush bearing tall spikes of showy blooms, and these flowers continue to appear from the end of June until mid October. A colourful addition to the border but there are drawbacks. Shelter is needed in windy, frost-prone areas and staking may be necessary.

VARIETIES: A number of varieties and hybrids of **L. olbia** and **L. thuringiaca** are available. The basic one is **L. 'Rosea'** — a 7 ft (2.1 m) giant with lobed leaves and pale pink saucer-shaped flowers. Other tall ones include **L. 'Barnsley'** (pinkish-white with a red eye) and **L. 'Burgundy Wine'** (dark pink flowers). For 4-5 ft (1.2-1.5 m) plants try **L. 'Ice Cool'** (white) or the rather tender **L. maritima** (purple-veined lilac).

SITE & SOIL: Any well-drained soil will do — thrives best in full sun.

PROPAGATION: Plant cuttings outdoors in late autumn.

L. 'Rosea'

Lavatera 'Burgundy Wine'

LEPTOSPERMUM New Zealand Tea Tree

Flowering shrub
•
Evergreen

The catalogue description of this shrub makes it sound a most desirable subject for the garden. The purplish stems bear small lance-shaped leaves and then masses of white, pink or red flowers in early summer. These saucer-shaped blooms are long-lasting and clothe the stems, but this plant is distinctly disappointing if you live in a cold area.

VARIETIES: **L. scoparium** is the popular species — a twiggy upright bush which can reach 8 ft (2.4 m) or more. The varieties are much more widely available than the basic species and offer a range of sizes and colours. **'Red Damask'** has double red flowers and purple-tinged leaves, and **'Snow Flurry'** has double white flowers. **'Huia'** and **'Kiwi'** are dwarfs for the rockery. **L. lanigerum** has white cup-shaped flowers and is hardier than the other Leptospermums.

SITE & SOIL: Well-drained, sandy or loamy soil in full sun — needs shelter of a west- or south-facing wall.

PROPAGATION: Plant cuttings in a cold frame in summer.

Leptospermum scoparium

L. scoparium

LEUCOTHOE Leucothoe

**Leafy shrub/
flowering shrub**
•
**Evergreen or
semi-evergreen**

Many evergreens are dull for much of the year, but the two popular varieties of Leucothoe provide year-round interest. The main feature is the colourful leaf display, although one of these varieties bears clusters of white, urn-shaped flowers in spring. Plant Leucothoe in acid soil with some shade and it will quickly spread to form a dense ground cover which will suppress weeds.

VARIETIES: There are two varieties from which to make your choice — both are varieties of **L. fontanesiana** (**L. walteri**). This 3 ft (90 cm) high shrub has lance-shaped green leaves which turn bronzy-purple in winter. The variety **'Rainbow'** is even more colourful with foliage which is green splashed with yellow, pink and cream — drooping flower heads appear in May. **'Scarletta'** foliage changes from purple to green and then to bronze as the year progresses.

SITE & SOIL: Fertile, non-alkaline soil and light shade are necessary.

PROPAGATION: Layer stems or plant cuttings in a cold frame in summer.

*Leucothoe fontanesiana
'Scarletta'*

L. fontanesiana

LEWISIA Lewisia

Rock garden plant
•
Evergreen

Lewisia is one of the most attractive plants you could choose for a gap between the stones in the rockery. The rosettes of fleshy leaves do not spread to threaten surrounding plants and from May until midsummer clusters of starry flowers appear on upright stalks. The petals of these blooms are usually striped and a wide range of colours is available. Place grit under the leaves to protect from soggy soil in winter.

VARIETIES: The varieties which you will see at the garden centre are hybrids of **L. cotyledon**. This species bears 1½ in. (4 cm) wide white-edged pink flowers on 8 in. (20 cm) high stalks — the popular hybrids include the **'Sunset'** strain in many colours, **'George Henley'** (brick red) and **'Rose Splendour'** (pink). **L. tweedyi** is the star with 2½ in. (6 cm) wide pink-tinged white flowers, but it is more difficult to overwinter than the L. cotyledon hybrids.

SITE & SOIL: Well-drained, gritty soil in full sun or light shade is necessary.

PROPAGATION: Sow seeds under glass in early spring.

Lewisia tweedyi

L. cotyledon

LIBERTIA Libertia

Border perennial
•
Evergreen

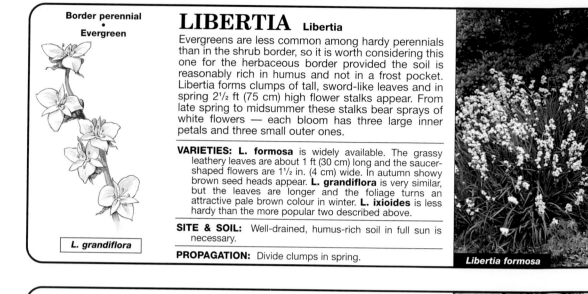

L. grandiflora

Evergreens are less common among hardy perennials than in the shrub border, so it is worth considering this one for the herbaceous border provided the soil is reasonably rich in humus and not in a frost pocket. Libertia forms clumps of tall, sword-like leaves and in spring 2½ ft (75 cm) high flower stalks appear. From late spring to midsummer these stalks bear sprays of white flowers — each bloom has three large inner petals and three small outer ones.

VARIETIES: L. formosa is widely available. The grassy leathery leaves are about 1 ft (30 cm) long and the saucer-shaped flowers are 1½ in. (4 cm) wide. In autumn showy brown seed heads appear. **L. grandiflora** is very similar, but the leaves are longer and the foliage turns an attractive pale brown colour in winter. **L. ixioides** is less hardy than the more popular two described above.

SITE & SOIL: Well-drained, humus-rich soil in full sun is necessary.

PROPAGATION: Divide clumps in spring.

Libertia formosa

LIGUSTRUM Privet

The days when privet was a prime choice for hedging are over. It belonged to the time when a plant was needed which could withstand smoky air and every tiny terrace-house garden wanted a hedge which could cope with dense shade. Nowadays we want something brighter than the dull green leaves of privet for hedging. We also want something showier than the insignificant display of small and pungent-smelling flowers of the Common Privet when looking for a specimen shrub for the border. Before rejecting privet, however, you should consider the colourful varieties which are available these days. There are varieties with large glossy leaves, others with all-yellow or variegated foliage and several with large flower heads which would grace any border.

VARIETIES: The Common Privet (**L. vulgare**) is the species which will grow into a 10 ft (3 m) semi-evergreen shrub if left unpruned but was much more widely used in the past for hedging. There are a few colourful varieties such as **'Aureum'** which has golden yellow leaves, but **L. ovalifolium** is a better choice for hedging as it is evergreen, has larger leaves and branches more freely. Varieties include **'Aureum'** (green-centred yellow) and **'Argenteum'** (cream-edged green). Among the privets grown for their flowers the showiest (L. quihoui) is unfortunately deciduous, but there are a number of good evergreens. **L. japonicum** is a compact 6 ft (1.8 m) high shrub with camellia-like leaves and large sprays of white flowers in summer. **L. sinense 'Variegatum'** is a tall semi-evergreen with white-splashed leaves and **L. lucidum 'Excelsum Superbum'** has late summer flowers and cream-edged leaves.

SITE & SOIL: Any reasonable garden soil will do — thrives in sun or partial shade.

PROPAGATION: Plant cuttings in the open in late autumn.

Ligustrum ovalifolium 'Aureum'

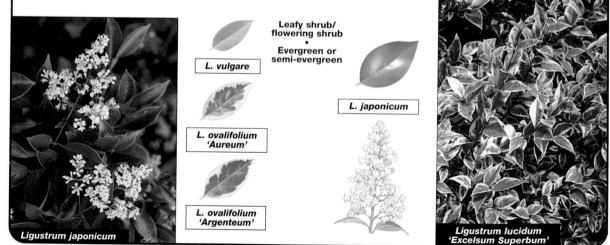

Leafy shrub/
flowering shrub
•
Evergreen or
semi-evergreen

L. vulgare

L. ovalifolium 'Aureum'

L. japonicum

L. ovalifolium 'Argenteum'

Ligustrum japonicum

Ligustrum lucidum 'Excelsum Superbum'

LIMONIUM Sea Lavender

Limonium produces rosettes of leaves at ground level and provides summer-long displays of small papery blooms. The 'everlasting' flowers are borne on wiry stems and can be cut at the opening bud stage and dried for indoor decoration. It will thrive in infertile and stony soil and is easy to grow, but you should cut down the stems in autumn.

VARIETIES: The popular species is the Broad-leaved Sea Lavender (**L. latifolium**). The sprays of 1/4 in. (0.5 cm) lavender-blue flowers rise about 2 ft (60 cm) high above the rosettes of oval leaves from July to September. Varieties include **'Violetta'** (deep violet) and **'Robert Butler'** (lavender). For the rockery there is **L. bellidifolium** — a mound-forming dwarf which grows about 6 in. (15 cm) high. The tiny white/violet flowers open in early summer.

SITE & SOIL: Any well-drained garden soil will do — thrives best in full sun.

PROPAGATION: Sow seeds under glass in spring or take root cuttings in winter.

Border perennial/
rock garden plant
•
Evergreen

L. latifolium

Limonium latifolium

LIRIOPE Lily Turf

This ground cover plant looks like an oversized Grape Hyacinth when in flower. The arching grassy leaves grow in clumps or mats and in late summer or autumn the upright stems bear spikes of tiny bell-shaped flowers. It can be used as edging in the herbaceous border, but it is invasive and you will have to lift and divide the clumps every few years to limit its spread. Dead-head when flowers fade.

VARIETIES: The species you are most likely to find is **L. muscari** with clumps of 1 ft (30 cm) long dark green leaves and flower spikes of about the same height from September to November. The usual flower colour is mauve or violet, but there are varieties in other colours — look for **'Monroe White'** (white flowers), **'Royal Purple'** (purple flowers) and **'John Burch'** (gold-splashed leaves). **L. spicata** is a mat-forming semi-evergreen species.

SITE & SOIL: Any lime-free garden soil will do — thrives in sun or light shade.

PROPAGATION: Divide clumps in spring.

Border perennial
•
Evergreen or
semi-evergreen

L. muscari

Liriope muscari

Mowing right up to the base of trees is a tricky and sometimes damaging operation. A band of evergreen ground cover such as Pachysandra instead of grass around the trunk saves both time and trouble, but do not cover this area until the tree is well established. Growing turf or an evergreen right up to the base of a young tree will slow down its development.

LONICERA Honeysuckle

The word 'Honeysuckle' conjures up a picture of a twining climber which loses its leaves in winter. The range of Honeysuckles, however, is more extensive. There are in fact three groups. Firstly there are the leafy shrubs which do not have a significant flower display and are used for ground cover and hedging. Next there are the flowering shrubs and finally the well-known flowering climbers. These climbers are best allowed to clamber over fences or pergolas rather than being tied against a wall. There are evergreens in each of these three groups — prune the flowering shrub types if necessary after flowering and with climbing evergreens cut out unwanted growth and a few old stems in spring.

Lonicera nitida 'Baggesen's Gold'

VARIETIES: The leading evergreen in the *Leafy Shrub* group is **L. nitida** — a 6 ft (1.8 m) small-leaved bush which is usually kept clipped as a hedge. The leaves are glossy and dark green — for more colour grow the yellow-leaved variety **'Baggesen's Gold'** or the white-edged **'Silver Beauty'**. The best ground cover is **L. pileata** — a spreading shrub with horizontal branches and box-like foliage. The popular choice in the *Flowering Shrub* group is **L. fragrantissima** which is a spreading 6 ft (1.8 m) high bush with ½ in. (1 cm) long creamy-white scented flowers from January to March and red berries in May. Only a few members of the *Flowering Climber* group keep their leaves in winter. The best-known evergreen is **L. japonica** which bears fragrant purple-flushed white flowers in summer — the variety **'Aureoreticulata'** has yellow-netted foliage. **L. henryi** (yellow-throated purple flowers) is another evergreen — semi-evergreens include **L. brownii 'Dropmore Scarlet'** (red) and **L. sempervirens** (orange).

SITE & SOIL: Well-drained, humus-rich soil is necessary — tolerates sun but climbers prefer light shade.

PROPAGATION: Layer shoots or plant cuttings in a cold frame in summer.

Climber/
flowering shrub/
leafy shrub
•
Evergreen or
semi-evergreen

Lonicera fragrantissima

L. pileata

L. brownii 'Dropmore Scarlet'

Lonicera henryi

Flowering shrub
•
Semi-evergreen

LOTUS Canary Clover

Most species of Lotus are too tender to spend the winter outdoors but the Hairy Canary Clover is hardy enough to be a year-round resident in a shrub or mixed border. In mild areas nearly all the leaves will remain on the stems, but the usual practice is to cut back the previous year's growth to the woody base each spring. The new stems which arise bear closely-packed leaflets which are greyish-green and covered with silvery hairs.

VARIETIES: The Hairy Canary Clover is **L. hirsutus**, sometimes sold as **Dorycnium hirsutum**. It grows about 2 ft (60 cm) high with a spread of 3 ft (90 cm) and is an excellent and unusual addition to the border if the conditions are right — free-draining sandy soil in full sun. At the top of each erect stem the flower clusters appear from July to September. The pea-like flowers are pink-tinged white and are followed by brown seed pods.

SITE & SOIL: Well-drained, light soil in full sun is essential.

PROPAGATION: Plant cuttings in a cold frame in summer.

L. hirsutus

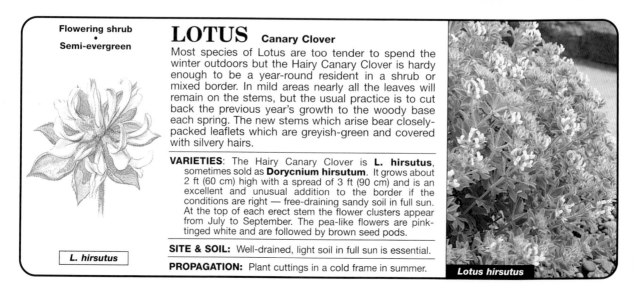

Lotus hirsutus

LUPINUS Tree Lupin

It is strange that the hardy perennial Lupin is a universally popular feature of the herbaceous border but the shrubby form is a rarity. It is not difficult to grow but it has fussier requirements than the ordinary Lupin. It needs both well-drained soil and sun, so it is not suitable for clayey gardens but is an excellent choice for a coastal site.

VARIETIES: L. arboreus is a rounded bush reaching about 5 ft (1.5 m) high and with a spread of 4 ft (1.2 m). The silky shoots are soft and the evergreen or semi-evergreen leaves are greyish-green with silky hairs on the underside. Each leaf is made up of 6-9 lance-shaped leaflets and from June to August the flower spikes appear. The pea-like blooms are fragrant and the usual colour is yellow. Varieties include **'Snow Queen'** (white) and **'Mauve Queen'** (pale purple).

SITE & SOIL: Well-drained soil in full sun is necessary.

PROPAGATION: Sow seeds in spring or plant cuttings in a cold frame in summer.

Flowering shrub
•
Evergreen or semi-evergreen

L. arboreus

Lupinus arboreus

LUZULA Woodrush

The popularity of ornamental grasses has increased in recent years but there are not many evergreen ones. Luzula is worth considering if you are looking for a ground cover plant to grow in damp and shady soil — it will grow under trees. It is not a true grass — this genus belongs to the rush family. It is grown either for its tiny flowers or for its coloured foliage.

VARIETIES: The Snowy Woodrush (**L. nivea**) is chosen for its clusters of minute white blooms which appear in summer above the clumps of narrow dark green leaves. The leafy flower stems grow to about 2 ft (60 cm) and are suitable for drying for indoor decoration. The Greater Woodrush (**L. sylvatica**) also has dark green basal leaves but the minute brown flowers are not decorative. Some varieties have decorative leaves — look for **'Aurea'** (yellow) and **'Marginata'** (cream-edged green).

SITE & SOIL: Well-drained, humus-rich soil in partial shade is necessary.

PROPAGATION: Divide clumps in spring.

Grass
•
Evergreen

L. sylvatica 'Aurea'

Luzula nivea

LYSIMACHIA Creeping Jenny

The tall Loosestrifes which produce white or yellow flowers on top of 2-3 ft (60-90 cm) stems lose their leaves in winter but the old favourite Creeping Jenny is evergreen. This lowly plant will spread quickly and is a useful ground cover for a damp and shady patch of bare ground. It is rather too invasive for most rockeries, but there is a less vigorous variety.

VARIETIES: Creeping Jenny (**L. nummularia**) grows about 2 in. (5 cm) high and produces a mat of creeping stems and rounded 1 in. (2.5 cm) leaves which suppress weeds. Masses of yellow ½ in. (1 cm) flowers appear in May-August along the stems — it prefers moist soil and some shade, but it will grow in dry ground and full sun. Its variety **'Aurea'** has yellow leaves and is much less invasive, but you must choose a shady site.

SITE & SOIL: Thrives best in well-drained, humus-rich soil in partial shade.

PROPAGATION: Divide clumps in autumn or plant cuttings in a cold frame in spring.

Rock garden plant/ border perennial
•
Evergreen

L. nummularia

Lysimachia nummularia 'Aurea'

Flowering shrub
•
Evergreen

M. grandiflora

MAGNOLIA Magnolia

A large and well-grown Magnolia is a showpiece in any border, but nearly all species lose their leaves in winter. The evergreen Magnolia is the largest of the popular garden types. The glossy oval leaves are about 8 in. (20 cm) long and the tree grows to 20 ft (6 m) or more. Few plants have larger or more stunning flowers, but think twice before you plant one. Lots of space is needed and so is shelter from cold winds.

VARIETIES: **M. grandiflora** is a slow-growing tree with large leaves which are dark green and leathery above but felted and reddish-brown below. The blooms in July-September are up to 10 in. (25 cm) across — large open cups with creamy-white petals. With the species you will have to wait up to 20 years before the first flowers appear. For flowers at an earlier age choose the variety **'Exmouth'** or **'St. Mary'**.

SITE & SOIL: Any reasonable soil will do — best against a warm wall. Thrives in sun or light shade.

PROPAGATION: Buy from a reputable supplier.

Magnolia grandiflora

MAHONIA Mahonia

Mahonia is one of the basic building blocks of the shrub or mixed border. It can be relied upon to provide year-round colour — green glossy leaves which are sometimes tinged bronze or purple in winter, yellow fragrant flowers in winter or spring depending on the variety and these blooms are followed by purple or black berries. Many types are available so choose with care. Heights range from 3-8 ft (90 cm-2.4 m) and some of the unusual ones are not fully hardy. All of the popular Mahonias are hardy and easy to grow — they are not fussy about soil type and will grow in quite dense shade. Pruning of mature plants is not essential, but M. aquifolium may need cutting back after flowering to stop it becoming too invasive.

VARIETIES: The old favourite with round clusters of yellow flowers in March and April is the Holly-berried Berberis or Oregon Grape (**M. aquifolium**). The dark green leaves are similar to holly and the 3 ft (90 cm) high plant with a 6 ft (1.8 m) spread is used extensively for ground cover. It suckers freely and can spread rapidly — the variety **'Apollo'** does not become invasive. **'Atropurpurea'** has purple leaves in winter and **'Smaragd'** has more compact growth but larger flower clusters than the species. A popular Mahonia in the 6-8 ft (1.8-2.4 m) specimen shrub group is **M. japonica** with flower spikes radiating from the stem tip like the spokes of a wheel. There are a number of excellent hybrids grouped under **M. media**. **'Charity'** is a highly recommended one with shuttlecock-like flower spikes in winter — **'Lionel Fortescue'** has unusually long flower spikes. For glossy, wavy-edged leaves grow **M. wagneri 'Undulata'**.

SITE & SOIL: Any reasonable garden soil will do — thrives best in shade.

PROPAGATION: Plant rooted suckers of M. aquifolium — for others plant cuttings in a cold frame in summer.

Mahonia aquifolium
'Atropurpurea'

Flowering shrub
•
Evergreen

Mahonia japonica

M. aquifolium

M. media
'Charity'

Mahonia media
'Lionel Fortescue'

MILIUM Milium

Grass
•
Semi-evergreen

Several evergreen or semi-evergreen ornamental grasses are described in this book and this one is the favourite choice where a yellow-leaved variety is required. In recent years Hakonechloa has increased in popularity, but this green-striped yellow rival is deciduous and lacks the nodding tiny yellow flower heads which Milium bears in spring and summer. Grow it if you like grasses and want to brighten up a shady and moist patch in the garden.

VARIETIES: You will find just one variety at the garden centre or in the catalogues — **M. effusum 'Aureum'** (Bowles' Golden Grass). It forms tufts of narrow, arching golden yellow leaves which are about 1 ft (30 cm) long. These tufts spread to about 1 ft (30 cm) and in May the slender flower stalks appear, reaching about 2 ft (60 cm) and bearing heads of golden panicles. It tolerates poorly-drained soil and is useful for flower arranging.

SITE & SOIL: Moisture-retentive soil in partial shade.

PROPAGATION: Divide clumps in spring.

Milium effusum 'Aureum'

M. effusum
'Aureum'

MORINA Morina

Border perennial
•
Evergreen

An unusual member of the scabious family with flowers which are quite unmistakable. The stems are about 3 ft (90 cm) tall and in midsummer each one bears a spike of showy flowers. The waxy blooms are borne in whorls with a collar of spiny green bracts below — these whorls of flowers are borne in tiers. Worth looking for, but only if you can provide cover against rain for the crown in winter.

VARIETIES: M. longifolia produces a basal rosette of 1 ft (30 cm) long thistle-like leaves — the leaves on the stems are smaller. The blooms are white when they open — waxy tubes with a five-lobed mouth. As they mature the colour changes to pink and finally to crimson. This species (common name Whorlflower) is widely available but **M. persica** is a rarity. The leaves are lobed, it grows about 4 ft (1.2 m) high and the final flower colour is pink and not red.

SITE & SOIL: Well-drained soil is essential — thrives best in full sun.

PROPAGATION: Sow seeds in a cold frame in spring.

Morina longifolia

M. longifolia

MYRTUS Myrtle

Flowering shrub
•
Evergreen

Myrtle has been grown as a garden shrub or tree for hundreds of years. Its oval leaves are glossy and fragrant when crushed, and the flowers in mid and late summer look like small single roses. These blooms are sweetly scented and are followed by purple-black berries in autumn. Despite its charms Myrtle is not a popular garden plant. The problem is its susceptibility to hard frosts and icy winds in winter.

VARIETIES: M. communis (Common Myrtle) is the most popular and hardiest species. When mature it is a 10 ft (3 m) high densely-leaved shrub. The July-September flowers have a central boss of fluffy stamens. The variety **'Tarentina'** grows only 3 ft (90 cm) high and produces white berries in autumn. There are also variegated varieties but these are not as hardy as the species. **M. luma** has flaking bark and bears edible fruits.

SITE & SOIL: Any reasonable garden soil — thrives best against a south- or west-facing wall in full sun.

PROPAGATION: Plant cuttings in a propagator in summer.

Myrtus communis

M. communis

Flowering shrub
•
Evergreen or
semi-evergreen

N. domestica

NANDINA Heavenly Bamboo

Heavenly Bamboo is not really a bamboo — it belongs to the berberis family. Nandina has become much more popular in recent years, and one of the reasons is the change in colour as the year progresses. In spring the new foliage is tinged with red and in autumn the green leaves are flushed with orange or purple. In midsummer white flowers appear and these are followed by red berries.

VARIETIES: The large and attractive leaves of **N. domestica** spread outwards and are evergreen, although they may fall in winter if the site is exposed to cold winds and heavy frosts. The cone-shaped flower heads in July are made up of crowded ½ in. (1 cm) starry blooms. It grows to about 4 ft (1.2 m) or more — for a more compact plant with more colourful leaves choose the variety **'Firepower'**.

SITE & SOIL: Any well-drained garden soil will do — thrives best in full sun.

PROPAGATION: Divide clumps in spring.

Nandina domestica
'Firepower'

Border perennial/
rock garden plant
•
Semi-evergreen

N. mussinii

NEPETA Catmint

An old favourite for the front of the herbaceous border — the flowers which appear from late spring to early autumn are loved by bees and the foliage of most species is attractive to cats. The leaves are borne in pairs along the stems and are generally grey-green and aromatic. The small tubular flowers are borne on upright spikes — dead-heading prolongs the flowering season.

VARIETIES: One of the popular species is **N. mussinii** (**N. faassenii**) — it grows about 1 ft (30 cm) high and produces pale purple flowers above lance-shaped or oval leaves. **N. racemosa** is very similar but the leaves are heart-shaped — its dwarf variety **'Little Titch'** (6 in./15 cm) is suitable for the rockery and its tall variety **'Superba'** grows up to 3 ft (90 cm) high. The most widely available Catmint is **N. 'Six Hills Giant'** (2 ft/60 cm, violet flowers).

SITE & SOIL: Any well-drained garden soil will do — thrives best in full sun.

PROPAGATION: Divide clumps in spring.

Nepeta 'Six Hills Giant'

Flowering shrub
•
Evergreen

O. scilloniensis

OLEARIA Daisy Bush

The origin of the common name is obvious when Olearia is in bloom — the bush is covered in small daisy-like flowers. When not in bloom this Australian plant can look gaunt if neglected — trim after flowering to maintain compact growth. All species are sun-lovers and only the most popular varieties are fully hardy. Nearly all are white-petalled.

VARIETIES: The June-flowering tall (8 ft/2.4 m) **O. macrodonta** is a popular choice — the flowers are white and the holly-like leaves are sage green above and silver felted below. The other popular species is **O. haastii**. It has flat heads of white flowers in summer like O. macrodonta but it is smaller (5 ft/1.5 m) and the leaves are quite different — they are box-like. Less hardy than the popular types are **O. scilloniensis**, **O. phlogopappa 'Comber's Pink'** and **'Comber's Blue'**.

SITE & SOIL: Any well-drained garden soil will do — thrives best in full sun.

PROPAGATION: Plant cuttings in a cold frame in summer.

Olearia macrodonta

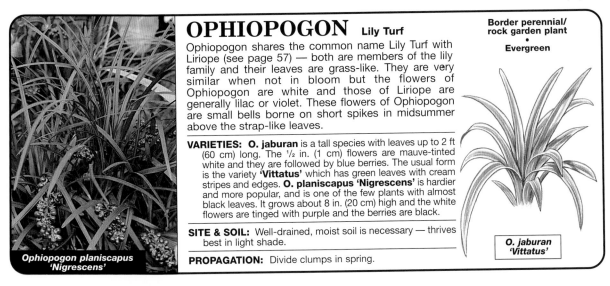

OPHIOPOGON Lily Turf

Border perennial/
rock garden plant
•
Evergreen

Ophiopogon shares the common name Lily Turf with Liriope (see page 57) — both are members of the lily family and their leaves are grass-like. They are very similar when not in bloom but the flowers of Ophiopogon are white and those of Liriope are generally lilac or violet. These flowers of Ophiopogon are small bells borne on short spikes in midsummer above the strap-like leaves.

VARIETIES: **O. jaburan** is a tall species with leaves up to 2 ft (60 cm) long. The ¹/₂ in. (1 cm) flowers are mauve-tinted white and they are followed by blue berries. The usual form is the variety **'Vittatus'** which has green leaves with cream stripes and edges. **O. planiscapus 'Nigrescens'** is hardier and more popular, and is one of the few plants with almost black leaves. It grows about 8 in. (20 cm) high and the white flowers are tinged with purple and the berries are black.

SITE & SOIL: Well-drained, moist soil is necessary — thrives best in light shade.

PROPAGATION: Divide clumps in spring.

Ophiopogon planiscapus 'Nigrescens'

O. jaburan 'Vittatus'

OSMANTHUS Osmanthus

Osmanthus is grown for both its year-round display of attractive foliage and its flowers in either spring or autumn. The shape of the leaves depends on the species — like Olearia on the previous page they may look like box or holly, although these two plants are not related. The white or creamy tubular flowers are small, measuring ¹/₄-¹/₂ in. (0.5-1 cm) across the lobed mouths, but they do have a jasmine-like fragrance. Osmanthus can be used in several ways — its most popular role is as a neat green foil between more colourful shrubs in the border, but it can also be used for hedging, as a woodland plant and for growing against a wall. Pruning is not necessary, but it can be cut back if required.

VARIETIES: You might confuse **O. heterophyllus** with a small holly bush but rabbits do not — holly is ignored but this Osmanthus is readily eaten. It is slow growing but can reach 8 ft (2.4 m) or more in time and it blooms in autumn. Look for the varieties **'Variegatus'** (creamy white-edged leaves), **'Gulftide'** (very spiny leaves) and **'Purpureus'** (purple-tinged leaves). The popular **O. delavayi** is quite different. It is a 5 ft (1.5 m) shrub with arching stems and box-like leaves — the flowers appear in April. One of its hybrids is **O. burkwoodii (Osmarea burkwoodii)**. Like its parents the oval leaves are very finely serrated and its profuse blooms appear in spring. It is, however, more vigorous and may reach 10 ft (3 m) when mature. If you want something different then search the catalogues for **O. yunnanensis** — it grows to 20 ft (6 m) high and the glossy lance-shaped leaves are 8 in. (20 cm) long.

SITE & SOIL: Any well-drained soil will do — thrives in sun or light shade.

PROPAGATION: Layer branches in autumn or plant cuttings in a cold frame in summer.

Osmanthus heterophyllus 'Variegatus'

Flowering shrub
•
Evergreen

Osmanthus delavayi

O. burkwoodii

O. heterophyllus

Osmanthus burkwoodii

**Border perennial/
rock garden plant
•
Evergreen**

OSTEOSPERMUM Osteospermum

This South African daisy has become a popular bedding plant in recent years. The 2-3 in. (5-7.5 cm) wide flowers appear from early June to September and almost cover the plant when soil and light conditions are right. These bedding types are half hardy plants and do not belong in this book, but there is a perennial evergreen species which is reasonably hardy.

VARIETIES: The hardy variety for the border is **O. jucundum**. It grows about 1 ft (30 cm) high — the lance-shaped leaves are pale green and the late spring to autumn flowers are pink or purple with a gold central disc. For the rockery there is the variety **'Compactum'** which grows about 6 in. (15 cm) high — **'Compactum Blackthorn'** has deep purple flowers.

SITE & SOIL: Any well-drained soil will do — thrives best in full sun.

PROPAGATION: Plant cuttings in a cold frame in summer.

O. jucundum

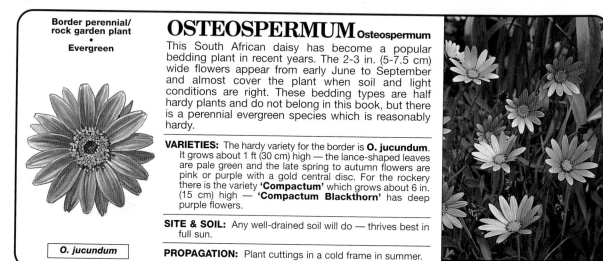

Osteospermum jucundum

**Border perennial
•
Evergreen**

OZOTHAMNUS Ozothamnus

An unusual plant — you will find this one in numerous catalogues but not at the garden centre. The problem is that it is often listed as a rather tender plant suitable only for regions with a mild climate, but there are two species which are reasonably hardy. It is closely related to Helichrysum (page 46) and shares the need for good drainage and full sun and the production of 'everlasting' flowers. It differs from Helichrysum by having reddish-brown flower buds which open to form white flowers with red or brown bracts beneath.

VARIETIES: O. ledifolius is the Kerosene Bush, so called because the leaves and stems are inflammable. In early summer the 2 in. (5 cm) wide flower clusters appear and are followed by decorative seed heads. It grows about 3 ft (90 cm) high — **O. rosmarinifolius** is larger and has rosemary-like leaves.

SITE & SOIL: Requires light, well-drained soil — full sun is essential.

PROPAGATION: Plant cuttings in a cold frame in summer.

O. rosmarinifolius

Ozothamnus ledifolius

**Leafy shrub
•
Evergreen**

PACHYSANDRA Japanese Spurge

It is surprising that Pachysandra is so often ignored when people are looking for ground cover to put in the dense shade under trees and shrubs. This wide-spreading evergreen grows only a few inches high and its densely-packed leathery leaves provide a bright green mat which thrives in sunless conditions. It is remarkably successful in preventing the growth of weeds.

VARIETIES: P. terminalis is the only species you are likely to find and it may not be available at your local garden centre. It is, however, listed in many catalogues and it is an easy plant to propagate. The 4 in. (10 cm) long glossy leaves are borne in clusters on top of the short stems — height is about 8 in. (20 cm). Tiny white blooms on short spikes appear in spring but are of little decorative value. Varieties include **'Green Carpet'** which is even more compact and **'Variegata'** with cream-edged leaves.

SITE & SOIL: Thrives best in moist soil — choose a site in partial or full shade.

PROPAGATION: Divide clumps in autumn.

**P. terminalis
'Variegata'**

Pachysandra terminalis

PARAHEBE Parahebe

Unlike its popular relative Hebe you will not find this one at your local garden centre. It is, however, listed in the catalogues of numerous nurseries and do not be put off by its reputation as a tender plant — several species are reasonably hardy and these are described below. Use Parahebe for ground cover or as a specimen plant in the rockery — cut back straggly shoots in spring.

VARIETIES: **P. catarractae** is the usual one — a spreading plant which grows about 1 ft (30 cm) high and has flowers which are white or pale purple with a central crimson ring. **P. hookeriana** has similar flowers but the blooms of **P. lyallii** are white with pink veins. **P. bidwillii** is a 4 in. (10 cm) dwarf with red-veined white flowers. All the Parahebes are summer-flowering.

SITE & SOIL: Any well-drained garden soil will do — thrives best in full sun.

PROPAGATION: Plant cuttings in a cold frame in early summer.

Flowering shrub
•
Evergreen

P. catarractae

Parahebe catarractae

PENSTEMON Penstemon

Penstemons are excellent plants for the herbaceous border — the colourful tubular flowers on upright spikes add interest all summer long. Choose with care — some are killed by winter frosts. There are a number of species which are both hardy and evergreen or semi-evergreen — the secrets of success are to make sure that the soil is free-draining and to dead-head faded blooms.

VARIETIES: **P. barbatus** is a good example of a hardy border Penstemon with an evergreen or semi-evergreen basal rosette of leaves. It grows about 3 ft (90 cm) high and bears pendent red flowers. Others include **P. 'Hidcote Pink'**, **P. 'Evelyn'** (pink), **P. glaber** (blue), **P. 'Garnet'** (dark red) and **P. digitalis** (white). The most popular shrubby Penstemon is **P. fruticosus** — there are white and purple varieties.

SITE & SOIL: Well-drained soil is essential — thrives best in full sun.

PROPAGATION: Plant cuttings in a cold frame in late summer.

Border perennial/ flowering shrub
•
Evergreen or semi-evergreen

P. 'Evelyn'

Penstemon 'Garnet'

In spring and summer the white-flowered Pyracantha can be overshadowed by its more glamorous neighbours, but in winter it comes into its own. When the roses, lilacs, clematis and so on are brown and lifeless this P. coccinea displays its glossy green leaves and masses of bright berries, the visual effect being enhanced by the snow.

Flowering shrub
•
Evergreen

P. mucronata
'Alba'

PERNETTYA   Prickly Heath

Choose this one if you want a low-growing prickly bush with showy berries which the birds leave alone. Masses of creamy flowers appear in early summer and these are followed in November by large porcelain-like fruits. Male and female flowers are nearly always borne by separate varieties, so you will have to plant more than one type to make sure of berry production.

VARIETIES: **P. mucronata** is now sometimes listed as **Gaultheria mucronata** — **'Bell's Seedling'** (dark pink berries) is the only variety which bears both male and female flowers. Female varieties include **'Cherry Ripe'** (red berries), **'Lilian'** (pink) and the white-berried **'Alba'**, **'Snow White'** and **'White Pearl'**. For male plants look for **'Thymifolia'** or **'Male'** on the label.

SITE & SOIL: Non-alkaline soil is essential — add peat at planting time. Thrives in sun or partial shade.

PROPAGATION: Remove rooted suckers and plant in autumn.

Pernettya mucronata
'Cherry Ripe'

Leafy shrub
•
Evergreen

P. latifolia

PHILLYREA   Phillyrea

Phillyrea is grown in the shrub border or woodland garden to provide a year-round display of strap-shaped or oval leaves on a rounded bush. Unlike its close relative Osmanthus the floral display is usually insignificant and so it is much less popular. These small white or greenish-white flowers are borne in clusters in spring or early summer and are followed by round blue-black berries. In colder areas grow Phillyrea against a south-facing wall.

VARIETIES: **P. angustifolia** is a dense shrub with 3 in. (7.5 cm) narrow dark green leaves — it reaches about 10 ft (3 m) when mature. **P. latifolia** grows to about the same height, but its drooping branches bear glossy oval leaves. With both these two species the flower heads and berries are small — for a much showier floral and berry display grow **P. decora**.

SITE & SOIL: Any well-drained soil will do — thrives best in a sunny and sheltered site.

PROPAGATION: Plant cuttings in a cold frame in summer.

Phillyrea decora

Flowering shrub
•
Evergreen

P. fruticosa

PHLOMIS   Jerusalem Sage

An easy plant to recognise — whorls of hooded flowers are borne on the stems above the foliage. These grey-green leaves are woolly and the flowers appear in mid or late summer. A showy and drought-tolerant plant but it will die in waterlogged soil in winter and with age the plant becomes unattractive. Cut the stems back to 4 in. (10 cm) above the ground each spring.

VARIETIES: **P. fruticosa** is the hardiest and most widely-available species — it soon forms a 3 ft (90 cm) high spreading bush with 2 in. (5 cm) wide whorls of flowers in June and July. For a larger bush and August-September flowers choose **P. 'Edward Bowles'** and buy **P. chrysophylla** if you want yellow leaves. **P. italica** (2 ft/60 cm) bears pale lilac flowers in midsummer.

SITE & SOIL: Any well-drained soil will do — thrives best in a sunny and sheltered site.

PROPAGATION: Plant cuttings in a cold frame in summer.

Phlomis 'Edward Bowles'

Phormium tenax 'Purpureum'

PHORMIUM New Zealand Flax

An architectural plant with sword-like leaves — use it where you want to add a tropical touch in green, yellow, bronze or purple. There are no stems — just a bold clump of leaves which are 2-5 ft (60 cm-1.5 m) long when the plant is mature. It is a slow starter, putting on little growth in the first year, but after a few years Phormium provides an excellent focal point. Mulch the crown in winter.

VARIETIES: **P. cookianum** has arching 2-3 ft (60-90 cm) leaves and small yellow flowers on long stalks — look for **'Tricolor'** (white, red and green leaves), **'Cream Delight'** (green-edged cream) and **'Maori Sunrise'** (red, yellow and bronze). **P. tenax** is taller with small red flowers — look for **'Purpureum'** (purple). Others include **P. 'Sundowner'** (pink and copper), **P. 'Yellow Wave'** (yellow and green) and **P. 'Bronze Baby'** (coppery bronze).

SITE & SOIL: Requires well-drained, moist soil in full sun.

PROPAGATION: Divide mature clumps in spring

Leafy shrub • Evergreen

P. cookianum 'Cream Delight'

Photinia fraseri 'Red Robin'

PHOTINIA Photinia

Photinia fraseri 'Red Robin' arrived from New Zealand after World War II and has become a firm favourite — it is an attractive glossy-leaved shrub all year round and in spring it bears young foliage which is bright red. Cut back once the young foliage has lost its colour — new red leaves will appear. Heads of small white flowers appear on the tips and along the sides of shoots in spring. Red fruits form if the weather is warm and sunny. Plant in a sheltered spot.

VARIETIES: **P. fraseri** is the only species which is widely available and the most popular variety is **'Red Robin'**. The shrub is clothed with dark green oval leaves which are sharply toothed and it grows about 8 ft (2.4 m) high. There are red new leaves in spring like Pieris, but this one will grow in alkaline soil. For a taller-growing plant choose **'Robusta'** — for dark red new growth pick **'Birmingham'**.

SITE & SOIL: Any reasonable soil will do — thrives best in full sun.

PROPAGATION: Plant cuttings in a cold frame in summer.

Leafy shrub • Evergreen

P. fraseri 'Robusta'

For much of the 20th century ferns have been regarded by many gardeners as one of the less desirable features of the Victorian garden and not suitable for a modern setting, but these plants are making a comeback. In a shady setting evergreen types such as Polypodium and Polystichum provide year-round feathery greenery — the one used here for ground cover is Polypodium interjectum.

PHYGELIUS Cape Figwort

Phygelius is a shrub which is in the unusual class because it is susceptible to frost. This should not stop you buying one for your garden. If you live in a relatively mild area plant it against a south-facing wall and in spring trim away any side shoots which have been damaged in winter. In other areas grow it as a border perennial, pruning to ground level in April.

Flowering shrub
•
Evergreen or semi-evergreen

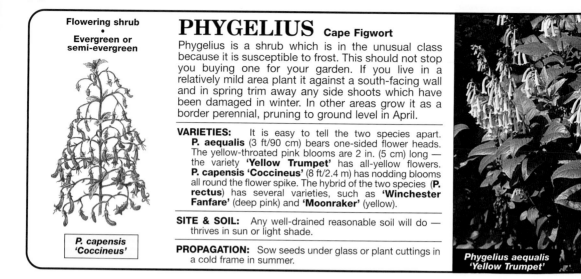

P. capensis 'Coccineus'

VARIETIES: It is easy to tell the two species apart. **P. aequalis** (3 ft/90 cm) bears one-sided flower heads. The yellow-throated pink blooms are 2 in. (5 cm) long — the variety **'Yellow Trumpet'** has all-yellow flowers. **P. capensis 'Coccineus'** (8 ft/2.4 m) has nodding blooms all round the flower spike. The hybrid of the two species (**P. rectus**) has several varieties, such as **'Winchester Fanfare'** (deep pink) and **'Moonraker'** (yellow).

SITE & SOIL: Any well-drained reasonable soil will do — thrives in sun or light shade.

PROPAGATION: Sow seeds under glass or plant cuttings in a cold frame in summer.

Phygelius aequalis 'Yellow Trumpet'

PICEA Spruce

The typical spruce is shaped like a Christmas Tree — a conical plant with branches arranged neatly up the stem in whorls. It may reach no more than a metre high when mature (e.g Picea glauca 'Albertiana Conica') or it may become a woodland giant reaching 50 ft (15 m) or more if P. omorika is chosen. As with Abies (Silver Fir) the leaves are narrow and are borne singly along the stems, and so the two genera are sometimes confused. It is not difficult to tell them apart. Look at a branch which has lost some of its leaves — the leaf base on the branch of a fir is a sunken scar but on a spruce it is a raised peg. It is even easier to spot the difference when cones are present — the fir cone stands upright but the oval or cylindrical spruce cone is always pendent. Not all varieties of Picea conform to the Christmas Tree pattern — there are weeping trees and squat bushes with foliage which may be blue or gold as well as green. These leaves are short and stiff and are often pointed — they are narrower than fir leaves and are often more needle-like than strap-shaped. They tend to be more numerous at the top of a branch than at the base. Spruce is often regarded as a tolerant plant which can be relied upon in difficult situations. Nearly all will thrive in cold and wet soil when they are mature but some are much less tolerant of poor conditions when young. The one area to avoid is dry and chalky soil especially if it is shallow — P. omorika will grow in alkaline soil but the others need neutral or acid soil in order to thrive.

SITE & SOIL: Any reasonable garden soil will do, but avoid a shallow chalky site. Thrives best in full sun.

PROPAGATION: Buy from a reputable supplier. If you have patience raise from seeds sown in a cold frame in spring.

Wait

Picea abies 'Nidiformis'

Conifer
•
Evergreen

P. omorika

Picea abies

Picea abies 'Reflexa'

PICEA continued

VARIETIES: P. abies (Norway Spruce, Common Spruce) is the best known species and countless specimens are sold each year as Christmas Trees. It is not a good garden plant — conical and attractive when young but columnar and often gaunt when mature. Choose a variety instead. **'Nidiformis'** (Bird's Nest Spruce) is a flat-topped bush with horizontal branches arranged in layers — it will reach about a metre when fully grown. **'Reflexa'** is a wide-spreading prostrate shrub which can be used for ground cover — **'Acrocona'** has pendent branches which bear bright red male cones at the tips. If you want a narrowly conical spruce which will grow into a large tree your best choice is the Serbian Spruce (**P. omorika**), and a favourite rockery spruce is **P. glauca 'Albertiana Conica'** which forms a neat dense cone about 3 ft (90 cm) high after 10 years. **P. breweriana** is perhaps the most eye-catching of all — it is a tall broadly conical tree with branches which bear pendulous branchlets. This weeping plant may reach 40 ft (12 m) when fully mature, but it will be no more than 5 ft (1.5 m) tall after 10 years. The shape of P. breweriana may attract more attention than any other spruce but for colour **P. pungens** is unrivalled. This is the Blue Spruce and several varieties are available. **'Koster'** is the most popular one — a conical tree which can reach 25 ft (7.5 m) in time. The foliage is steely blue — if you want the palest blue grow **'Hoopsii'**. Both of these Blue Spruces require staking during the first few years to ensure an even conical shape, but not all the blue varieties are cone-shaped. There are **'Globosa'** (round, irregular) and **'Glauca Prostrata'** (ground cover). An excellent choice for the rockery is **P. mariana 'Nana'** — a dwarf form of Black Spruce which forms a tight ball of foliage reaching 1 ft (30 cm) when fully grown. Very few Picea varieties have yellow foliage — the choice is between two varieties of the tall columnar **P. orientalis**. **'Aurea'** has yellow spring leaves and **'Skylands'** is golden all year round.

Picea omorika

Picea glauca 'Albertiana Conica'

Picea breweriana

Picea pungens 'Globosa'

Picea pungens 'Glauca Prostrata'

Picea mariana 'Nana'

Picea orientalis 'Aurea'

PIERIS Andromeda

In recent years Pieris has increased in popularity and you will now find a range of varieties in most garden centres. Its appeal is obvious — colours change as the seasons progress and there is interest all year round. The glossy oval or lance-shaped leaves may be green or variegated and they clothe the neat and slow-growing bush. In spring the new leaves appear and these are usually brightly coloured — red, pink or white. In addition to this bright foliage display in spring there are the sprays of flowers between March and May. These urn-shaped blooms are ¼-½ in. (0.5-1 cm) long and the white or occasionally pink or red flower heads have a Lily-of-the-Valley look. Grow this one if you have a bare spot in the shrub border, but only if your soil is lime-free.

VARIETIES: The brightest displays of spring foliage are borne by varieties of **P. formosa forrestii**. These are large bushes reaching 8-10 ft (2.4-3 m) when fully grown — the white flowers are borne on 6 in. (15 cm) long tassels. The most popular one is **'Wakehurst'** with bright red young leaves — **'Jermyns'** has deeper red new foliage and red flower buds are present all winter. For earlier flowers (March/April) and petal colours other than white pick a variety of **P. japonica** — examples include **'Blush'** (pink flowers) and **'Valley Valentine'** (red flowers). However, most varieties of P. japonica have white flowers (**'Red Mill'**, **'Purity'** etc) and some such as **'Flaming Silver'** and **'Variegata'** have silver-edged leaves. In addition there are several dwarfs — **'Debutante'** grows about 3 ft (1 m) high and **'Little Heath'** is even more compact. Finally there is the interesting hybrid **P. 'Forest Flame'** — young foliage changes from red to pink, cream and then green.

Pieris formosa forrestii
'Wakehurst'

SITE & SOIL: Acid soil is essential — add peat at planting time. Thrives best in partial shade.

PROPAGATION: Layer shoots in summer.

Flowering shrub
•
Evergreen

Pieris japonica 'Blush'

P. formosa forrestii

P. japonica

Pieris japonica
'Flaming Silver'

Climber
•
Evergreen

P. viburnoides

PILEOSTEGIA Pileostegia

You are unlikely to have heard of this plant if you are not a keen and knowledgeable gardener as it is not often seen and does not appear in many catalogues. It is neither fully hardy nor particularly showy, but it is included here because evergreen flowering climbers are few and far between. It is closely related to Hydrangea, and like H. petiolaris it is self-clinging and so can be used to cover walls.

VARIETIES: P. viburnoides is the only species available — it is a slow-growing climber which will eventually reach a height of 20 ft (6 m) or more. The leathery dark-green leaves are lance-shaped and about 6 in. (15 cm) long — in late summer and autumn the flower heads appear. These are 4-6 in. (10-15 cm) wide and are made up of numerous tiny creamy-white flowers. Cut back if necessary in late winter.

SITE & SOIL: Any well-drained garden soil will do — thrives in sun or partial shade.

PROPAGATION: Plant cuttings in a cold frame or layer shoots in summer.

Pileostegia viburnoides

Pinus sylvestris

PINUS Pine

Most pines are tall trees which are at home in woodland or large gardens but not in the average plot. Grow P. sylvestris, P. nigra, P. ponderosa etc if you really have the space, but choose one of the more compact types if space is limited. The long needles borne by pines make a welcome change from the scale-like foliage or short strap-like leaves which cover the shoots of most other conifers. Pine needles are 2-9 in. (5-22.5 cm) long and are grouped in bundles of 2-5 — young foliage often forms a candle-like structure. The woody cones are 2-3 in. (5-7.5 cm) long and are usually oval. They remain on the tree for several years. Nearly all pines will flourish in sandy soil and make excellent windbreaks near the coast. Some conifers such as Junipers will thrive in partial shade, but pines need a sunny site.

VARIETIES: The Scots Pine **P. sylvestris** will reach 50 ft (15 m) or more when mature. Conical at first but later irregular, this tree has reddish bark and grey-green leaves borne in pairs. Slow-growing varieties include **'Beuvronensis'**, **'Watereri'**, **'Fastigiata'** and **'Aurea'**. The Austrian Pine (**P. nigra nigra**) and the Corsican Pine (**P. nigra laricio**) are good specimen trees for the country estate but for an average garden choose the dwarf **P. nigra 'Hornibrookiana'**. One of the most attractive of all the tall pines is the Bhutan Pine **P. wallichiana** which unlike the others retains its lower branches when mature. The most important of the dwarf species is **P. mugo** — the Mountain Pine. The shape is bushy or prostrate, and the leaves are borne in pairs — look for the varieties **'Gnom'** (squat 2 ft/60 cm high bush) and **'Mops'** (globular 1½ ft/45 cm bush). **P. strobus 'Nana'** is a spreading plant which is about 6 ft/1.8 m high when mature — the foliage is silvery blue-green.

SITE & SOIL: Any well-drained garden soil will do — full sun is necessary.

PROPAGATION: Buy from a reputable supplier — if you have patience sow seeds of species in a cold frame in spring.

Pinus sylvestris 'Aurea'

Conifer
•
Evergreen

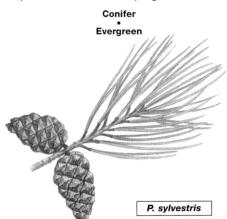

P. sylvestris

Pinus nigra 'Hornibrookiana'

Pinus wallichiana

Pinus mugo

Pinus strobus 'Nana'

Flowering shrub
•
Semi-evergreen

P. laburnifolius

PIPTANTHUS Evergreen Laburnum

The leaves of this shrub are made up of three leaflets and the flower heads bear numerous yellow pea-like blooms, which is what you would expect from a plant with this common name. Despite these similarities it differs in a number of ways from its much better known herbaceous relative. It keeps most of its leaves in winter, the flower heads are erect and it is somewhat tender.

VARIETIES: **P. laburnifolius** (**P. nepalensis**) is the only species. Plant it in the shelter of a wall and it will grow to 10 ft (3 m) or more. The dark green glossy leaflets are about 4 in. (10 cm) long — the bright yellow 1½ in. (3.5 cm) flowers appear in May and June. Pruning is not essential, but some leaves will drop in a cold winter and frost-damaged shoots should be removed in spring.

SITE & SOIL: Well-drained fertile soil is necessary — thrives best in full sun.

PROPAGATION: Layer branches in early summer or plant cuttings in a cold frame in summer.

Piptanthus laburnifolius

Leafy shrub
•
Evergreen

P. tenuifolium

PITTOSPORUM Pittosporum

If you are a flower arranger you may be tempted to buy this shrub when you see it at the garden centre — the branches with attractive green or variegated leaves seem ideal for cutting. It is also a good hedging plant, but only buy Pittosporum if the situation is suitable. It needs a mild location — otherwise grow it against a wall or put it in a pot which can be moved under glass in winter.

VARIETIES: The most popular and one of the hardiest species is **P. tenuifolium**. This slow-growing shrub will reach 12 ft (3.6 m) or more when fully grown — the wavy-edged leaves are grey-green and small purple flowers may appear in May. Varieties include **'Limelight'** (dark green/lime green leaves) and **'Purpureum'** (purple leaves). **P. tobira** has fragrant white flowers in May — **P. 'Garnettii'** has white-edged leaves.

SITE & SOIL: Well-drained soil in a warm and sheltered spot is necessary.

PROPAGATION: Plant cuttings in a cold frame in late summer.

Pittosporum tobira

Conifer
•
Evergreen

P. andinus

PODOCARPUS Podocarpus

You will find this conifer in few nurseries and in even fewer garden books, but in a book on evergreens even rarities like this one find a place. The podocarps grow as shrubs rather than trees and some are yew-like — there are small flattened leaves and fleshy fruits. Grow it in a large rock garden or plant it in a container — all are slow-growing.

VARIETIES: There are several hardy species. **P. nivalis** is a low spreading bush with ½ in. (1 cm) long narrow leaves — female plants bear oval red fruits in autumn. **P. andinus** is another yew-like species, but the fruits look like small pale green plums — with both these species the male plants bear yellow cones. **P. salignus** is quite different from yew — the strap-like leaves are 4 in. (10 cm) long.

SITE & SOIL: Well-drained soil is necessary — thrives best in full sun.

PROPAGATION: Plant cuttings in a cold frame in summer.

Podocarpus salignus

POLYGALA Milkwort

Polygala calcarea

The milkworts are plants for the rockery — low-growing, spreading and in late spring and early summer covered with colourful pea-like flowers. Both the species described below are hardy, but these plants are hard to find despite their attractive appearance and evergreen growth habit. Perhaps the blooms are a little too small for popular appeal, but they are borne in large numbers.

VARIETIES: **P. calcarea** forms a creeping mat with small leathery leaves and blue flowers — choose the variety **'Lillet'** for the brightest display. This species thrives in gritty soil and full sun — for peaty soil and partial shade choose **P. chamaebuxus**. The flowers of this dwarf shrub have purple wings and yellow lips — choose the variety **'Grandiflora'**.

SITE & SOIL: Depends on the species — see above.

PROPAGATION: Plant cuttings in a cold frame in early summer.

Rock garden plant
•
Evergreen

P. chamaebuxus
'Grandiflora'

POLYPODIUM Polypody

Polypodium vulgare

Ferns provide effective ground cover in the border or in the shade of woodland gardens, but there are not many evergreen types from which to make your choice. Two are described on this page. Polypodium does not like wet soil so choose it if the ground is sandy or pick a Polystichum species if the site is moist and humus-rich.

VARIETIES: Common Polypody (**P. vulgare**) is a creeping fern with fronds which are about 1½ ft (45 cm) long. These dark green leaf-like structures have a herring-bone arrangement of pinnae (leaflets) along the mid-rib. The pinnae on the best variety **'Cornubiense'** are divided up again to give a lacy effect. P. vulgare tolerates chalk and provides good ground cover in dry soils — for wetter situations use **P. interjectum**. The roots of **P. glycyrrhiza** have a liquorice taste.

SITE & SOIL: Any well-drained, sandy or gritty soil will do — thrives in sun or partial shade.

PROPAGATION: Divide clumps in spring.

Fern
•
Evergreen

P. vulgare
'Cornubiense'

POLYSTICHUM Shield Fern

Polystichum setiferum
'Divisilobum'

The growth habit of the Shield Fern (Holly Fern) is quite different to the Polypody described above — Polystichum has fronds which form a shuttlecock-like clump and it is not invasive. The ends of the leaflet lobes are sometimes sharply pointed. There are small ones for the rock garden and large ones for the border and woodland garden. Cover the crowns with peat in winter and remove old fronds when new ones appear.

VARIETIES: **P. setiferum** has soft arching fronds which grow up to 4 ft (1.2 m) high — the leaflets are shallowly or deeply cut so that the effect may be feathery or lacy. There are many varieties with widely differing heights and shapes. They include **'Congestum'** (8 in./20 cm) and **'Divisilobum'** (feathery foliage and bulbils on the mid-ribs).

SITE & SOIL: Well-drained, humus-rich soil and partial shade are necessary.

PROPAGATION: Divide clumps in spring.

Fern
•
Evergreen

P. setiferum

Rock garden plant
•
Semi-evergreen

P. auricula

PRIMULA Auricula

There is one group, the auriculas, which can be grown outdoors and retain at least some of their leaves during winter. In Victorian and Edwardian times they were great favourites but have now been relegated to an occasional appearance in rock gardens. There are hundreds of varieties of show and alpine auriculas grown primarily under glass and for exhibition, but here we are concerned with border auriculas which are the easiest and most reliable class to grow outdoors.

VARIETIES: The border auricula class of **P. auricula** hybrids has fleshy spoon-shaped leaves and in March and April there are clusters of fragrant flowers on 4-8 in. (10-20 cm) stalks. Varieties include **'Old Yellow Dusty Miller'** (yellow flowers), **'McWatt's Blue'** (grey-blue) and **'Old Suffolk Bronze'** (red/brown/yellow).

SITE & SOIL: Well-drained, moisture-retentive soil in light shade.

PROPAGATION: Divide clumps after flowering.

Primula auricula
'Old Yellow Dusty Miller'

Flowering shrub
•
Evergreen

P. cuneata

PROSTANTHERA Mint Bush

A neat bush densely covered with tiny leaves for the border or rockery. The white-flowering Prostanthera is available at many garden centres but it has never been a popular plant. The problem is its inability to withstand heavy and prolonged frost in winter but do not let this deter you — grow it against a south-facing wall for an unusual display of white or purple flowers.

VARIETIES: **P. cuneata** is the species you are most likely to find. When fully grown it is a rounded shrub about 1-2 ft (30-60 cm) high with masses of tiny leaves. The edges of these leaves are rolled and they are aromatic when crushed. The $^1/_2$ in. (1 cm) wide white flowers appear in spring. **P. rotundifolia** is a taller and more tender plant with purple bell-shaped flowers in late spring.

SITE & SOIL: Any well-drained, reasonable soil will do — thrives best in full sun.

PROPAGATION: Plant cuttings in a cold frame in summer.

Prostanthera cuneata

Border perennial/
rock garden plant
•
Evergreen

P. grandiflora

PRUNELLA Self-heal

Self-heal is a vigorous ground cover which will spread quite quickly to blanket a large area of bare earth. It will effectively keep down weeds but it will also soon swamp smaller plants, so site it in the border or rockery with care. In midsummer the flower spikes appear, each one bearing a cluster of tubular hooded blooms. Lift and divide the clumps every two or three years.

VARIETIES: **P. grandiflora** grows about 9 in. (22.5 cm) high and bears pale purple flowers during June and July — these blooms are about 1 in. (2.5 cm) long and are dark-lipped. There are a number of varieties in colours other than pale purple. The most popular one is **'Pink Loveliness'** (clear pink) — others include **'Loveliness'** (mauve), **'Alba'** (white) and **'White Loveliness'** (white).

SITE & SOIL: Any reasonable soil will do — thrives in sun or light shade.

PROPAGATION: Divide clumps in autumn or spring.

Prunella grandiflora

Prunus laurocerasus 'Otto Luyken'

Prunus laurocerasus 'Camelliifolia'

PRUNUS Laurel

Most of the species and varieties of Prunus do not belong in this book — they are the flowering cherries, almonds and plums which lose their leaves before the onset of winter. Here we are concerned with the evergreen Prunus species and varieties — these are the laurels which are so popular for screening and hedging. The large glossy leaves and dense growth of tall varieties effectively hide undesirable views and deter intruders — with dwarf varieties the leaves provide excellent weed suppression. In spring or early summer there is a display of white flowers and these are followed by berries. Prune bushes if necessary in late winter and trim hedges in late summer. Use secateurs and not a hedge trimmer — dispose of all clippings as they are poisonous.

VARIETIES: P. laurocerasus (Common or Cherry Laurel) is seen everywhere as it is a favourite shrub for tall hedges. Left unpruned it will reach 15 ft (4.5 m) or more, but it can be cut back hard if required. Candles of small white flowers appear in April and berries in September — red at first and then black. There are numerous varieties. 'Rotundifolia' is chosen for its excellent hedging properties — others include 'Schipkaensis' (best floral display), 'Castlewellan' (white-splashed leaves), 'Otto Luyken' and 'Zabeliana' (ground cover) and 'Camelliifolia' (twisted leaves). P. lusitanica differs in a number of ways from Cherry Laurel — the leaves are smaller and red-stalked and the flower spikes appear in early summer and are longer. It is a better choice for alkaline soil and is the one to grow if you want a smaller hedge or if you plan to trim the shrub into a formal shape. 'Variegata' has white-edged leaves.

SITE & SOIL: Any well-drained, reasonable soil will do — thrives in sun or partial shade.

PROPAGATION: Plant cuttings in a cold frame in summer.

Flowering shrub
•
Evergreen

P. laurocerasus

P. lusitanica

Prunus lusitanica 'Variegata'

Pseudotsuga menziesii 'Fletcheri'

PSEUDOTSUGA Douglas Fir

The Douglas Fir has no place in the garden as a specimen tree — it will reach about 60 ft (18 m) in twenty years. Narrow and conical at first but flat-topped when old, its only garden use is as a tall hedge as it is not harmed by regular clipping. It can easily be mistaken for a Silver Fir (Abies) but the oval cones hang downwards and the soft needles do not have a sucker-like base.

Conifer
•
Evergreen

VARIETIES: P. menziesii (Douglas Fir) is an impressive sight. The corky trunk is deeply furrowed and the graceful lower branches bend upwards. The 1 in. (2.5 cm) leaves are borne in two ranks and have white bands below. A mighty tree, but there are a few slow-growing and dwarf varieties. 'Glauca' (Blue Douglas Fir) reaches 20 ft (6 m) in 20 years — 'Fletcheri' is only 5 ft (1.5 m) high when fully grown.

SITE & SOIL: Well-drained, non-chalky soil in full sun.

PROPAGATION: Buy a pot-grown specimen. If you have patience raise from seeds sown outdoors in spring.

P. menziesii

PULMONARIA Lungwort

Border perennial
•
Evergreen

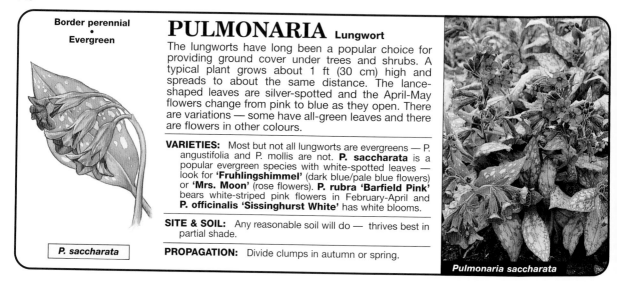

The lungworts have long been a popular choice for providing ground cover under trees and shrubs. A typical plant grows about 1 ft (30 cm) high and spreads to about the same distance. The lance-shaped leaves are silver-spotted and the April-May flowers change from pink to blue as they open. There are variations — some have all-green leaves and there are flowers in other colours.

VARIETIES: Most but not all lungworts are evergreens — P. angustifolia and P. mollis are not. **P. saccharata** is a popular evergreen species with white-spotted leaves — look for **'Fruhlingshimmel'** (dark blue/pale blue flowers) or **'Mrs. Moon'** (rose flowers). **P. rubra 'Barfield Pink'** bears white-striped pink flowers in February-April and **P. officinalis 'Sissinghurst White'** has white blooms.

SITE & SOIL: Any reasonable soil will do — thrives best in partial shade.

PROPAGATION: Divide clumps in autumn or spring.

P. saccharata

Pulmonaria saccharata

PYRACANTHA Firethorn

Few evergreen wall shrubs can match Pyracantha for year-round colour. The attractive oval leaves are 2-3 in. (5-7.5 cm) long and are borne on spiny shoots — this foliage is shiny and the edges are usually toothed. In late spring or early summer the flower heads appear, each one made up of masses of small white flowers — so numerous that with some modern hybrids there are sheets of white covering the stems. These flowers are followed from October until January by a colourful display of berries — yellow, orange or red. Growing against a wall is not its only use — Pyracantha can be planted as a hedge or specimen shrub and the low-growing ones provide useful ground cover. Trim in late winter.

VARIETIES: Firethorns are usually chosen on the basis of the colour of their berries, but you should also think about resistance to disease as some varieties are particularly prone to scab or fireblight infection. Red-berrying types are the most popular choice and **P. coccinea 'Lalandei'** (12 ft/3.6 m) used to be the favourite one but not any more. It produces masses of orange-red berries on its upright branches but it is prone to scab. Recommended reds and orange-reds include **P. rogersiana**, **P. coccinea 'Red Column'** and **P. 'Mohave'** for walls and **P. coccinea 'Red Cushion'** (3 ft/90 cm) for ground cover. **P. 'Orange Glow'** (10 ft/3 m) is perhaps the best of the orange-berrying types — **P. 'Orange Charmer'** is equally vigorous and **P. 'Teton'** has good fireblight resistance. The popular yellows are **P. 'Soleil d'Or'**, **P. atalantioides 'Aurea'** and **P. 'Golden Charmer'**. The variegated-leaf types produce fewer flowers and berries than the all-green ones above.

SITE & SOIL: Any reasonable soil will do. Thrives in sun or partial shade.

PROPAGATION: Plant cuttings in a cold frame in summer.

Pyracantha rogersiana

Flowering shrub
•
Evergreen

P. coccinea 'Lalandei'

P. atalantioides 'Aurea'

Pyracantha 'Orange Glow'

Pyracantha 'Soleil d'Or'

QUERCUS Oak

The oak is a basic feature of parks and large country gardens — tall and broad-headed with acorns in the autumn and lobed leaves which fall in winter. Not all oaks follow this pattern and there is a small group of evergreen and semi-evergreen species. These types which keep some or all of their leaves in winter are generally grown as specimen trees but a few can be used for hedging.

VARIETIES: By far the most popular evergreen species is the Holm Oak (**Q. ilex**). It is an imposing rounded tree with grey bark — white new shoots are attractive in spring and the silvery new foliage matures into lance-shaped, glossy and dark green leaves which are grey below. It can be kept trimmed as a hedge. **Q. coccifera** is another evergreen — semi-evergreens include **Q. lucombeana**.

SITE & SOIL: Any deep reasonable soil will do — thrives in sun or light shade.

PROPAGATION: Plant acorns as soon as they are ripe.

Q. ilex

Quercus ilex

RHAMNUS Buckthorn

This shrub is worth considering if you want a neat pyramidal shape with oval grey-green leaves which are edged in creamy-white. Tiny greenish-white flowers in spring are usually followed by a crop of berries in late summer. It has one snag — some shoots may be killed if the temperature falls below -5°C in winter, so it is a plant which is only fully reliable in the milder areas of the country.

VARIETIES: The variety described above is **R. alaternus 'Argenteovariegata'** and is the only Rhamnus which is widely available. It will reach about 10 ft (3 m) when mature but it can be kept trimmed as a formally-shaped container plant. Provide winter protection if a heavy frost is expected — the green-leaved **R. alaternus** is hardier but less attractive.

SITE & SOIL: Any well-drained reasonable soil will do — thrives in sun or light shade.

PROPAGATION: Plant cuttings in a cold frame in summer.

R. alaternus
'Argenteovariegata'

Rhamnus alaternus
'Argenteovariegata'

The Rhododendron is regarded by many as the queen of the flowering evergreens — glossy leaves all year round and then a spectacular display of blooms in late spring. The usual choice is a large-flowered hybrid, but the Species Rhododendrons should not be ignored. If you have the space there are several tree-like types which can reach 30 ft (9 m) or more, such as R. arboreum 'Roseum' illustrated here.

RHAPHIOLEPIS Rhaphiolepis

Flowering shrub • Evergreen

This is a plant for people who like to grow unusual shrubs. It is an attractive member of the rose family with clusters of starry white, pink or red blooms in spring or summer above oval glossy leaves. It is slow-growing and not fussy about soil type, but it is not fully hardy so a sheltered site is needed. Pruning is not necessary — remove unwanted or damaged branches in spring.

VARIETIES: **R. delacourii** grows to about 6 ft (1.8 m) in time. The pink flowers are borne in 4 in. (10 cm) clusters and provide a showy display, but it is a rather tender plant and needs the shelter of a sunny wall. **'Coates' Crimson'** is a red-flowering variety, but the best Rhaphiolepis to choose is **R. umbellata** which bears heads of ¾ in. (1.5 cm) wide white flowers.

SITE & SOIL: Any well-drained garden soil will do — thrives in sun or light shade.

PROPAGATION: Plant cuttings in a cold frame in summer.

R. delacourii

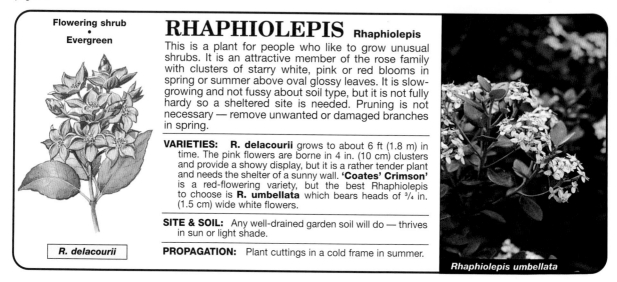

Rhaphiolepis umbellata

RHODODENDRON Rhododendron, Azalea

The number of different species and varieties of Rhododendron is enormous. There are 60 ft (20 m) giants and prostrate ground covers, and flowers from ¼ in. (0.5 cm) to 4 in. (10 cm) across. These blooms may be saucer-, trumpet- or bell-shaped and the leaves may be ¼ in. (0.5 cm) up to 3 ft (90 cm) long. Still, there are a number of common features. All need acid soil to thrive and all are shallow-rooting. Nearly all have oval leaves and as a general rule prefer partial shade to full sun. The usual split is into rhododendrons and azaleas. Azaleas are usually the more compact ones with smaller leaves and daintier flowers but do not take this as an absolute rule — there are 10 ft (3 m) high azaleas and ground-hugging rhododendrons. It seems that rhododendrons have ten stamens and azaleas have a smaller number, but some authorities believe that the separation is wholly artificial. An important point to remember is that not all members of this genus are evergreen. There are three major groups but only two keep their leaves in winter — the rhododendrons and the evergreen (or Japanese) azaleas. The remainder are the deciduous azaleas which include the Ghent, Knap Hill, Exbury and Mollis hybrids. The whole of the floral colour range is covered by the rhododendrons and azaleas apart from true blue and true black. May is the usual flowering time but there are varieties which bloom as early as February and others which do not open until August. Mulch with peat in autumn and water thoroughly in dry weather. Break off dead blooms from large-flowered types — do not damage buds at the base of the flower.

Rhododendron 'John Walter'

SITE & SOIL: Acid soil is essential. Thrives best in partial shade.

PROPAGATION: Layer branches in autumn.

Flowering shrub • Evergreen

Rhododendron 'Fastuosum Flore Pleno'

R. 'Pink Pearl'

R. macabeanum

R. 'Elizabeth'

R. 'Blue Danube'

Rhododendron 'Sappho'

RHODODENDRON continued

VARIETIES: Dealing with the rhododendrons first, the most popular ones are the *Hardy Hybrids* or *Iron-Clad Varieties*. The usual height range is 5-8 ft (1.5-2.4 m) and the flowering season is between April and July depending on the variety. Red-flowering varieties include **'Britannia'**, **'Cynthia'**, **'Doncaster'**, **'Kluis Sensation'**, **'Vulcan'** and the late-flowering **'Lord Roberts'** and **'John Walter'**. Pinks are popular — look for the old favourite **'Pink Pearl'** as well as **'Alice'**, **'Mrs. G.W. Leak'** and **'Gomer Waterer'**. Lavenders and purples range from the pale mauve **'Fastuosum Flore Pleno'** to the blackish-purple **'Purple Splendour'**, and the whites and yellows are represented by many excellent varieties including **'Sappho'** (dark-eyed white) and **'Odee Wright'** (yellow). These Hardy Hybrids are often too tall for a small garden and so the *Dwarf Hybrids* have become popular. These shrubs grow 2-3 ft (60-90 cm) high and bear masses of small flower clusters in April-May. **'Elizabeth'** (red) is the leading one — others include **'Baden-Baden'** (red), **'Blue Diamond'** (lavender), **'Bow Bells'** (pink), **'Carmen'** (red), **'Princess Anne'** (yellow) and **'Snow Lady'** (white). For something more unusual pick a plant from the *Species Rhododendrons*. The most important one is **R. yakushimanum**, a dome-shaped 3 ft (90 cm) bush with pink flowers fading to white. Look out for its excellent hybrids, including **'Surrey Heath'**, **'Percy Wiseman'**, **'Silver Sixpence'**, **'Doc'**, **'Dopey'** and **'Sleepy'**. You will find other species in the catalogues — **R. macabeanum**, **R. arboreum** etc. Finally, the *Evergreen* or *Japanese Azaleas* — 2-4 ft (60 cm-1.2 m) high with sheets of bell-shaped flowers in April or May. These blooms are 1-3 in. (2.5-7.5 cm) across. Examples include **'Addy Wery'** (red), **'Blue Danube'** (violet), **'Hino-mayo'** (pink), **'Mother's Day'** (red), **'Orange Beauty'** (orange), **'Palestrina'** (white), **'Rosebud'** (pink) and **'Vuyk's Rosyred'** (pink).

Rhododendron 'Elizabeth'

Rhododendron 'Blue Diamond'

Rhododendron yakushimanum

Rhododendron macabeanum

Rhododendron 'Blue Danube'

Rhododendron 'Hino-mayo'

Rhododendron 'Orange Beauty'

Flowering shrub
•
Evergreen or semi-evergreen

R. speciosum

RIBES Ornamental Currant

It may seem strange that Ribes is included in a book on evergreens as the old favourite Flowering Currant loses its leaves in winter. However, there are two less popular ones which keep some or all of their leaves all year round. They are worth considering if you want to add a novel touch to the shrub border.

VARIETIES: The one to choose is the semi-evergreen Fuchsia-flowered Currant (**R. speciosum**) — an attractive bush which should be more widely grown. It is not completely hardy but will flourish in the protection provided by a wall or surrounding plants. The upright stems reach about 5 ft (1.5 m) and are clothed with 1 in. (2.5 cm) glossy leaves. In spring clusters of 1 in. (2.5 cm) red fuchsia-like blooms hang down. The hardy evergreen **R. laurifolium** bears greenish-yellow flowers.

SITE & SOIL: Any reasonable soil will do — thrives in sun or partial shade.

PROPAGATION: Plant cuttings outdoors in autumn.

Ribes speciosum

Flowering shrub
•
Semi-evergreen

R. 'Felicite Perpetue'

ROSA Rose

Of all the plants in this book the rose is perhaps the most surprising entry — we all know roses and we all know that the leaves die in winter. This is true for the floribundas, hybrid teas etc which are so popular, but there is a small group of Victorian and new introductions which keep most of their green leaves over winter.

VARIETIES: In Victorian times **R. sempervirens** was used to provide green foliage cover against walls or scrambling over the ground. It is no longer available — its best known hybrid **'Felicite Perpetue'** is a creamy-white rambler with the semi-evergreen properties of its parent. The semi-evergreen habit nowadays has passed to some of the small-leaved patio and ground cover roses as well as a few climbing miniature roses — **'Flower Carpet'** is an example.

SITE & SOIL: Any well-drained, reasonable soil will do — thrives best in full sun.

PROPAGATION: Buy from a reputable supplier.

Rosa 'Flower Carpet'

Flowering shrub
•
Semi-evergreen

R. officinalis

ROSMARINUS Rosemary

Rosemary would be a good plant to grow in the shrub border even if its leaves did not have a use in the kitchen. The upright stems are densely clothed with strap-like leaves which are white-felted below. Masses of small flowers appear along the stems in spring. Use tall varieties for hedging and small ones for ground cover.

VARIETIES: **R. officinalis** (5 ft/1.5 m high, leaves grey-green, flowers lilac-blue) has a number of varieties. The favourite blue one is the tall **'Miss Jessopp's Upright'** (**'Fastigiatus'**) and **'Benenden Blue'** is a smaller arching plant. For a change in flower colour there are **'Albiflorus'** (white) and **'Roseus'** (pink). Low-growing ones (2 ft/ 60 cm) include **'Severn Sea'** and **'Tuscan Blue'**, and there is the 6 in. (15 cm) rockery dwarf **'Prostratus'**.

SITE & SOIL: Well-drained, non-heavy soil is necessary — thrives best in full sun.

PROPAGATION: Plant cuttings in a cold frame in summer.

Rosmarinus officinalis 'Miss Jessopp's Upright'

RUBUS Ornamental Bramble

Most of the ornamental brambles such as the large-flowered R. tridel 'Benenden' and the white-stemmed R. cockburnianus are deciduous but there are also a few interesting evergreens. These are either shrubs or climbers with bristly stems which arch or scramble. The flowers look like single roses and may be pink or white. Cut back ground cover types in spring.

VARIETIES: **R. tricolor** is the most popular evergreen Rubus. This shrub grows about 2 ft (60 cm) high and spreads widely. The creeping stems have red bristles and the 1 in. (2.5 cm) white flowers open in summer — the red fruits which follow are edible but tasteless. **R. 'Betty Ashburner'** is another white-flowered ground cover. **R. henryi bambusarum** is quite different — it is a climber with pink flowers. For double flowers grow the semi-evergreen **R. ulmifolius 'Bellidiflorus'**.

SITE & SOIL: Any reasonable garden soil will do — thrives in sun or partial shade.

PROPAGATION: Plant cuttings in a cold frame in summer.

Flowering shrub
•
Evergreen or semi-evergreen

Rubus tricolor

R. ulmifolius 'Bellidiflorus'

RUTA Rue

Sub-shrub or woody perennial — it depends on which catalogue you read. Rue is a rounded bush which grows about 2-3 ft (60-90 cm) high — it was once widely grown as a herb for medicinal purposes but its place is now in the border or as a low hedge. It is grown for its foliage rather than for its flowers. Wear gloves when handling the leaves — the sap can cause a severe rash.

VARIETIES: **R. graveolens** is the only species you are likely to find — the aromatic leaves are deeply divided which gives a filigree effect of small blue-green lobes. It is grown for this foliage display — the greenish-yellow flowers in early summer are not particularly decorative. A variety is usually chosen rather than the species — **'Jackman's Blue'** (steely blue foliage) or **'Variegata'** (cream-blotched foliage).

SITE & SOIL: Any well-drained reasonable soil will do — thrives in sun or partial shade.

PROPAGATION: Plant cuttings in a cold frame in summer.

Leafy shrub
•
Evergreen

Ruta graveolens 'Jackman's Blue'

R. graveolens

SALVIA Sage

There are several types of Salvia — there are the well-known red-flowered annuals and the blue-flowered border perennials, but these lose their leaves in winter. Here we are concerned with the aromatic types grown for their leaves in the herb garden or border. Lilac-blue flowers appear in early summer but the decorative feature is the soft downy foliage in various colours.

VARIETIES: The basic species is the Common Sage (**S. officinalis**) — height 2 ft (60 cm), spread 3 ft (90 cm), grey-green leaves 3 in. (7.5 cm) long. A coloured-leaf variety is usually chosen — examples include **'Icterina'** (yellow-edged green), **'Kew Gold'** (yellow), **'Purpurascens'** (reddish-purple) and the multicoloured **'Tricolor'** (pink/purple/cream/grey-green).

SITE & SOIL: Any well-drained reasonable soil will do — thrives in sun or light shade.

PROPAGATION: Plant cuttings in a cold frame in summer.

Leafy shrub
•
Evergreen

Salvia officinalis 'Tricolor'

S. officinalis 'Icterina'

Flowering shrub
•
Evergreen

| S. rosmarinifolia |

SANTOLINA   Cotton Lavender

A dual purpose plant — all year round the mounded bush provides an attractive display of narrow, finely-divided leaves which are aromatic, and in summer there is a mass of button-like flowers. Grow it as a specimen plant or a low hedge — both leaf colour and bush shape are improved if the flower buds are removed. Every few years prune back hard in April.

VARIETIES: The popular variety is **S. chamaecyparissus** — height 1½ ft (45 cm), spread 3 ft (90 cm), silvery-grey foliage and yellow flowers in June-August. The varieties **'Nana'** and **'Small-Ness'** are denser and more compact, and **S. neapolitana** is taller. For creamy-white flowers grow **S. chamaecyparissus 'Edward Bowles'**. The green-leaved species is **S. rosmarinifolia** (**S. virens**).

SITE & SOIL: Any well-drained reasonable soil will do — full sun is essential.

PROPAGATION: Plant cuttings in a cold frame in summer.

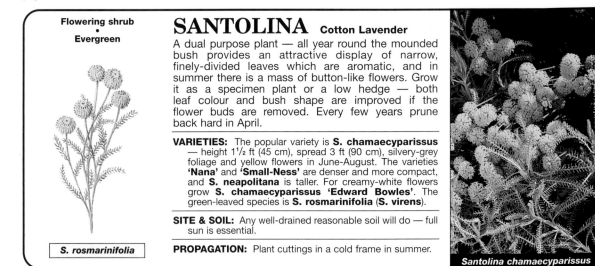

Santolina chamaecyparissus

Flowering shrub
•
Evergreen

| S. hookeriana 'Digyna' |

SARCOCOCCA   Christmas Box

A shrub much loved by flower arrangers — its branches provide useful material for late winter arrangements. In February and March clusters of white- or cream-petalled male flowers and tiny female flowers are borne along the stems. These fragrant blooms are followed by red or black berries. Most varieties sucker freely and so spread may have to be contained.

VARIETIES: **S. confusa** grows about 2½ ft (75 cm) high. The oval leaves are glossy and dark green, and the cream-coloured flowers are followed by black berries. This species is a rounded bush — for a taller suckering variety choose **S. hookeriana 'Digyna'**. A good dwarf for ground cover is **S. humilis** and for broad leaves and red berries choose **S. ruscifolia**.

SITE & SOIL: Any well-drained soil including chalky ones will do — thrives in sun or partial shade.

PROPAGATION: Plant suckers in autumn or cuttings in a cold frame in summer.

Sarcococca humilis

The brilliant leaf colour of some evergreens can light up a bed or border all year round. This is especially welcome in winter, but even in summer this Choisya ternata 'Sundance' rivals any yellow-flowered shrub in full bloom. Behind the Choisya is the variegated evergreen Elaeagnus pungens 'Dicksonii' and the purple-leaved deciduous shrub Cotinus coggygria 'Royal Purple'.

SAXIFRAGA Saxifrage

There are border Saxifrages with 3 in. (7.5 cm) long leaves and at the other end of the scale there are mossy mounds of tiny leaves. Most Saxifraga species are rockery plants which form either leafy rosettes or a mossy mat. From this mound or mat upright flower stalks bearing loose clusters of starry flowers appear in spring or early summer. The range of colours includes white, yellow, pink, red and purple. This extensive genus is divided into 14 or more groups, but for garden purposes only four need be considered.

VARIETIES: The *Border* group consists of large plants with rosettes or clumps of leaves from which arise branching slender stems with masses of starry flowers. The best known evergreen is London Pride (**S. urbium**) which grows 1 ft (30 cm) high and flowers between May and July. **S. umbrosa primuloides** is a larger-leaved and less invasive species. The *Encrusted* or *Silver* group is made up of plants with rosettes of lime-encrusted leaves and starry flowers in May-July. Examples are **S. paniculata** (1 ft/30 cm, white), **S. cotyledon** (2 ft/60 cm, white), **S. cochlearis** (8 in./20 cm, white) and **S. 'Esther'** (6 in./15 cm, cream). The *Mossy* group contains plants which form moss-like hummocks and bear star- or saucer-shaped flowers in April-May. The single species **S. moschata** (3 in./7.5 cm) has many varieties, such as **'Cloth of Gold'** (white, leaves yellow), **'Hi-Ace'** (pink) and **'Pixie'** (rose red). Finally there is the *Cushion* group which form a low mound of lime-encrusted leaves and flowers in February-April. **S. burseriana** (2 in./5 cm, white) is a late-winter variety — for early spring flowers try **S. apiculata** (4 in./10 cm, yellow). Other evergreens include **S. 'Elizabethae'** (yellow), **S. 'Jenkinsiae'** (pink) and **S. 'Cranbourne'** (pink).

SITE & SOIL: All require well-drained soil. Choose a moist spot with some shade — only the Encrusted group will thrive in full sun.

PROPAGATION: Separate rosettes or divide clumps. Plant in a cold frame in summer.

Rock garden plant/
border perennial
•
Evergreen

Saxifraga urbium

Saxifraga moschata 'Cloth of Gold'

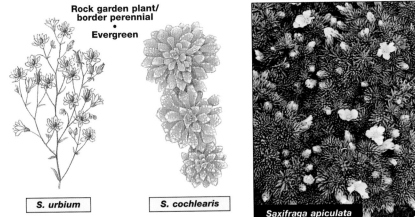
S. urbium | S. cochlearis

Saxifraga apiculata

SCHIZOSTYLIS Kaffir Lily

Despite its common name this bulbous plant belongs to the iris and not the lily family. Use it in the middle of the border where its miniature gladioli-like flowers will add colour at the end of the season. Schizostylis cannot tolerate dryness at the roots, so it is a plant for humus-rich soil and thorough watering during prolonged dry spells. It is an evergreen, but the usual practice is to cut down the stems when flowering is over and to cover the crowns with leaf mould or peat.

VARIETIES: **S. coccinea** (height 2 ft/60 cm, flowers 1½ in./3.5 cm wide, flowering period September-November) has numerous varieties. **'Mrs. Hegarty'** is a pink one which blooms earlier than the others but **'Viscountess Byng'** (pink) does not bloom until November. Look for **'Sunrise'** (salmon-pink), **'Alba'** (white) and **'Major'** (large, deep red).

SITE & SOIL: Well-drained but moist soil is necessary — thrives in sun or light shade.

PROPAGATION: Divide clumps in spring.

Bulb
•
Evergreen

S. coccinea

Schizostylis coccinea 'Mrs. Hegarty'

Conifer
•
Evergreen

| S. verticillata |

SCIADOPITYS Japanese Umbrella Pine

This rarity from Japan is not for the garden centre shopper — you will have to search through the catalogues to find a supplier. There is just one species and the leaf form is quite different from other conifers. The leaves look like pine needles but they are arranged in whorls of 10-30 around the stem like the spokes of an umbrella — hence the common name. Another feature of this unusual conifer is its peeling red bark.

VARIETIES: **S. verticillata** is an extremely slow-growing conifer which becomes an attractive broadly conical specimen tree in time, reaching 20 ft (6 m) perhaps but only about 3 ft (90 cm) after 10 years. The needles are about 5 in. (12.5 cm) long and the 4 in. (10 cm) cones are green at first and brown when mature. The main shoot will have to be staked for the first few years.

SITE & SOIL: Well-drained, non-alkaline soil is necessary and so is partial shade.

PROPAGATION: Buy from a reputable supplier.

Sciadopitys verticillata

SEDUM Stonecrop

The Sedums are a large genus of fleshy-leaved plants. A few grow to 1-2 ft (30-60 cm) and bear flower heads which are large plates of tiny flowers. These are the ice plants which belong in the herbaceous border and lose their leaves in winter. Here we are concerned with the much larger section — the stonecrops which belong in the rockery and are usually evergreen. They sprawl or form a mat of small leaves and are generally easy to grow, thriving in infertile and dry soil. Five-petalled starry flowers, borne either singly or in flat heads, appear in midsummer. They are easy to propagate and deserve their popularity as carpeters for cracks and crevices.

Sedum acre

VARIETIES: The best known member of the evergreen stonecrop group is the Common Stonecrop (**S. acre**). It grows about 2 in. (5 cm) high and has yellow flowers in 1 in. (2.5 cm) heads in June-July — even more colourful is the yellow-leaved variety **'Aureum'**. This species is useful if you have a large area of poor ground to cover, but in a rockery it is better to choose a plant which is less invasive. There are **S. album 'Coral Carpet'** (height 4 in./10 cm, spread 10 in./25 cm) with red leaves and pink flowers, and the old favourite **S. spathulifolium** with small rosettes of silver-grey leaves and flat heads of yellow flowers. The variety **'Purpureum'** has purple leaves and the foliage of **'Cape Blanco'** is powdery white. For white, red or purple flowers choose a variety of **S. spurium** (height 3 in./7.5 cm, spread 1 ft/30 cm). Perhaps the most colourful of all the stonecrops is **S. kamtschaticum 'Variegatum'** — yellow and orange flowers above cream- and red-edged leaves.

SITE & SOIL: Any well-drained soil will do — thrives best in full sun.

PROPAGATION: Divide clumps in autumn or spring.

Rock garden plant
•
Evergreen

Sedum spathulifolium 'Purpureum'

S. kamtschaticum 'Variegatum'

S. spathulifolium

Sedum spurium

SEMPERVIVUM Houseleek

The days when houseleeks were used to cover roofs of houses are over, but this succulent remains a popular resident in the rockery. It is grown for the ball-like rosettes of fleshy leaves, and the many varieties show a wide range of colour, texture, hairiness etc. Yellow, red or purple flowers appear on thick stalks in summer — the rosette at the base dies when flowering comes to an end.

Rock garden plant
•
Evergreen

VARIETIES: The Common Houseleek (**S. tectorum**) produces 4 in. (10 cm) wide rosettes made up of purple-tipped leaves — rosy purple flowers appear in July. For more colourful leaves try **S. 'Commander Hay'** (green-tipped purple) or **S. 'Rubin'** (reddish-bronze). The Cobweb Houseleek (**S. arachnoideum**) has small rosettes which are densely covered with white threads.

SITE & SOIL: Any well-drained soil will do — full sun is necessary.

PROPAGATION: Remove and plant offsets in spring.

Sempervivum arachnoideum

S. tectorum

SENECIO Senecio

Senecio is an extensive and extremely varied genus. There are annuals, shrubs, succulent house plants etc and leaves vary from green balls to silver filigree. The range of evergreens for growing outdoors is much more limited, but there is still a wide variation. First of all there are the Dusty Millers. These are mound-forming plants with felted grey or silvery leaves — they are usually grown as half-hardy annuals but these plants are really shrubby evergreens which will survive winter frosts in most areas. Flowers are insignificant and should be removed at the bud stage — the senecios grown for their flowers as well as their attractive felted leaves include the popular S. 'Sunshine' which is the hardiest of all the garden senecios.

VARIETIES: All the evergreen senecios have alternative names, which is a source of confusion for the gardener. There are several latin names for Dusty Miller — it will be listed as **Senecio maritimus**, **S. cineraria**, **S. bicolor**, **S. candicans** or **Cineraria maritima**. The range of varieties is more limited — most catalogues list only **'Silver Dust'** which has silvery-white lace-like leaves and grows about 1 ft (30 cm) high. **'White Diamond'** is the variety which is usually grown as a border perennial rather than an annual — it will reach about 1½ ft (45 cm) and has less divided and greyer leaves. **'Cirrhus'** has notched rather than deeply-divided leaves and the leaf colour changes from silvery-green to silvery-white. The flowering senecios have leathery leaves covered with silvery down and bright yellow daisy-like flowers in June. Common Senecio is **S. 'Sunshine'** (**Brachyglottis 'Sunshine'**) and grows about 3 ft (90 cm) high. **S. monroi** has crinkle-edged leaves and **S. hectoris** (8 ft/2.4 m) is a rather tender white-flowered species.

SITE & SOIL: Any well-drained soil will do — full sun and a sheltered site are necessary.

PROPAGATION: Plant cuttings in a cold frame in summer or sow seeds under glass in early spring.

Flowering shrub
•
Evergreen

Senecio maritimus 'White Diamond'

Senecio maritimus 'Cirrhus'

S. maritimus

S. 'Sunshine'

Senecio 'Sunshine'

Conifer
•
Evergreen

S. sempervirens

SEQUOIA Californian Redwood

The world's tallest tree — the record stands at over 360 ft (108 m) in the U.S. A column-like giant with drooping branches and spongy bark — a specimen for a large park or woodland area but totally unsuitable for the garden. It does, however, have a couple of dwarf forms. These small varieties are slow growing at first but will often revert and become tall trees if not pruned each year.

VARIETIES: There is just one species — **S. sempervirens** which grows to 20 ft (6 m) or more in about 10 years. The strap-like pointed needles are about ½ in. (1 cm) long and small globular cones are borne at the ends of the branches. The variety **'Adpressa'** has creamy-white growing tips and reaches about 4 ft (1.2 m) in 10 years — **'Prostrata'** is even more compact. Cut both back regularly.

SITE & SOIL: Any well-drained soil will do — thrives in sun or light shade.

PROPAGATION: Buy from a reputable supplier.

Sequoia sempervirens 'Adpressa'

Conifer
•
Evergreen

S. giganteum

SEQUOIADENDRON Wellingtonia

Another thick-barked American giant like Sequoia above — a popular specimen tree for planting in grand gardens in Victorian times but its popularity declined in the 20th century. Shorter but broader than the Californian Redwood, it is the world's largest living thing and is a tree to admire but not to plant. Slower-growing varieties are available, but they are hard to find.

VARIETIES: **S. giganteum** is the Wellingtonia or Big Tree, and specimens reaching 60 ft (18 m) or more are to be seen around many stately homes. The size may be similar to the Sequoia but the branches look quite different. The leaves are small and awl-shaped and the colour is blue-green — the cones are oval and about 3 in. (7.5 cm) long. The variety **'Pendulum'** grows much more slowly.

SITE & SOIL: Any well-drained soil will do — thrives in sun or light shade.

PROPAGATION: Buy from a reputable supplier.

Sequoiadendron giganteum 'Pendulum'

Rock garden plant/
border perennial
•
Evergreen or
semi-evergreen

S. schafta

SILENE Campion

Silene is an easy plant to grow in the rockery or in the crevices of a wall if the conditions are right. Sun and sandy soil are essential — poor drainage and shade will lead to death or a disappointing display. It is a carpeting plant with leaves which are soft, narrow and hairy. The flat-faced tubular flowers appear in late spring, midsummer or autumn, depending on the species you choose.

VARIETIES: Moss Campion (**S. acaulis**) forms a dense mat about 2 in. (5 cm) high — the pink flowers with notched petals are almost stemless and appear in May-June. **S. alpestris** is a taller plant with loose clusters of starry white flowers in June-August — choose the double-flowered variety **'Flore Pleno'**. The Sea Campion (**S. maritima 'Flore Pleno'**) has double white flowers and **S. schafta** provides a pink July-October display. **S. dioica** is a 2½ ft (75 cm) semi-evergreen for the border.

SITE & SOIL: Well-drained soil and full sun are essential.

PROPAGATION: Plant cuttings in a cold frame in summer.

Silene acaulis

SISYRINCHIUM Sisyrinchium

Border perennial/ rock garden plant
•
Evergreen or semi-evergreen

This member of the iris family shows its relationship by developing rhizomes in the soil and by producing erect fans of sword-like leaves. The flowers, however, are quite different to the iris — the simple Sisyrinchium blooms are star- or cup-shaped. The flowers are not long-lived but they appear over a long period. The only problem is that the taller types sometimes die after a few years.

VARIETIES: Two 9 in. (22.5 cm) high rockery species are called Blue-eyed Grass — both of them (**S. angustifolium** and **S. bermudianum**) bear blue flowers between June and September. Grow **S. 'Mrs. Spivey'** for white flowers — **S. brachypus** is a 4 in. (10 cm) yellow-flowered dwarf. **S. striatum** is the one for the border, with whorls of pale yellow flowers on 2 ft (60 cm) stalks in early summer. The variety **'Aunt May'** has yellow-striped leaves.

SITE & SOIL: Requires well-drained, humus-rich soil in full sun.

PROPAGATION: Divide clumps in autumn or spring.

S. angustifolium

Sisyrinchium striatum

SKIMMIA Skimmia

Flowering shrub
•
Evergreen

One of the best choices you can make for the small border or the front of a large shrub border if your soil is neutral or acid. All year round there is a display of shiny aromatic leaves and in March and April there are prominent clusters of tiny white flowers. On female plants there is the added interest of glossy berries in autumn and winter. Pruning is not necessary.

VARIETIES: Nearly all the Skimmias offered for sale are varieties of **S. japonica** (2-4 ft/60 cm-1.2 m) — you will need one male plant for every three or four females. Popular females include **'Bowles' Dwarf Female'** (compact), **'Veitchii'** (large heads of red berries) and **'Fructu Albo'** (white berries). Males to try are **'Fragrans'** (very fragrant) and **'Rubella'** (red flower buds all winter). If you can only have one grow the bisexual **S. reevesiana**.

SITE & SOIL: Any well-drained, non-alkaline soil will do — thrives in partial shade.

PROPAGATION: Plant cuttings in a cold frame in summer.

S. japonica

Skimmia japonica 'Fructu Albo'

SOLANUM Perennial Nightshade

Climber
•
Semi-evergreen

Flowering climbers which are evergreen or semi-evergreen are hard to find so this plant is worth looking for. It is not fully hardy, but with the most reliable species (S. crispum) you should not have a problem if you can provide some shelter and grow it against a south- or west-facing wall. The small blooms are borne in large clusters from June to October. Cut back any unwanted growth in April.

VARIETIES: The usual choice and the hardiest species is **S. crispum**, the Chilean Potato Vine. It is a fast-growing, weak-stemmed shrub rather than a true climber and so some tying-in will be necessary. It will reach 15 ft (4.5 m) or more. Flowers are yellow-centred mauve — choose the variety **'Glasnevin'**. **S. jasminoides** is a blue-flowered true climber which is less hardy — **'Album'** is a white-flowered variety.

SITE & SOIL: Any well-drained soil will do — plant in full sun.

PROPAGATION: Layer stems in summer.

S. crispum

Solanum crispum 'Glasnevin'

Flowering shrub
• Evergreen

S. tetraptera

SOPHORA Sophora

A showy shrub or tree which can reach 15 ft (4.5 m) or more when fully grown. However it develops slowly and reaches only about 5 ft (1.5 m) after 10 years. It is well worth planting if you live in a reasonably mild area and can give the plant the protection of a south-facing wall. It bears attractive leaves, flowers and seed pods, and does not require regular pruning.

VARIETIES: The usual choice is the New Zealand Laburnum (**S. tetraptera**). Like laburnum it is a member of the pea family and bears masses of yellow pendent flowers in spring, but these blooms are tubular rather than pea-like. The 1 ft (30 cm) long leaves are made up of scores of tiny leaflets and the seed pods have prominent wings. **S. microphylla** is hardier and the leaves and flowers are smaller.

SITE & SOIL: Well-drained, light soil is necessary — full sun is essential.

PROPAGATION: Plant cuttings in a cold frame in summer.

Sophora microphylla

Border perennial
• Evergreen

S. byzantina
'Silver Carpet'

STACHYS Lambs' Ears

You can do no better than Stachys if you want a dense silvery ground cover which will provide maximum weed suppression. The thick oval or lance-shaped leaves are densely covered with white and grey wool. Most but not all varieties bear woolly flower spikes in summer — the small purple blooms are borne in whorls around these stems but add little to the display.

VARIETIES: The basic species is **S. byzantina (S. lanata, S. olympica)**. It grows about 1½ ft (45 cm) high with a 2 ft (60 cm) spread and 4 in. (10 cm) long leaves. For large (10 in./25 cm) leaves choose the variety **'Big Ears'** — for leaves with a yellow tinge grow **'Primrose Heron'**. The non-flowering **'Silver Carpet'** (4 in./10 cm high) is a grey-green carpeter.

SITE & SOIL: Any well-drained soil will do — thrives in sun or partial shade.

PROPAGATION: Divide clumps in autumn or spring.

Stachys byzantina

Grass
• Evergreen or semi-evergreen

S. gigantea

STIPA Feather Grass

If you are one of the growing band of grass enthusiasts then Stipa should be at the top of your list if you are looking for a bold specimen plant which is evergreen and bears feathery flower heads. The leaves are narrow and the tall stems bear arching panicles of tiny silvery, purple, green or golden flowers. Choose carefully — not all species are evergreen.

VARIETIES: **S. arundinacea** is a golden-leaved species which grows about 3 ft (90 cm) high and bears drooping heads of purple-tinged grass flowers in late summer. **S. gigantea** (Golden Oats) is a bigger plant — the oat-like flower heads are 6 ft (1.8 m) high, rising above the rolled green leaves and changing from purplish-green to yellow as they ripen. Stipa flower heads can be dried for flower arranging.

SITE & SOIL: Any well-drained soil will do — thrives best in full sun.

PROPAGATION: Divide clumps in late spring.

Stipa arundinacea

STRANVAESIA Stranvaesia

Flowering shrub
•
Evergreen

Some books and catalogues have accepted the scientists' view that this plant should now be listed as a species of Photinia. In this book and most garden centres the Stranvaesia name has been retained. It is a spreading shrub with lance-shaped leaves — hawthorn-like flower heads appear in May and these are followed by bunches of bright berries all winter long.

VARIETIES: S. davidiana is the only species you will find. It is a tall shrub reaching 10 ft (3 m) or more with narrow leathery leaves — old foliage turns bright red in winter. It is grown mainly for its winter display of red berries, and so it looks more like Cotoneaster than Photinia. **'Fructu Luteo'** (6 ft/1.8 m) is a yellow-berried form and **'Prostrata'** (1 ft/30 cm) is used for ground cover.

SITE & SOIL: Any well-drained soil will do — thrives in sun or partial shade.

PROPAGATION: Layer branches in spring.

S. davidiana

Stranvaesia davidiana 'Fructu Luteo'

SYMPHYTUM Comfrey

Border perennial
•
Evergreen

Comfrey was widely grown in earlier times as a medicinal herb but these days it is used either for the compost-activating properties of its leaves or as a vigorous ground cover in woodland areas or on shady sites. Two words of warning — it can be invasive and contact with the coarse hairy leaves can result in a rash. Drooping heads of tubular flowers appear in spring or summer.

VARIETIES: S. grandiflorum (*S. ibericum*) grows about 1 ft (30 cm) high — the lance-shaped leaves are about 10 in. (25 cm) long and the creamy-yellow flowers open in May. **S. 'Hidcote Pink'** and **S. 'Hidcote Blue'** offer other colours. For yellow-edged leaves grow **S. 'Goldsmith'** and for white-edged ones pick **S. uplandicum 'Variegatum'** (3 ft/90 cm, purplish-pink flowers).

SITE & SOIL: Any reasonable soil in sun or partial shade.

PROPAGATION: Divide clumps in spring.

Symphytum 'Hidcote Pink'

S. grandiflorum

Evergreens can offer more than a display of attractive green leaves during the winter months. Many bear flowers and some produce an eye-catching display of berries — a few possess all three features. The example in the photograph is Skimmia japonica 'Bowles Dwarf' with white flowers and over-wintered red berries showing among the dark green foliage in spring. Other foliage/flower/fruiting types include varieties of Berberis, Pieris, Cotoneaster and Pyracantha.

TAXUS Yew

Yew is more tolerant of unfavourable conditions than most other conifers. It can cope with chalky soil, shade and air pollution but it cannot tolerate badly-drained soil which is waterlogged in winter. The ¾-1½ in. (1.5-3.5 cm) long needles are borne in two rows and the male and female flowers are borne on separate plants. The females bear ¾ in. (1.5 cm) red fleshy fruits which contain a single seed. It is a slow-growing conifer and the usual leaf colour is dark green — a plant we associate with churchyards and formal hedging. It is unfortunate that we regard yews in such a limited way — there are other colours than dark green and other shapes than the shrubby form which is kept trimmed as a hedge. Finally, a word of warning — leaves and fruits are poisonous.

Taxus baccata

VARIETIES: The Common or English Yew (**T. baccata**) is an upright and dense small tree or large shrub which has been grown as a garden plant for centuries. If you want a specimen tree or bush it is better to choose one of the many varieties. The usual selection for a column-like tree is **'Fastigiata'** (Irish Yew) which has an ultimate height of about 15 ft (4.5 m) — for coloured leaves there are the yellow-splashed **'F. Aurea'**, the yellow-edged **'F. Aureomarginata'** and the dwarf yellow **'F. Standishii'**. The most popular of the low-growing yews are the yellow-leaved variety **'Summergold'** and the brightest of all the Golden Yews — the male variety **'Semperaurea'**. The best of the wide-spreading ground covers is **'Repandens'** which reaches only 2 ft (60 cm) after 10 years. T. baccata is the most popular but not the only species — **T. media 'Hicksii'** is a dark green rounded bush and **T. cuspidata 'Nana'** is a slow-growing spreading yew.

SITE & SOIL: Any well-drained soil will do — thrives in sun or partial shade.

PROPAGATION: Buy from a reputable supplier.

Conifer
•
Evergreen

Taxus baccata 'Fastigiata'

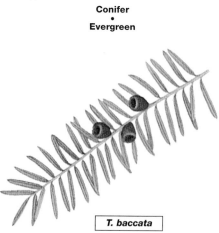
T. baccata

Taxus baccata 'Fastigiata Aurea'

Taxus baccata 'Semperaurea'

Taxus baccata 'Repandens'

Taxus media 'Hicksii'

TELLIMA Fringecup

Like its close relative Tiarella this ground-covering plant has lobed leaves with prominent veins. They may look similar at first glance but Tellima has bell-shaped flowers which are pale green and not white frothy stars like Tiarella. Choose this plant for ground cover or to edge the border if you live in a dry area — it withstands drought much better than most garden plants.

VARIETIES: T. grandiflora is the only species you can buy. It grows as a 1½ ft (45 cm) high clump of hairy maple-like leaves and spreads to 1½-2 ft (45-60 cm). In May and June the 2 ft (60 cm) flower stalks appear — each ½ in. (1 cm) bloom on the spike is fringed and turns reddish with age. The variety **'Purpurea'** has purplish leaves and pink-edged flowers.

SITE & SOIL: Any well-drained soil will do — thrives in sun or partial shade.

PROPAGATION: Divide clumps in autumn or spring.

Tellima grandiflora

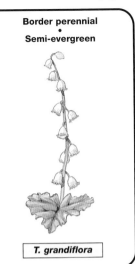

T. grandiflora

TEUCRIUM Germander

The germanders are shrubs or sub-shrubs which bear heads of two-lipped flowers throughout the summer. The stems are square in cross-section and all need sun and free-draining soil. Not many types are widely available, but they do range from tall woody shrubs to low-growing leafy mounds, and from plants which are completely hardy to tender ones needing winter protection.

VARIETIES: The Shrubby Germander (**T. fruticans**) is a 5 ft (1.5 m) shrub with stems and undersides of leaves covered with silvery down. The pale blue flowers appear from June to October — **'Azureum'** is the best variety and **'Compactum'** is the smallest. It needs winter protection, unlike the fully hardy Wall Germander **T. chamaedrys** (1½ ft/45 cm, pink flowers) and **T. aroanium** (3 in./7.5 cm, purple flowers).

SITE & SOIL: Requires well-drained soil and full sun.

PROPAGATION: Plant cuttings in a cold frame in summer.

Teucrium fruticans

T. chamaedrys

There are several evergreen trees and shrubs which can be used to add a Mediterranean touch to your garden. Palms are an obvious choice, but only Trachycarpus fortunei is hardy enough for our climate. As shown here its fan-like leaves are impressive, but they need the protection of a site sheltered from cold winds. Other exotic evergreens include Cordyline, Phormium and Yucca.

THUJA Arbor-vitae

This group of conifers has several uses in the garden. There are dwarfs for the rockery and also fine specimen trees for the border or lawn. In addition there are types suitable for hedging — trim Thuja hedges in spring and again in late summer. The tiny, scale-like leaves are grouped in fours around the stems and these leafy branchlets form flattened sprays like the more popular Chamaecyparis. To tell the difference crush a branchlet — most Thujas are aromatic. A more reliable way of telling them apart is to look at the cones — the Thuja ones are small and elongated with scales which curl outwards when ripe. All require free-draining soil — yellow varieties need full sun.

VARIETIES: **T. occidentalis** (White Cedar) is one of the three basic species. There are a number of excellent dwarfs with **'Rheingold'** topping the list. This deep gold conical bush reaches about 3 ft (90 cm) after 10 years — another yellow variety which grows to the same height is the spherical **'Golden Globe'**. For a green sphere choose **'Little Champion'** and for a narrow cone pick **'Holmstrup'**. The smallest variety is the true miniature **'Hetz Midget'** — a dark green globe which reaches only 9 in. (22.5 cm) in 10 years and a tall one for hedging is **'Smaragd'**. **T. orientalis** (Chinese Arbor-vitae) bears its branches in flattened sprays — the popular one is the dwarf **'Aurea Nana'** with golden yellow leaves which change to bronzy green in winter. **'Rosedalis'** is even more colourful, changing from spring yellow to summer pale green and then autumn/winter purple. **T. plicata** (Western Red Cedar) is a tall pyramidal tree suitable for hedging — the variety **'Zebrina'** has yellow banded leaves.

Thuja occidentalis 'Rheingold'

SITE & SOIL: Any well-drained soil will do — thrives in sun or light shade.

PROPAGATION: Buy from a reputable supplier.

Conifer
•
Evergreen

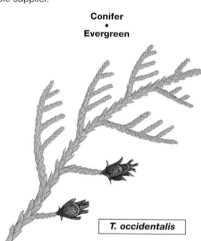

T. occidentalis

Thuja occidentalis 'Hetz Midget'

Thuja orientalis

Thuja orientalis 'Aurea Nana'

Thuja orientalis 'Rosedalis'

Thuja plicata 'Zebrina'

Thujopsis dolabrata

THUJOPSIS Thujopsis

Conifer
•
Evergreen

This slow-growing Japanese conifer is related to the much more popular Tsuga, but despite the close family link it is quite easy to tell them apart. The leaves and branches of Thujopsis are larger and these shiny leaves are silvery grey below. The cones are also different. The Thujopsis cone is a ½ in. (1 cm) sphere with fleshy grey-green scales ripening to brown — each of these scales is pointed at the tip.

VARIETIES: The only species which is available is **T. dolabrata** (Hiba Arbor-vitae). It provides a good specimen tree in a sheltered site — a densely-leaved wide pyramid which will reach about 8 ft (2.4 m) in about 10 years and about 25 ft (7.5 m) when fully mature. Choose the dwarf variety **'Nana'** if you want a 3 ft (90 cm) flat-topped bush or **'Aurea'** if you prefer yellow leaves.

SITE & SOIL: Requires well-drained, humus-rich soil in a sheltered site. Thrives best in full sun.

PROPAGATION: Buy from a reputable supplier.

T. dolabrata

THYMUS Thyme

Thyme is a basic feature of most herb gardens but is much less widely used as a decorative garden plant. It should be more widely grown as there is a profusion of flowers in early summer on an easy-to-grow plant. The carpeting varieties can be used to provide sheets of colour in the rock garden or to fill cracks between paving stones. It has few rivals in this latter function — thyme can happily withstand foot traffic and has the bonus of being fragrant when crushed in this way. In addition to the carpeters there are dwarf bushy varieties which can be grown in the border or the rock garden. There are a couple of cultural points — thyme will not succeed if your soil is acid or heavy, and remember to cut back the stems of bushy types in spring.

Thymus serpyllum
'Albus'

VARIETIES: The major carpeting species is **T. serpyllum**. The mat of trailing stems and small oval leaves spreads for about 2 ft (60 cm) but grows no more than 1-3 in. (2.5-7.5 cm) high and in May-July ½ in. (1 cm) rounded heads of flowers appear. There are numerous varieties from which to make your choice. **'Pink Chintz'** (flesh pink flowers) is the most popular one, but you will also find **'Snowdrift'** (white), **'Albus'** (white), **'Annie Hall'** (pink), **'Minor'** (pink), **'Minimus'** (pink), **'Goldstream'** (mauve) and **'Coccineus'** (red). **T. 'Bressingham'** is a widely available pink-flowered carpeter — another popular carpeting hybrid is **T. 'Doone Valley'**. Most popular dwarf bushy thymes are varieties of **T. citriodorus**, the Lemon-scented Thyme. It grows about 1 ft (30 cm) high with lance-shaped leaves and oval flower heads — there are several variegated varieties including **'Silver Queen'** (silver/green leaves), **'Golden King'** (gold-edged green) and **'Bertram Anderson'** (yellow-splashed green).

SITE & SOIL: Requires well-drained light soil in full sun.

PROPAGATION: Divide clumps in autumn or spring, or plant cuttings in a cold frame in summer.

Rock garden plant/
border perennial
•
Evergreen

Thymus 'Bressingham'

T. serpyllum

Thymus citriodorus
'Golden King'

TIARELLA Foam Flower

Border perennial • Evergreen or semi-evergreen

T. cordifolia

Tiarella forms a mound of lobed and toothed leaves which are prominently veined and turn bronze or red in winter. In early summer spikes of small frothy flowers appear which give the plant its common name. Some species are invasive and all provide an effective weed-suppressing ground cover. It will grow happily under trees and the flowering period is usually prolonged.

VARIETIES: **T. cordifolia** grows about 8 in. (20 cm) high and spreads quite rapidly to produce an evergreen carpet of tightly-packed 4 in. (10 cm) long leaves. In May and June there are upright flower stalks bearing tiny white starry blooms. **T. wherryi** is taller (1 ft/30 cm), blooms later, has pink-tinged flowers and is not invasive. **T. polyphylla** is even taller (1½ ft/45 cm).

SITE & SOIL: Any moisture-retentive soil will do — thrives best in partial shade.

PROPAGATION: Divide clumps in autumn or spring.

Tiarella wherryi

TRACHELOSPERMUM Star Jasmine

Climber • Evergreen

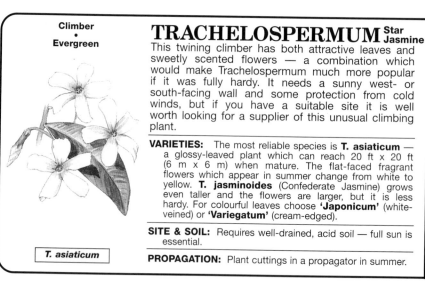

T. asiaticum

This twining climber has both attractive leaves and sweetly scented flowers — a combination which would make Trachelospermum much more popular if it was fully hardy. It needs a sunny west- or south-facing wall and some protection from cold winds, but if you have a suitable site it is well worth looking for a supplier of this unusual climbing plant.

VARIETIES: The most reliable species is **T. asiaticum** — a glossy-leaved plant which can reach 20 ft x 20 ft (6 m x 6 m) when mature. The flat-faced fragrant flowers which appear in summer change from white to yellow. **T. jasminoides** (Confederate Jasmine) grows even taller and the flowers are larger, but it is less hardy. For colourful leaves choose **'Japonicum'** (white-veined) or **'Variegatum'** (cream-edged).

SITE & SOIL: Requires well-drained, acid soil — full sun is essential.

PROPAGATION: Plant cuttings in a propagator in summer.

Trachelospermum jasminoides

TRACHYCARPUS Windmill Palm

Tree • Evergreen

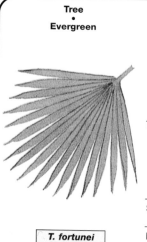

T. fortunei

There is nothing to rival a palm tree if you want to give a tropical touch to the garden, but there is only one which can be considered hardy. This is the Chusan or Windmill Palm, and even though it can withstand winter frosts in most areas it will require some protection from icy winds. Each leaf is large and fan-shaped with a stalk which is toothed. Remove dead leaves to display the stem.

VARIETIES: **T. fortunei** has a stout unbranched trunk which reaches about 10 ft (3 m) when mature. The stiff leaves measuring up to 3 ft (90 cm) across are borne on the top of the trunk and large flower heads of small yellow blooms appear in early summer — these are followed by round black fruits in autumn. T. fortunei is widely available, but varieties are hard to find.

SITE & SOIL: Well-drained soil is necessary — choose a sunny, sheltered site.

PROPAGATION: Buy from a reputable supplier.

Trachycarpus fortunei

TSUGA Hemlock

Hemlock is not one of the popular conifers like Spruce, Juniper, Chamaecyparis etc which you can find in great variety at most garden centres. The range on offer is usually very small and you will have to look through the catalogues for most varieties. It is still a plant worth considering as it has a charm of its own. The yew-like branches are thin and arch at the tips and this gives the tree or bush an unusually graceful appearance. The short, flat needles are borne in two ranks and are generally white-banded below — a point of recognition is that these needles are variable in size. The cones which are borne at the tips of the branchlets are small and egg-shaped. All types are fully hardy and shade-tolerant.

VARIETIES: About seven species of Tsuga are available but you are likely to find only two — the Eastern Hemlock (T. canadensis) and Western Hemlock (T. heterophylla). **T. canadensis** is an elegant tree which usually has several trunks arising from near the base. It is too tall for the average garden and so one of the more compact varieties is usually chosen. **'Pendula'** forms a low spreading mound of overlapping and drooping branches — it is slow-growing but the eventual spread may be 15 ft (4.5 m) or more. **'Jeddeloh'** is a dome-shaped shrub with a mature height of 5 ft x 5 ft (1.5 m x 1.5 m) — **'Bennett'** grows to a similar size. **T. heterophylla** is even taller than T. canadensis, capable of reaching 100 ft (30 m) or more. It is a slender, glossy-leaved giant which will not grow in chalky ground like T. canadensis — its prime requirement is moist soil. A fine specimen tree for the large estate but not for the ordinary garden.

SITE & SOIL: Well-drained, humus-rich soil is necessary — thrives in sun or partial shade.

PROPAGATION: Buy from a reputable supplier.

Tsuga canadensis

Tsuga canadensis 'Pendula'

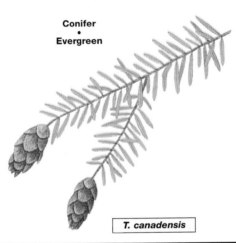

Conifer
•
Evergreen

T. canadensis

Tsuga heterophylla

ULEX Gorse

The yellow pea-like flowers and spiny stems of Ulex are to be seen in spring in dry-soil areas throughout the country — a common wild flower but an uncommon garden plant. Its problem in the garden is its fussy requirements — sandy or stony soil, free drainage, low fertility and no lime. It does not like transplanting — buy a small, container-grown specimen.

VARIETIES: **U. europaeus** is the Gorse, Furze or Whin seen in the countryside, but you will have to buy a plant if you want one and not dig up a shrub which is growing wild. It grows about 6 ft (1.8 m) high, flowering in March-May and then on and off throughout the year. A better choice is the semi-double variety **'Flore Pleno'** (4 ft/1.2 m). **U. gallii 'Mizzen'** (2 ft/60 cm) flowers in autumn.

SITE & SOIL: Avoid fertile and humus-rich soils. Thrives best in full sun.

PROPAGATION: Plant cuttings in a cold frame in summer.

Flowering shrub
•
Evergreen

U. europaeus
'Flore Pleno'

Ulex gallii 'Mizzen'

Flowering shrub
•
Evergreen

V. nummularia

VACCINIUM Vaccinium

Vaccinium is a plant with special needs. It will fail if the soil is not acid and moist, so it is a plant for humus-rich soil in which shrubs like rhododendron flourish. Some species are bushy and upright and others are low and spreading — some but not all are evergreen. Urn-shaped pendent flowers are borne in clusters and are followed by berries in autumn.

VARIETIES: **V. ovatum** is an example of the tall species. It grows to 4 ft (1.2 m) and in early summer white flowers open above the glossy oval leaves — the black berries are edible. **V. floribundum** (3 ft x 6 ft/90 cm x 1.8 m, pink flowers, red berries) is another large vaccinium. Low-growing ones include **V. vitis 'Koralle'** (Cowberry) and **V. nummularia**.

SITE & SOIL: Well-drained, acid and moist soil is essential — thrives best in light shade.

PROPAGATION: Plant cuttings in a cold frame in summer.

Vaccinium floribundum

Border perennial/ rock garden plant
•
Evergreen or semi-evergreen

V. phoeniceum

VERBASCUM Mullein

Verbascum is a familiar sight at the back of the herbaceous border — tall spires of densely-packed yellow flowers above a basal rosette of woolly leaves. This is not the whole story as there are dwarf species for the rockery and there are other colours than yellow. Many types are evergreen or semi-evergreen and some are short-lived. Stake tall varieties.

VARIETIES: Yellow-flowered giants reaching 6 ft (1.8 m) or more include **V. bombyciferum, V. 'C. L. Adams'** and **V. olympicum**. There is a larger selection in the 3-4 ft (90 cm-1.2 m) range — examples include **V. chaixii** (yellow flowers), **V. densiflorum** (yellow), **V. 'Gainsborough'** (yellow) and **V. phoeniceum** (purple). The most popular rockery species is **V. 'Letitia'** (1 ft/30 cm, yellow).

SITE & SOIL: Any well-drained garden soil will do — thrives best in full sun.

PROPAGATION: Strike root cuttings in winter.

Verbascum bombyciferum

Border perennial/ rock garden plant
•
Evergreen or semi-evergreen

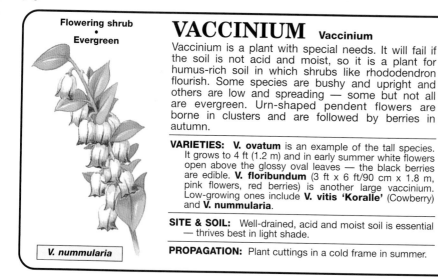

V. spicata

VERONICA Speedwell

The speedwells are a large genus of white-, blue-, purple- or pink-flowered plants which usually bear their small flat-faced blooms on tall and narrow spikes. They range in height from 1 in. (2.5 cm) to 5 ft (1.5 m) so read the label before you buy, and remember that most types are not evergreen. An easy plant to grow if the soil drains freely and you water in prolonged dry weather.

VARIETIES: The most popular semi-evergreen species for the border is **V. spicata** and its silvery-leaved subspecies **V. spicata incana** (height 1½ ft/45 cm, flowering period June-July). There are several evergreen and semi-evergreen types which grow to 6 in. (15 cm) or less — look for **V. pectinata** (dark blue), **V. cinerea** (silvery leaves, dark blue), **V. beccabunga** (blue) and **V. prostrata** (white, blue or pink).

SITE & SOIL: Well-drained soil is necessary — thrives in full sun or light shade.

PROPAGATION: Divide clumps in autumn or spring.

Veronica cinerea

VIBURNUM Viburnum

Viburnums are one of the basic building blocks of the shrub or mixed border. There are spring-flowering and winter-flowering species as well as autumn-berrying ones, and in each of these three major groups you will find at least one evergreen species. Nearly all are easy to grow and they will do well in most soils including chalky ones. Pruning is not necessary — cut back damaged or unwanted branches on evergreens in May. There is no standard leaf form nor flower head pattern although nearly all are pink in bud and white in flower. Depending on height and shape you will find viburnums which can be used for hedging, growing against a wall, spreading as ground cover or planting as specimen shrubs.

Viburnum tinus

VARIETIES: By far the most popular evergreen in the winter-flowering group is Laurustinus (**V. tinus**). This dense and upright shrub with glossy oval leaves grows about 10 ft (3 m) high — between December and April the clusters of pink buds which cover the bush open into small white flowers. Grow it as a specimen bush or use it for hedging — there are several excellent varieties, including **'Eve Price'** (red buds, pink and white flowers) and **'Gwenllian'** (pale pink flowers). The favourite spring-flowering evergreen is **V. burkwoodii** (6 ft/1.8 m, white fragrant flowers in April-May) — for large heads of pink flowers choose the variety **'Park Farm Hybrid'**. The autumn-berrying group is dominated by the deciduous V. opulus — the popular evergreen is **V. davidii** (3 ft/ 90 cm, blue berries if a male plant is nearby). At large garden centres you will find several other evergreen viburnums, such as **V. rhytidophyllum** (10 ft/3 m, large leaves) and **V. 'Pragense'** (10 ft/3 m, deeply-veined glossy leaves).

SITE & SOIL: Requires well-drained soil — thrives best in humus-rich ground in sun or light shade.

PROPAGATION: Layer branches in autumn or plant cuttings in a cold frame in summer.

Flowering shrub
•
Evergreen

Viburnum tinus 'Gwenllian'

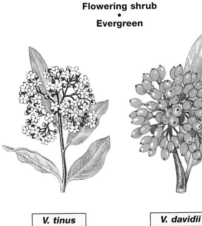

V. tinus

V. davidii

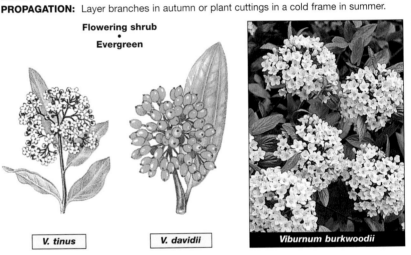

Viburnum burkwoodii

Viburnum davidii

Viburnum rhytidophyllum

Viburnum 'Pragense'

VINCA Periwinkle

The lowly periwinkle may not seem appealing when surrounded by showy plants at the garden centre, but it can play an important role. The trailing stems root into the soil as they spread and the tangled mat of shoots and oval leaves forms a splendid ground cover around shrubs. Above this carpet of green or variegated leaves starry or saucer-faced flowers appear on short stalks between May and September. The main flush of blooms occurs before midsummer, but there will be occasional flowers all summer long in a sunny site. Vinca is a grow-anywhere plant which will survive if not thrive in deep shade and poor soil. The only problem is that some varieties can be very invasive — trim back the shoots of all Vincas in spring.

VARIETIES: **V. major** is the Large Periwinkle with 2 in. (5 cm) long leaves and 1 in. (2.5 cm) wide mauve flowers. The variegated varieties are **'Variegata'** (cream-edged green leaves) and **'Maculata'** (yellow-edged green). This species can be very invasive so avoid planting close to small plants. It grows about 1 ft (30 cm) high — for a lower-growing and less invasive plant choose **V. minor** (Lesser Periwinkle). It reaches about 4 in. (10 cm) but will spread to 3 ft (90 cm) or more. The leaves are narrower and the petals are smaller than V. major and there is a greater choice of colours. The flowers of the species are mauve — variety colours include **'Gertrude Jekyll'** (white), **'Bowles' Variety'** (blue) and **'Atropurpurea'** (purple). For variegated leaves choose **'Aureovariegata'** (yellow-edged green leaves) or **'Alba Variegata'** (cream-edged green). **V. difformis** is similar in size to V. major but the lilac flowers appear in October-December.

SITE & SOIL: Any well-drained soil will do — thrives in sun or partial shade.

PROPAGATION: Divide plants or remove rooted shoots in autumn or winter.

Vinca major 'Variegata'

Flowering shrub
•
Evergreen

Vinca minor 'Atropurpurea'

V. major

V. minor

Vinca minor 'Alba Variegata'

Border perennial/
rock garden plant
•
Evergreen or
semi-evergreen

V. cornuta

VIOLA Violet

Violets have lost the popularity they enjoyed in Victorian times — their place has been taken by the large-flowered violas and pansies which are bedded out each year. But the small-flowered evergreen species of Viola have their own special charm for the front of the border, the rockery or as ground cover. The 1/2-1 in. (1-2.5 cm) wide blooms should be dead-headed regularly — water in dry weather.

VARIETIES: There are two species for the herbaceous border. **V. cornuta** (Horned Violet) grows 6-9 in. (15-22.5 cm) high and blooms in May-August — varieties include **'Alba'** (white) and **'Lilacina'** (lilac). **V. odorata** (Sweet Violet) is smaller and blooms earlier. Violas for the rock garden include **V. gracilis**, **V. labradorica**, **V. jooi**, **V. lutea** and the yellow-flowered **V. aetolica** and **V. biflora**.

SITE & SOIL: Requires well-drained soil in sun or light shade.

PROPAGATION: Divide clumps in autumn or plant cuttings in a cold frame in summer.

Viola odorata

WALDSTEINIA Waldsteinia

Border perennial/ rock garden plant
•
Semi-evergreen

A low-growing, spreading plant for the woodland garden, front of the border or the rockery. It is a member of the rose family, and the ½ in. (1 cm) wide 5-petalled yellow flowers are similar to the blooms of Potentilla. These flowers are borne in loose clusters above the lobed leaves in late spring and early summer. It can be invasive so do not plant close to small or delicate alpines.

VARIETIES: The only species you are likely to find at the garden centre is **W. ternata** which grows about 4 in. (10 cm) high but spreads to 2 ft (60 cm) or more. The 3-lobed leaves are toothed and about 2 in. (5 cm) long. You may find **W. geoides** in a few catalogues — the leaves have 5 lobes and the flowers are larger. The downy-leaved **W. fragarioides** is even harder to find.

SITE & SOIL: Any well-drained soil will do — thrives in sun or partial shade.

PROPAGATION: Divide clumps in spring.

W. ternata

Waldsteinia ternata

YUCCA Yucca

Flowering shrub
•
Evergreen

Several leafy plants described on the previous pages are used to give an exotic touch to the garden — Cordyline, Phormium, Trachycarpus etc, but Yucca has an added advantage. After a couple of years tall flower stalks clothed with 2-3 in. (5-7.5 cm) long bell-shaped blooms appear in summer.

VARIETIES: The most popular Yucca is Adam's Needle (**Y. filamentosa**) — the 2 ft (60 cm) stiff leaves at the base bear white threads along the edges and the flower stalks are 4-6 ft (1.2-1.8 m) high. For yellow-edged leaves grow the variety **'Bright Edge'** or **'Variegata'**. **Y. flaccida** is a very similar species, but the leaves are less rigid — the varieties **'Golden Sword'** (yellow-striped leaves) and **'Ivory'** (large flower heads) are popular. **Y. gloriosa** has bayonet-tipped foliage.

SITE & SOIL: Requires well-drained soil — thrives best in full sun.

PROPAGATION: Remove rooted offsets and plant in spring.

Y. filamentosa

Yucca gloriosa

ZENOBIA Zenobia

Flowering shrub
•
Semi-evergreen

The last plant in this book is also the last plant the gardener is likely to think of when choosing something for an acid bed to accompany Rhododendron or Camellia. Pieris, Calluna, Leucothoe and Kalmia are to be found at the garden centre but not Zenobia. There is no reason why it should not be more widely grown — it is hardy and displays a variety of colours as the season progresses.

VARIETIES: **Z. pulverulenta** is the only species. The young stems and leaves are silvery at first but this bloom disappears as the foliage matures. In autumn both stems and the 2 in. (5 cm) long oval leaves turn orange. In June-July there is the floral display — pendent ½ in. (1 cm) white bells with an aniseed-like fragrance. Remove flower stems when the blooms have faded.

SITE & SOIL: Acid soil is necessary — requires partial shade.

PROPAGATION: Layer shoots in spring or plant cuttings in a cold frame in summer.

Z. pulverulenta

Zenobia pulverulenta

CHAPTER 3

GROWING EVERGREENS

It is quite impossible to generalise about the proper way to buy, plant and care for evergreens. The range of types extends from bulbs to border plants and from giant trees to tiny alpines. The range of cultural needs extends from boggy ground to sandy soil and from shade to full sun. To ensure success, follow a simple two-step plan.

Firstly, if you are not experienced then read a basic guide on the care of the type of plant in question. There are many good reference books available these days — in the Expert series there are The Bulb Expert, Tree & Shrub Expert, Flower Expert etc. You will find that there is more to planting than just digging a hole and popping in a plant and you will discover that the correct way to water, prune, mulch etc are techniques which must be learnt if you want to be a successful gardener.

Secondly, check that the plant you intend to buy is suitable for the site you have in mind. Anticipated height and spread, space available, soil acidity, shade, exposure to strong winds, soil texture and the likelihood of heavy frosts can all be key points. Don't let a pretty picture be the deciding factor when making your choice — read the label carefully and look in a book if the instructions attached to the plant are too sketchy.

With woody evergreens such as conifers, shrubs and climbers it is necessary to take several measures in addition to the two basic steps outlined above. The reason for these extra measures is the simple fact that plants which keep their leaves in winter are more at risk during the season of frost and snow than are deciduous plants with similar cultural requirements. It is therefore essential that a newly-planted specimen should develop fresh roots as quickly as possible so that water uptake from the soil in the garden can take place.

The first impact of this need for quick rooting is at the buying stage. Conifers and evergreen shrubs are not bought as bare-rooted plants. These 'bare roots' are bought from the garden centre or mail order nursery — the popular form these days is a brightly-coloured pack containing a young plant from which the soil around the roots has been removed and then replaced by moist peat. An inexpensive way of buying plants, but not suitable for evergreens as the absence of any root activity after planting would result in leaf fall. Your choice of planting material is restricted to container-grown specimens or balled plants where the roots are growing in soil or compost — see page 101.

Planting time like planting material is also restricted. With deciduous trees and shrubs you can plant out at any time as long as the soil is neither frozen nor waterlogged. With evergreens there is the additional restriction of avoiding planting when the soil is too cold to allow root development — this means that you should not plant during the late autumn-early spring period. Staking at the planting stage is often essential, especially with tall and leafy plants which are sure to be dislodged by strong winds if left unsecured.

The extra care required by evergreens continues after planting. The first few months are critical and on no account should you allow the soil around the root ball to dry out. Copious watering every week is essential during dry weather and the likelihood of leaf browning of conifers can be reduced by spraying the foliage with water in the morning or evening if the weather is hot and dry. Mulching is another great help in the battle against drought.

With established plants winter can be a trying time as the foliage is exposed to the elements. The weight of snow can break branches and icy winds can scorch the foliage — read the section on winter protection on page 106.

You can increase your stock at home of nearly all the plants in this book, but the amount of work and skill involved varies enormously. In general leave conifers to the nurseryman, but at the other end of the scale dividing up clumps of border perennials and rock garden plants is a job which anyone can do, and so is taking hardwood cuttings — see page 109.

BUYING

Buying good quality stock is important, whether it is a bag of bulbs or a choice specimen plant. This is especially true with conifers and shrubs where the purchase can represent a considerable outlay. Wherever possible inspect the plants beforehand and look for both good and bad signs — see below. The size to choose is a complex point. Don't assume you should buy the biggest one you can afford. Large old shrubs and trees take a long time to establish and are often overtaken by young, vigorous and much less expensive specimens. The smallest size also has its drawbacks — although inexpensive a small plant can be a recently rooted cutting which may take some time to become established in the garden.

CONTAINER-GROWN PLANT

Bad Signs

Soil ball comes up easily when the plant is gently tugged. This usually indicates that the plant has recently been lifted from open ground

Thick root growing downwards from the base of the container into the bed. This indicates starvation or the plant has been in the container too long

Dry soil, thick exposed roots and/or dense weed growth on the surface

Splits or tears in the container

Good Signs

Absence of leaf discoloration or marginal scorch. No symptoms of disease or pest attack

Small roots peeping through the container and a few weeds or algal growth on the surface indicate that the plant is well-established

Growth is not one-sided and no indication that stems have been cut back

Stems well-clothed with leaves

BALLED PLANT

Bad Signs

Growth is lop-sided. This is usually associated with patches of brown foliage or stems where leaf fall has clearly occurred

Girdling roots growing horizontally around the stem at the top of the soil ball. You can feel these girdling roots through the wrapping

Soil ball is obviously broken or the surface soil below the hessian or netting is dry

Good Signs

The stem is sturdy and the plant is clothed with healthy leaves. No signs of drastic pruning are present, which might indicate the removal of damaged or diseased parts

Soil ball is large for the size of the plant and the wrapping of hessian, nylon netting or polythene sheeting is tight

Soil ball feels firm and has not been squashed out of shape. No signs of dryness

PLANTING

Poor planting rather than poor stock is often the reason for failure. If the site is starved and compacted then it is a good idea to dig over the area and incorporate a good supply of compost or rotted manure a week or two before you intend to plant. Incorporate a slow-acting fertilizer such as Bone Meal if you wish, but do not use a standard quick-acting one. The ideal time for planting conifers and evergreen shrubs is early September-mid October while the soil is still warm — if you miss the autumn planting date then try to choose April when the winter chill has left the soil. Follow the five steps to successful planting on page 103 — after planting put a mulch around the stem to reduce moisture loss, to keep the surface cool in summer and to reduce the weed problem.

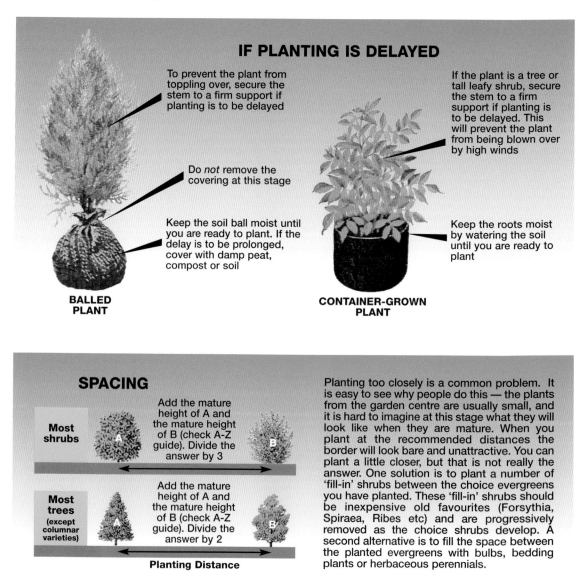

IF PLANTING IS DELAYED

To prevent the plant from toppling over, secure the stem to a firm support if planting is to be delayed

Do *not* remove the covering at this stage

Keep the soil ball moist until you are ready to plant. If the delay is to be prolonged, cover with damp peat, compost or soil

BALLED PLANT

If the plant is a tree or tall leafy shrub, secure the stem to a firm support if planting is to be delayed. This will prevent the plant from being blown over by high winds

Keep the roots moist by watering the soil until you are ready to plant

CONTAINER-GROWN PLANT

SPACING

Most shrubs
A B
Add the mature height of A and the mature height of B (check A-Z guide). Divide the answer by 3

Most trees (except columnar varieties)
A B
Add the mature height of A and the mature height of B (check A-Z guide). Divide the answer by 2

Planting Distance

Planting too closely is a common problem. It is easy to see why people do this — the plants from the garden centre are usually small, and it is hard to imagine at this stage what they will look like when they are mature. When you plant at the recommended distances the border will look bare and unattractive. You can plant a little closer, but that is not really the answer. One solution is to plant a number of 'fill-in' shrubs between the choice evergreens you have planted. These 'fill-in' shrubs should be inexpensive old favourites (Forsythia, Spiraea, Ribes etc) and are progressively removed as the choice shrubs develop. A second alternative is to fill the space between the planted evergreens with bulbs, bedding plants or herbaceous perennials.

THE PLANTING OPERATION

Planting Mixture
Make up the planting mixture in a wheelbarrow on a day when the soil is reasonably dry and friable — 1 part topsoil and 1 part moist peat. Keep this mixture in a shed or garage until you are ready to start planting.

① Choose a day when the soil is moist but not soaking wet. Squeeze a handful of soil — it should be wet enough to form a ball and yet dry enough to shatter when dropped on to a hard surface

④ Examine the exposed surface — cut away circling roots and gently tease out some of the roots at the sides, but do not break up the soil ball. Fill the space between the soil ball and the sides of the hole with planting mixture. Firm down the planting mixture with your hands

③ The container should have been watered thoroughly. Cut down the side of the container when it is stood in the hole. Remove the cover and its base very carefully

⑤ After planting there should be a shallow water-holding basin. Water in after planting

② The hole should be deep enough to ensure that the top of the soil ball will be about 1 in. (2.5 cm) below the soil surface after planting. The hole should be wide enough for the soil ball to be surrounded by a 3-4 in. (7.5-10 cm) layer of planting mixture. Put a 1 in. (2.5 cm) layer of planting mixture (see above) at the bottom of the hole

STAKING

Note that the information on staking is included in the Planting section. This is the time to secure a tree or tall shrub and not when it has been dislodged or blown over by strong winds. Driving in a stake next to the stem is the traditional way to secure a tree but it is not recommended for container-grown plants as the soil ball would be disturbed. It is better to use the angled stake method illustrated below, but this is not practical for a tree or shrub with foliage coming down to ground level. The recommended method here is to use three stout wires as shown on the right — these wires are secured to three posts and they are cushioned around the stem with short pieces of tubing or garden hose.

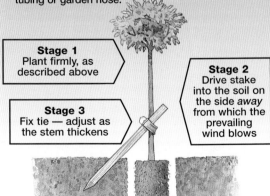

Stage 1
Plant firmly, as described above

Stage 2
Drive stake into the soil on the side *away* from which the prevailing wind blows

Stage 3
Fix tie — adjust as the stem thickens

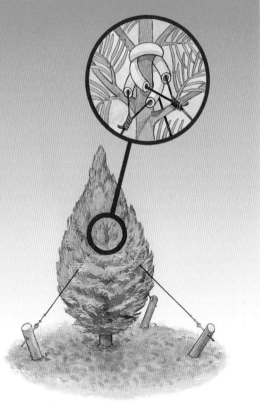

ROUTINE CARE

Evergreens need the routine treatment required by the other members of the types to which they belong — bulbs, border perennials, flowering shrubs etc. Watering, feeding, weeding and so on are necessary during the growing season to ensure success. Listed below are some general rules for the care of conifers, trees, shrubs and climbers, but do check in the A-Z guide to see if there are any special needs for the plant in question.

WATERING

The battle against water shortage should begin before the dry days of summer. Add organic matter to the soil before planting, water in thoroughly after planting and mulch the plant in spring every year. Copious watering will be necessary during a prolonged spell of dry weather in spring or summer for the first couple of years of an evergreen's life in your garden.

Once established the plant will need watering less often, but the need to water cannot be ignored. If the weather is dry, look at the trouble spots. Climbers growing next to the house, shrubs in tubs and all plants growing in very sandy soil will probably need watering. Then there are the shallow-rooted evergreens which can quite quickly suffer even in good soil once the dry spells of summer arrive.

Once you decide to water, then water thoroughly — a light sprinkling can do more harm than good. As a rough guide use 1 gallon (4.5 litres) for each small shrub and 4 gallons (18 litres) for each large one. A watering can is often used, but a hosepipe is a much better idea unless your garden is very small. Remember to water slowly close to the base of the plant.

Trickle irrigation through a perforated hose laid close to the bushes is perhaps the best method of watering. A quick and easy

technique is to build a ridge of soil around each bush and then fill the basin with a hose.

MULCHING

The benefits of using an organic mulch are numerous and remarkable, but most gardeners still do not bother to mulch their plants. There

are four basic reasons for using this underrated technique:

- The soil below is kept moist during the dry days of summer.
- The soil surface is kept cool during the hot days of summer. This moist and cool root zone promotes more active growth than in unmulched areas.
- Annual weeds are kept in check — the ones that do appear can be easily pulled out.
- Some mulches provide plant foods and soil structure is improved by the addition of humus.

Many materials are suitable for mulching — you can use moist peat, pulverised bark, leaf mould, well-rotted manure and garden compost. Grass clippings are sometimes recommended, but a word of caution is necessary. Add a thin layer and stir occasionally — do not use them if they are weedy nor if the lawn has been treated with a weedkiller.

The standard time for mulching is May. Success depends on preparing the soil surface properly before adding the organic blanket. Remove debris, dead leaves and weeds, and then water the surface if it is dry. Apply a spring feed if required, hoe in lightly and you are now ready to apply the mulch. Spread a 2-3 in. (5-7.5 cm) layer over the area which is under the branches and leaves. Do not take the mulch right up to the stems — a build-up of moist organic matter around the crown may lead to rotting. This layer can be lightly forked into the soil in October but it is better to leave it undisturbed if the shrubs (e.g Azalea) are shallow-rooted. Renew the mulch in spring.

WEEDING

Weeding is a season-long chore and in most gardens it is tackled badly. Hours are spent hoeing, forking and hand pulling with each bed in turn, only to find that the first bed is full of weeds before the last one is reached.

There is no single answer but you can break this frustrating cycle by using several methods. The first step is to try to prevent weeds appearing by growing ground-cover plants around shrubs, conifers etc or by applying a mulch. Some weeds will still get through, and these should be tackled promptly while they are still small. Hand pulling may be sufficient if you have used a mulch or ground-cover plants, but if there are lots of weeds on bare ground around the evergreens it will be necessary to use a weedkiller or hoe.

The range of weedkillers which can be used close to plants is limited — use diquat for annual weeds (chickweed, groundsel etc) and glyphosate for perennial ones (thistle, ground elder, dandelion, bindweed etc). The hoe remains the most popular method of killing

weeds around evergreens. It is quicker than hand pulling and will kill large numbers of annual weeds if the surface is dry, the blade is sharp and the depth of cut is kept shallow. Hoeing is not really effective against perennial weeds.

FEEDING

The production of stems, leaves and flowers is a drain on the soil's reserves of nitrogen, phosphates, potash and other nutrients. If one or more of these vital elements is in short supply then hunger signs such as stunted growth or discoloured leaves will appear.

For most plants the answer is to apply a fertilizer at some stage or stages of the plant's life. A lawn needs a nitrogen feed in spring and border perennials benefit from an annual dressing of a balanced nitrogen/phosphate/potash feed. With large-flowered perennials regular liquid feeding during the season will improve the display. Most rock garden plants need little or no feeding — once every couple of years with a potash-rich feed is ample.

Most shrubs and trees develop an extensive root system which effectively taps the nutrient resources in the soil, and this means that regular feeding is not always necessary. This ability to thrive without regular feeding is even more apparent with conifers and leafy evergreen shrubs as there is no annual leaf fall to replace. There are exceptions — large-flowered evergreen shrubs and those with a prolonged flowering season will benefit from an annual feed, and lime-hating evergreens may need an iron chelate dressing in non-acid soil — see Chlorosis on page 111.

TRAINING & SUPPORTING

Supporting and training are not quite the same thing. Supporting involves the provision of a post, stake or framework to which weak stems can be attached. Training involves the fixing of

branches into desired positions so that an unnatural but desirable growth habit is produced.

Some shrubs with lax spreading stems may require some means of support after a few years. Use three or four stakes with a band joining their tops — never rely on a single pole and twine.

Climbers must be grown against a support from the outset to ensure that they remain attached to it and grow in the desired direction. Use trellis work, posts, pillars, pergolas, fences etc. Make sure that all fence posts are well-anchored. For covering walls use plastic-covered straining wire stretched horizontally at 1½ ft (45 cm) intervals — there should be at least 3 in. (7.5 cm) between the wire and the wall. Many plants can be grown against walls in this way, including weak-stemmed non-climbers such as Winter Jasmine and Perennial Nightshade. The wire ties used to attach the main stems to the supports should not be tied too tightly. Plant the climber about 1-1½ ft (30-45 cm) away from the base of the wall. When growing climbers up a pillar, wind the stems in an ascending spiral rather than attaching to one side of the support.

The main stems need not all be trained vertically — spreading them horizontally to form an espalier or at an angle to form a fan can dramatically increase the display.

SPECIFIC CARE

On pages 104 and 105 several cultural operations are described — these apply to all plants in the garden and not just to evergreens. With some tasks such as weeding the fact that the plant is an evergreen is irrelevant, but with others (e.g feeding) the evergreen factor may affect the work which has to be done. In addition there are two operations which are strongly influenced by whether the plant retains or loses its leaves in winter. Both of these are dealt with in this section.

WINTER PROTECTION

In winter deciduous plants are devoid of foliage, so there is no water loss to dry out the tissues — in addition there are no leaves to be damaged by wind, rain, frost or snow. The situation is different with evergreens. Most established ones can quite happily withstand the rigours of winter, but others may be susceptible to damage and so need some form of protection.

Newly-planted conifers and leafy evergreen shrubs are most at risk, and it is the drying effect of strong winds which is more likely than frost to be the cause of browning or death in winter. The easiest answer is to plant in a spot which has the protection of other plants or a wall — failing that a screen as shown below may be necessary. Heavy frosts can be a problem with plants which are not completely hardy and a mulch will help — snow can cause damage with large leafy trees and tying up is sometimes needed.

SNOW PROTECTION
Plants most at risk: Cordyline, fir, cedar, cypress

The weight of snow on large conifer branches can cause them to break — if heavy snow is forecast it may be worth tying the branches of a choice evergreen or leafy palm-like plant with twine

In most cases all that is required is to knock off the snow from the branches with a cane — start at the bottom and work up

WIND PROTECTION
Plants most at risk: Newly-planted conifers and shrubs

Top of netting should be above the plant

Anchor stout posts firmly in the ground

Use windbreak netting or hessian — solid plastic sheeting is not recommended. Leave a 4 in. (10 cm) gap between plant and netting

Pin down base of netting

Small plants can be protected by draping horticultural fleece or placing a cloche over them

FROST PROTECTION
Plants most at risk: Evergreens which are not fully hardy

Cover the ground under the branches from December to early March with a 6 in. (15 cm) layer of leaves, bark or straw. Hold it down with netting or twigs

RAIN PROTECTION
Plants most at risk: Delicate evergreen rock garden plants

Place a sheet of rigid transparent plastic or glass over the plant on bricks. Secure with additional bricks. The top of the plant should not touch the surface. Remove when the weather turns mild in spring

If there are numerous plants to protect use cloches with open ends

PRUNING

It is clear from page 106 that the winter care of evergreens can be more complex and time consuming than the protection of deciduous plants, but the roles are reversed with pruning. With leaf-losing shrubs and trees the amount and timing of pruning vary widely from plant to plant, and mistakes can mean no flowers, or leggy unattractive branches. With evergreens, however, routine annual pruning is hardly ever required except for hedges — see page 116 for details.

Occasions will arise when some pruning is necessary, so it is a good idea to get to know what to do.

● Buy good quality tools and make sure they are sharp.
● Use the right tool for the job you have to do. Secateurs are suitable for stems up to $^1/_2$-$^3/_4$ in. (1-1.5 cm) wide. For branches $^1/_2$-1$^1/_2$ in. (1-3.5 cm) across use a long-handled pruner and for wider branches you will need a pruning saw.
● For trimming (see below) the usual tool is a pair of garden shears or a hedge trimmer if the amount to be pruned is large. Large-leaved plants such as laurel are an exception — use secateurs so as to avoid leaving cut leaves which turn brown.
● Learn the difference between trimming and thinning, and use the appropriate technique when the need arises.

TRIMMING

Trimming involves the removal of the ends of the branches. This stimulates the buds below the cuts to burst into growth. The long-term effect is to produce a plant which is smaller and denser than one left unpruned.

THINNING

Thinning involves the removal of entire branches back to the main stem. This diverts extra energy to the main stem. The long-term effect is to produce a plant which is larger and more open than one left unpruned.

DAMAGED GROWTH PRUNING

Even in the best of gardens there will be times when a branch breaks or the leaves on a stem are browned by icy winds. Cut the damaged stem back to a point which is close to the main stem from which it arose. If a branch has been dislodged by snow or strong winds in winter but has foliage which is still green then try to restore it to its former position with twine or netting rather than removing it by pruning.

UNWANTED GROWTH PRUNING

It is quite common for one or more branches on an evergreen shrub or conifer to grow long enough to be either unsightly or to exceed its allotted space. Cut these branches back to the main stem — don't snip away at the tips. Occasionally most or all of the branches have become overgrown and pruning is obviously essential. You can cut out some of the largest branches by thinning and then repeat the procedure each year — drastically cutting back all the branches at the same time can lead to the death of the plant. Trimming rather than thinning is practical with many shrubs and conifers, but this usually results in a formal appearance.

Root pruning is a useful but underused technique for slowing down the growth of an over-vigorous evergreen. Drive a spade into the ground to the depth of the blade, making several cuts directly below the outer reach of the branches.

All-green shoots on variegated evergreens should be cut off as soon as they are seen. Where practical carefully break off dead blooms on Rhododendron bushes.

ANNUAL ROUTINE PRUNING

Only a few evergreens need cutting back every year as a matter of routine. Erica, Calluna and Lavandula should be lightly trimmed as soon as the flowers have faded. Grey-leaved ground-cover evergreens such as Artemisia, Senecio and Santolina, as well as Vinca and Pachysandra, should be trimmed in early spring.

When to Prune

With nearly all evergreens, spring is the best season and March is the best month. Where winter-damaged branches are to be removed it is best to wait until late spring to see the full extent of the damage and to see if there has been any regrowth. With spring-flowering evergreen shrubs prune as soon as the blooms have faded. The worst time for pruning evergreens is August-October.

PROPAGATION

Not all evergreens can be raised at home and the ease with which new plants can be produced varies from child's play to near impossible. If you are really keen then you may wish to try to raise shrubs and trees from seed, but for everyone else there are other methods to use. Do at least try the easy outdoor techniques of layering, division and taking hardwood cuttings — there is nothing to lose and much to gain.

DIVIDING CLUMPS

The usual method of increasing the stock of border perennials, rock garden and ground-cover plants is to divide up mature clumps. Dig up the clump with a fork on a mild day in spring or autumn when the soil is moist. Break it up into well-rooted pieces — you may be able to do this with your hands, but if the clump is too tough then use two hand forks or garden forks as shown. Prise apart and select divisions which came from the outer part of the clump. Replant as soon as possible and water in thoroughly.

SUMMER CUTTINGS

Many border perennials and evergreen trees are propagated by this method. With perennials and small shrubs stem-tip cuttings are used — these are green at the tip and base, and are taken between early summer and midsummer. Heel cuttings are used for many larger shrubs — these are green at the top and partly woody at the base, and are taken between midsummer and early autumn. Examples of summer cuttings include Berberis, Ceanothus, Cotoneaster, Escallonia, Euonymus, Hebe, Laurus, Pernettya, Skimmia and Viburnum.

Stem-tip cutting

Cut off leaves from lower half of the cutting

1-6 in. (2.5-15 cm) depending on the size of the parent plant

Leaf joint

Straight cut

Dip bottom ½ in. (1 cm) of the cutting into a rooting hormone

Heel cutting

Cut off leaves from lower half of the cutting

Pull off side shoot with a heel attached. Dip bottom 1 in. (2.5 cm) of the cutting into a rooting hormone

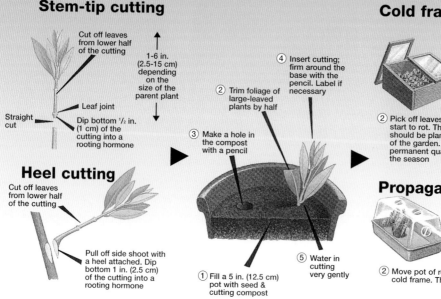

(1) Fill a 5 in. (12.5 cm) pot with seed & cutting compost
(2) Trim foliage of large-leaved plants by half
(3) Make a hole in the compost with a pencil
(4) Insert cutting; firm around the base with the pencil. Label if necessary
(5) Water in cutting very gently

Cold frame method

(1) Place pots in the cold frame — shade glass and ventilate on hot days. Water when necessary. In frosty weather cover glass with sacking
(2) Pick off leaves which turn yellow or start to rot. The rooted cuttings should be planted out in a corner of the garden. Move them to their permanent quarters at the end of the season

Propagator method

(1) Place pots in the propagator. Keep at 65°-75°F (18°-24°C). Shade and ventilate on hot days
(2) Move pot of rooted cuttings to a cold frame. Then as (2) above

PLANTING SUCKERS

Some woody evergreens spread by means of suckers. These are shoots which arise from underground shoots or roots — removing and then planting these daughter plants is an easy method of propagation. Lift the suckers and plant in April or September. Examples include Arundinaria, Danae, Elaeagnus, Mahonia and Pernettya.

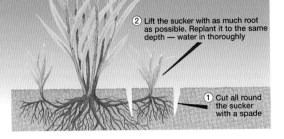

② Lift the sucker with as much root as possible. Replant it to the same depth — water in thoroughly

① Cut all round the sucker with a spade

LAYERING

Increasing the stock of evergreens by planting cuttings under glass is not for everyone — care, patience and equipment are needed. Outdoor propagation methods are easier, but the numbers of plants which can be raised by striking outdoor cuttings is limited. Layering is an excellent alternative — evergreen shrubs and climbers with flexible stems can be raised very easily by this method. A stem is pegged down in spring or autumn and left attached to the parent plant until roots have formed at the base of the layered shoot. This takes 6-12 months. Examples include Berberis, Calluna, Camellia, Carpenteria, Erica, Euonymus, Garrya, Ilex, Kalmia, Laurus, Lonicera, Osmanthus, Rhododendron and Viburnum.

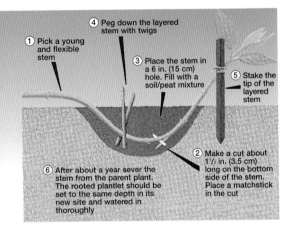

① Pick a young and flexible stem
② Make a cut about 1½ in. (3.5 cm) long on the bottom side of the stem. Place a matchstick in the cut
③ Place the stem in a 6 in. (15 cm) hole. Fill with a soil/peat mixture
④ Peg down the layered stem with twigs
⑤ Stake the tip of the layered stem
⑥ After about a year sever the stem from the parent plant. The rooted plantlet should be set to the same depth in its new site and watered in thoroughly

AUTUMN CUTTINGS

Cuttings planted outdoors in late autumn are easier to strike than the summer ones which require glass or plastic to maintain a moist atmosphere, but unfortunately not many evergreens can be propagated by this method. Hardwood cuttings of shrubs are used — well-ripened shoots from the current year's growth. November is the best month. Berberis, Buxus, Jasminum and Lavandula are usually propagated by means of summer cuttings indoors, but they are suitable for outdoor propagation as shown below.

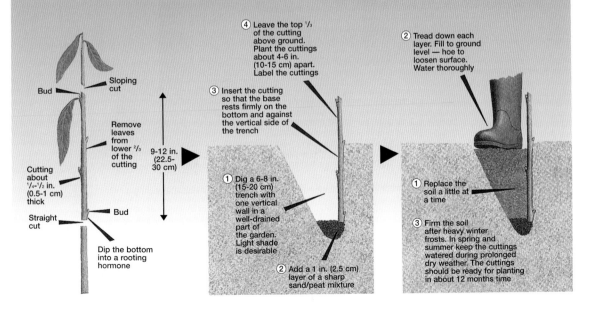

PROBLEMS

The non-specific pests, diseases and cultural problems which afflict leaf-losing perennials, bulbs, rockery plants, ferns and so on can affect the evergreen types. With woody evergreens the situation is different. As a general but by no means universal rule they suffer less from pests and diseases than their deciduous counterparts, but they are more prone to suffer from cultural problems when newly-planted and in winter.

For the non-specific problems which can affect an evergreen plant look in an appropriate text book. Described in this section are specific problems together with some general problems which are particularly serious with these plants.

DIE-BACK

A serious problem — begins at the tips and progresses slowly downwards. There are several possible causes, including diseases such as canker and coral spot. If no disease is present, waterlogging or drought is the likely cause. Cut out dead wood, feed with a foliar feed and improve the soil by mulching regularly each spring.

SPLIT BARK

A crack may appear in the bark at any time of the year. The cause can be a severe frost, and it is not uncommon for the base of Rhododendron bushes to split in this way. Another cause is poor growing conditions. Cut away any dead wood and paint with a sealing compound. Feed and mulch to restore good health.

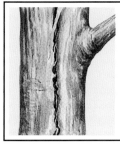

BUD BLAST

Infected flower buds of Rhododendron turn brown and are covered with black fungal bristles. They do not rot and remain firmly attached to the bush — flowering in future seasons may be affected. Remove and burn diseased buds. Do not confuse with frost-damaged buds, which are soft and easily pulled away. To prevent attack spray with a systemic insecticide in August to kill the disease-carrying leafhopper.

BUTT ROT

Butt rot (Fomes annosus) is a fatal disease of conifers. Other trees are rarely attacked. The first signs of infection are yellow and wilted leaves. The tree quickly deteriorates and finally dies. At the base of the trunk bracket-like toadstools may appear. Dig out and burn the tree — do not leave a stump. Do not replant a conifer on the same site.

ADELGID

Tiny aphid-like insects attack conifers and can seriously affect young trees. If present in large numbers spray with bifenthrin in April and again 3 weeks later. In summer dense tufts of white wool are produced, coating the underside of the leaves. Conspicuous galls may be produced — pick off and burn.

WITCHES BROOM

A dense clump of branching twigs can sometimes be seen on the trunks and main branches of conifers. The cause is usually a fungus, but it may be a virus or a change in the structure of a growth bud. These 'bird nest' clumps do no harm, but they can be cut off and the wounds painted with a sealing compound.

LEAF DROP

It is natural for an occasional leaf to fall during the growing season but a heavy drop which results in the stems looking bare means that something is wrong. Water shortage is an obvious cause but too little light is often the reason for this problem. Other possible causes (disease, insects and air pollution) are much less likely.

TOO RAPID GROWTH

A woody evergreen which has outgrown its site is an all-too-common problem in the garden. Cutting back is an immediate answer but it can be a regular chore and result in a misshapen plant. Root pruning (page 107) can be used to slow down the growth rate — for small shrubs and trees lifting and then replanting every few years is a better answer.

DROUGHT

In prolonged dry weather the soil reserves of moisture are seriously reduced. The first sign is wilting of the foliage and in the early stages the effect is reversible. The next stage is browning of the foliage and leaf drop which is extremely serious or fatal. Water before symptoms appear, and improve the water-holding capacity of the soil by adding humus *before* planting. Mulch in late spring.

WINTER DAMAGE

Many evergreens are at risk in a severe winter, especially if they are slightly tender or newly planted. They can be damaged in several ways — waterlogging in an abnormally wet season can lead to root rot, temperatures well below freezing point can cause frost damage (brown blotches on leaves, usually at the tips) and heavy snow can break or bend down the branches. See Winter Protection (page 106).

SPRING SCORCH

Bright sunny weather after a cold spell surprisingly leads to browning or death of evergreens instead of active growth. The cause is cold-induced drought — sunshine and drying winds stimulate water loss from the leaves, but the roots are not active and cannot replace the loss. Spray newly-planted evergreens with water in spring — provide protection from frosts and east winds.

RHODODENDRON BUG

Shiny brown insects with lacy wings feed on the undersurface of Rhododendron leaves. Foliage becomes mottled above, rusty brown below. Leaf edges curl downwards. At the first sign of trouble in May or June spray thoroughly with thiacloprid. Repeat the treatment about a month later.

LOSS OF VARIEGATION

Some shrubs bear yellow and green leaves ('variegata') or green, yellow and red leaves ('tricolor'). In dense shade the green areas spread and variegation is diminished. Even in good light there is often a tendency for the shrub to revert to the all-green form. Cut out such shoots immediately.

CHLOROSIS

Some shrubs such as Azalea and Camellia develop pale green or yellow leaves if grown in chalky soil. This is lime-induced chlorosis, and is helped but not always prevented by incorporating peat and by applying an iron chelate compound. Chlorosis of the lower leaves is often due to poor drainage.

How to reduce the risk

Choose wisely. Make sure that the plants you have picked are not too tender for the climatic conditions in your area, and check that the soil and light requirements can be satisfied

Buy good plants. Abundant roots and sound stems are essential

Prepare the ground thoroughly. A shrub in poorly-drained soil is likely to succumb to root-rotting diseases

Plant in the proper place and in the proper way. This will reduce the risk of problems due to drought, poor root development, waterlogging, windrock, frost damage and light deficiency. Stake if necessary

Avoid overcrowding. Do not plant too closely as this can encourage mildew and other diseases

Provide frost protection if necessary. Both snow and frost can cause a great deal of damage in a severe winter. Read the section on Winter Protection (page 106)

Why shrubs fail to survive

An evergreen shrub or tree planted in the manner described in this book should grow and flourish for many years. Failure to survive will almost certainly be due to one of the following causes:

Poor-quality planting material

Poor site preparation

Break-up of the soil ball of container-grown or balled plants

Windrock especially in exposed sites. Staking of tall specimens in such locations is essential

Waterlogged soil around the roots due to poor drainage

Winter damage and spring scorch — see above

Dry roots at planting time or during the first season

One of the fatal pests or diseases — die-back, honey fungus, canker or butt rot can kill a susceptible plant

CHAPTER 4

USING EVERGREENS

Articles on using evergreens often begin with the point that their basic role is to provide a display of living foliage among the lifeless stalks and over the bare ground in the winter garden. This, however, is far too simple an approach to the role of evergreens. They do indeed keep most or all of their leaves during the dead season of the year, but the all-year-round nature of their foliage is not always the main or even an important feature.

At one end of the scale are the plants which are grown solely for their flowers. We choose a particular Kniphofia for the colour and size of its poker-like blooms and not for the fact that the variety is an evergreen one. Ground-cover roses are selected on the basis of size, flower colour, disease resistance etc — the fact that the variety may be semi-evergreen is not even mentioned in the catalogues. Next there are the evergreens which are grown primarily for their flowers but which have leaves that remain on the plants as a bonus. Many of the popular ones belong here — evergreen Azaleas, Hypericum, Viburnum etc, and a number of these have foliage which is particularly attractive such as Bergenia, Rhododendron, Camellia and Choisya. These blend into the group where flowers and foliage are equally important (Pieris, Skimmia etc) and finally there is the group of plants where the evergreen nature of the foliage is all-important for winter colour and where flowers are missing or are not important. Here are the plants which are the first to spring to mind when we hear the word 'evergreen' — conifers in a wide variety of leaf colours, shapes and sizes together with others like Euonymus, Aucuba, Buxus, Hedera and Pachysandra. Thus among the evergreens there are plants for flowers and others for foliage and many which provide a fine display of both.

There are evergreens for every part of the garden, ranging from the grasses on the lawn to the Willow Moss growing under the water in the pond. On the following pages a number of areas where evergreens can be used are discussed and illustrated, but the role of evergreens as compared to deciduous types differs quite markedly from one site to another. The herbaceous border is a garden feature where plants are chosen for their in-season display of flowers, foliage and shape and not for the promise of green leaves in winter. There are evergreen varieties of Achillea, Digitalis, Kniphofia, Penstemon, Salvia etc but their winter foliage is not particularly attractive. It generally adds little to the overall appearance of the border between November and March when the leaves and stems of the deciduous species are brown or absent. The situation is rather different in the rock garden where spreading old favourites like Aubrieta, Arabis, Cerastium and Armeria together with dwarf conifers such as Abies balsamea 'Hudsonia' and Chamaecyparis lawsoniana 'Minima Glauca' clothe rocks and ground with patches of living green in winter. The low-growing non-woody perennials and sub-shrubs which have an all-important part to play are the ground-cover evergreens. These spreading types are used to provide mats of all-year-round foliage around shrubs and trees or over bare ground — these mats suppress weeds and give both colour and interest. These ground covers are chosen for their ability to grow horizontally or spread widely so as to cover the soil — at the other extreme there are evergreens chosen for their ability to grow upwards and so cover or screen walls or supports or be free-standing as a screen or hedge. It was said earlier that people didn't bother whether a herbaceous border plant was evergreen or not when making a choice and this sometimes applies to rockery plants, but the situation is different with hedging and screening plants. Here we want year-round foliage and so evergreens and semi-evergreens like conifers, Buxus, Laurus, Ligustrum and so on are the most popular choice. Another garden feature where year-round foliage is considered to be an important or vital feature is specimen planting in the lawn, open ground or container. Here the stand-alone specimen serves as either an architectural plant or an accent one — see page 114 for the difference. To complete the list of areas for evergreens there are conifer/heather beds and borders, shrub borders and mixed borders.

GROUND COVER PLANTING

A ground cover evergreen is a reasonably or highly decorative plant with a spread of leafy growth which is sufficiently dense to partly or completely suppress the growth of weeds. Most of them form a low blanket of leaves which hugs the ground, but there are also many low-growing conifers and shrubs which make excellent ground covers. The dividing line between ground cover and dwarf shrubs is not clear-cut — in this book the term 'ground cover' is restricted to those wide-spreading plants which have an ultimate height of 3 ft (90 cm) or less.

Several of the evergreen types described on pages 4-5 contain ground-covering plants. There are conifers, led by the low-growing Junipers such as Juniperus media 'Old Gold' and J. horizontalis 'Glauca' — J. squamata 'Blue Star' will quite quickly form an attractive steely blue carpet under trees and tall shrubs. These wide-spreading conifers should be more widely used. Numerous border perennials can be grown for ground cover — popular ones include Ajuga, Bergenia and Stachys. These have the bonus of being flowering plants, but some of the most popular ground-covering shrubs and sub-shrubs such as Euonymus, Hedera and Pachysandra are grown just for their foliage. Finally there are a few rock garden plants such as Cerastium which make effective ground covers.

There are two rules — choose carefully and plant carefully. Make sure you choose a species or variety which is right for the situation — that means that it can flourish in the soil texture, soil acidity, light and space you can provide. Remember that some can spread very quickly, which is fine for a large patch of bare ground but can be a menace between closely-planted shrubs. Before planting the ground cover you have bought it is necessary to remove every bit of perennial weed root from the soil.

Make more use of evergreen ground covers in your garden. They provide greenery beneath taller shrubs and trees, hide stumps and manhole covers, edge shrub borders, clothe low walls and cover banks, but do not regard them as eliminators of established weeds. When making your choice look up the following genera in the A-Z guide — Ajuga, Bergenia, Calluna, Cerastium, Cotoneaster, Erica, Euonymus, Hebe, Hedera, Hypericum, Iberis, Juniperus, Lamium, Lavandula, Pachysandra, Rosa, Sedum, Stachys and Vinca.

ROCKERY PLANTING

Evergreen rock garden plants together with dwarf conifers, compact evergreen shrubs and ferns give the rock garden a permanent living form in winter. Between these patches of permanence the rockery bulbs and deciduous alpines appear in spring for added interest. All year round these evergreens can provide upright columns of green, yellow or blue together with rounded shapes and flat sheets of colour.

Choose carefully. Small rooted cuttings are sometimes labelled as 'rockery conifers' whereas they are really immature forms of tall-growing varieties. The only answer is to lift and replace when such plants outgrow their sites. Not all rockery evergreens have such vigorous constitutions. Some alpines are quite delicate and need winter protection — see page 106.

There are numerous conifers and shrubs which are suitable for the rockery — occasional trimming may be necessary. Examples include Chamaecyparis lawsoniana 'Minima Aurea', Erica species, Hebe pinguifolia 'Pagei', Helianthemum species, Juniperus communis 'Compressa', Pinus mugo 'Gnom', Rhododendron 'Elizabeth', Rosmarinus prostratus and Thuja occidentalis 'Hetz Midget'.

Architectural plant

Accent plant

SPECIMEN PLANTING

A specimen evergreen is grown to be admired on its own as distinct from being part of a group of plants in a bed or border. The classical specimen plant is a tree, tall shrub or stately conifer in the lawn or at the end of a border. Such specimens provide the upright living framework for the garden — they give the plot its third dimension. Evergreens are the popular choice as they have branches which are always clothed with leaves — a clear sign of life when so much appears dead.

This love affair with specimen evergreens began hundreds of years ago. In the 17th century Cedar of Lebanon, Italian Cypress and Yew were widely planted in country estates and every self-respecting Victorian villa had to have its Monkey Puzzle Tree. Tall and stately trees, but specimen plants need not be giants. In small gardens plants such as Juniperus chinensis 'Pyramidalis' and Pieris japonica can serve as specimen shrubs, but like all specimen plants they must be in good condition.

The bare stems of a neglected shrub may be hidden by other plants when grown in a mixed border and the rather drab appearance of some varieties can be overcome by the bright display of its neighbours. But a specimen plant must stand on its own, acting as a focal point or adding to the interest of a nearby object. Because of the role it has to play there are rules for its selection and care.

Choose a plant which will be worth looking at for most if not all of the year. Attractive foliage and a pleasing shape are vital — an eye-catching floral display is a bonus, but a specimen tree or shrub should not be chosen for that feature alone. With many specimen plants the colour is obtained from variegated foliage, berries or coloured bark rather than from the flowers.

It is important to pick the right shape and size. A small shrub in a large lawn can look out of place. A large tree in a small lawn also looks out of place, but it may also be positively harmful by robbing the land of light, water and nutrients. If you want a tree rather than a bush for a small garden, consider a shrub grown as a standard. As a general rule, the taller the specimen is likely to grow, the narrower its growth habit should be.

Proper maintenance is important. Water regularly in dry weather and prune when necessary. Within these rules there will still be a wide choice from which to make your selection for the site you have in mind. Listed below are some trees and shrubs which are widely recommended.

Cedrus atlantica 'Glauca' (blue-green)
Chamaecyparis lawsoniana 'Columnaris' (column)
Chamaecyparis lawsoniana 'Stewartii' (golden/yellow)
Chamaecyparis pisifera 'Boulevard' (blue-green)
Cupressus sempervirens (column)
Elaeagnus pungens 'Maculata' (variegated)
Eucryphia nymansensis (floral display)
Ilex altaclerensis 'Golden King' (variegated)
Juniperus virginiana 'Skyrocket' (column)
Picea breweriana (weeping habit)
Picea pungens 'Koster' (blue-green)
Pieris formosa (red new growth)
Rhododendron species (floral display)
Taxus baccata 'Fastigiata Aureomarginata' (column)
Thuja occidentalis 'Rheingold' (golden/yellow)
Yucca filamentosa 'Variegata' (variegated)

Specimen conifers, trees, shrubs etc are sometimes separated into architectural plants and accent plants, although some varieties can fulfil either role. An architectural plant draws attention to itself — it is a focal point. An accent plant heightens the effect of a nearby structure or of a nearby plant or group of plants. Architectural plants or accent plants — specimen trees or shrubs are important in every garden.

CONTAINER PLANTING

Growing plants in containers has become much more popular in recent years as more and more people have discovered the many advantages. Plants not suited to your soil can be grown, plants can be put out on paths and patios, plants can be moved once the display is over, tender evergreens can be grown outdoors, eyesores can be hidden and so on. A colourful bush in a tub will add interest to a bare wall where direct planting is not possible, and doorways framed by trimmed Buxus or Laurus bushes are familiar sights.

Pick the right container. It must be sturdy and at least 9 in. (22.5 cm) wide and deep. For a leafy shrub the pot or tub should be at least 1 ft (30 cm) deep. Adequate drainage is essential — large containers should have at least one hole every 6 in. (15 cm). Fill with a soil-based compost, or a peat-based one if weight is a problem. Plant firmly and stake if necessary. Regular watering in dry weather is essential. With small and thin-walled pots there is a danger of the soil ball freezing in a severe winter — sacking or bubble plastic tied round the container should prevent this from happening.

A wide range of evergreens can be grown in containers. Ordinary shrubs and compact conifers can be used to give their normal display or you can grow varieties which tolerate regular pruning and grow them in geometric shapes — see Topiary Planting on page 120. Tender exotics such as Citrus, Callistemon, Nerium etc can spend their summer outdoors in tubs or pots. Some favourite evergreen tub plants for year-round display are listed below.

Arundinaria viridistriata
Buxus sempervirens
Chamaecyparis lawsoniana 'Elwoodii'
Chamaecyparis pisifera 'Boulevard'
Cordyline australis
Cotoneaster salicifolius (standard)
Euonymus fortunei 'Silver Queen'
Fatsia japonica
Juniperus chinensis 'Pyramidalis'
Juniperus media 'Old Gold'
Juniperus squamata 'Meyeri'
Laurus nobilis
Picea glauca 'Albertiana Conica'
Rhododendron species
Trachycarpus fortunei
Yucca filamentosa

SCREEN PLANTING

A screening plant is a variety which is grown primarily to protect the garden from an undesirable feature such as an unattractive view or the prevailing wind. There are three properties of a successful screening plant — it should be evergreen or semi-evergreen, it must be densely covered with leaves for most purposes (see below) and it must be quick-growing.

The usual way of blocking out an unattractive view is to plant Ilex, Ligustrum or a vigorous conifer such as Chamaecyparis lawsoniana or Cupressocyparis leylandii — do remember when planting tall-growing conifers that if left unchecked they can become a worse nuisance than the unpleasant view.

On exposed sites a line of screening plants is sometimes grown to provide a windbreak. For this purpose the dense growth required for hiding ugly objects or views is no longer a desirable property. A wall of dense foliage causes turbulence — a less solid growth habit absorbs the wind. The width of the wind-protected zone behind the screen is about six times the height. A wide band of screening plants can reduce the noise level from passing traffic but a single line of conifers will do virtually nothing to reduce the problem.

HEDGE PLANTING

PLANTING A HEDGE

The first job is to decide whether you need a single or double row of hedging plants and where the planting line or lines will be. Remember that the width of the hedge will be much greater than the planting material you have bought. The edge of the pavement or close to your neighbours' fence may seem the right place at planting time, but in a few years there may well be a serious problem of encroachment onto their property or the overhang onto the street.

Having decided on the area for planting, dig a 3 ft (90 cm) wide strip to house the plants. Remove the roots of perennial weeds and then mark out the position of the planting holes. Single row planting is recommended where economy is an important factor and quick cover is not essential. Mark out the planting line with string stretched along the centre of the cultivated area and use canes to mark out the planting sites. Set the canes 1¼-1½ ft (37.5-45 cm) apart for shrubs such as privet and 2-2½ ft (60-75 cm) for large shrubs and trees. Double row planting is recommended for spindly shrubs and where maximum cover is required as quickly as possible. Use string to mark out the planting lines 1¼ ft (37.5 cm) apart and put in the canes at 1½ ft (45 cm) intervals along these lines.

Plant out as described on pages 102-103. Stretch a wire tightly along the young plants and attach them with ties. Keep the plants well watered during the first season.

The usual reason for planting a hedge is to form a boundary between you and the road or your neighbour. It must be capable of providing some privacy and also a degree of protection against dogs, children etc. There are other roles a hedge can play — it can divide one area of the garden from another, it can edge beds and borders, and also serve as a screen against unsightly views and noise (see page 115).

CHOOSING A HEDGE

The job a hedge has to do is a vital factor in the correct choice of planting material — so is the degree of formality required and the desired height. The blessings of a tall and dense hedge for privacy are obvious, but do consider the drawbacks. If it is to serve as a boundary do discuss it with your neighbour before going ahead — over-vigorous boundary hedges are one of the commonest causes of disputes. Also think about the effect on your own garden — shade will be a problem for nearby plants and so will the drain on both the water and nutrient resources in the soil.

It is usual to grow just one variety but there are variations if you like to be a little different. With a privet or holly hedge you can mix an all-green variety with a variegated one or you can go even further by growing two or more quite different species or genera to produce a tapestry hedge — see page 9.

PRUNING A HEDGE

For a formal hedge it is essential to build up a plentiful supply of shoots at the base. This calls for hard pruning shortly after planting — cut back the plants to about $2/3$ of their original height. Do not prune again during the first growing season.

In the second year clip lightly on three or four occasions between May and August. Do not leave it untrimmed because it has not yet reached the required height — the purpose of this second year pruning is to increase shoot density and to create the desired shape before the ultimate height is reached. Use a pair of shears or an electric hedge trimmer. Lay down a sheet of plastic at the base — this will make the removal of fallen clippings a much easier task.

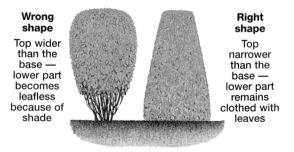

Wrong shape

Top wider than the base — lower part becomes leafless because of shade

Right shape

Top narrower than the base — lower part remains clothed with leaves

Once the hedge has reached the desired height, trimming should take place between May and August each year (unless otherwise stated on page 117) when the plants look untidy. This may involve a single clipping during the season or trimming every 6 weeks to maintain a neatly manicured box. Cut back to a little above the last cut, leaving about ½ in. (1 cm) of new growth.

FORMAL HEDGES

Cupressocyparis

Cupressocyparis leylandii (Leyland Cypress) has become the most popular as well as the quickest-growing hedging plant — it can reach 10 ft (3 m) in 5 years. Keep staked at first and trim regularly.

Ilex

Ilex aquifolium (Common Holly) is relatively slow to start but in time forms a dense impenetrable hedge. It will grow in shade but variegated ones need sun. Trim in late summer.

Ligustrum

Much despised, but the privet hedge is quick-growing, tolerant of poor conditions and hardy. Choose a variety of Ligustrum ovalifolium. New plants should be cut back hard after planting.

Prunus

Prunus lusitanica (Portugal Laurel) and P. laurocerasus (Cherry Laurel) make fine tall hedges with dense shiny leaves. They need a lot of space. Trim in August.

Taxus

Yew is an old favourite. It need not be dull — there are bright golden varieties as well as the dark green ones. Not as quick as some, but not as slow as its reputation. Trim in late summer.

Thuja

Thuja plicata (Western Red Cedar) is the one to grow if you want cypress-like foliage without the Cupressocyparis menace of over-rapid growth. Trim in August.

INFORMAL HEDGES

Berberis

Berberis stenophylla, B. darwinii and B. julianae make excellent hedges. Yellow flowers appear in spring — trim when they fade. Spiny stems provide some protection.

Escallonia

Escallonia macrantha is grown in coastal areas as it tolerates salt-laden air — it grows quickly when established. Red flowers appear in June — trim when they fade to induce a second flush.

Osmanthus

For milder regions Osmanthus heterophyllus can be used to produce an unusual hedge with holly-like leaves and small, white fragrant flowers in autumn. Trim in spring.

Pyracantha

Pyracantha coccinea (Common Firethorn) can be used but the species recommended for hedging is P. rogersiana. Grown for its berries — cut back in August to expose them.

Rhododendron

Where space permits and the soil is acid you can use Rhododendron ponticum as a tall and wide hedge with large oval leaves and pale purple flowers. Trim when blooms fade.

Viburnum

Viburnum tinus (Laurustinus) is a good winter-flowering informal hedge for difficult sites — it will thrive in clay, chalk and shade. It will grow to 6 ft (1.8 m) or more — trim in May.

DWARF HEDGES

Buxus

Buxus sempervirens (Common Box) has long been the favourite plant for formal dwarf hedging. It is slow-growing and not fussy about soil type. Trim in July or August.

Lavandula

Like box, Lavandula spica (Common Lavender) has been a popular dwarf hedge plant for centuries. Cut off the flower stalks once the purple flowers fade — trim back the plants in April.

Rosmarinus

Rosmarinus officinalis (Rosemary) can be used as an alternative to lavender — more unusual but also more likely to fail. Trim when the pale blue flowers have faded.

Santolina

Santolina chamaecyparissus (Cotton Lavender) has silvery foliage and yellow button-like flowers in summer. Remove the faded flower heads and trim back the plants in April.

BED & BORDER PLANTING

BED OR BORDER?

Unfortunately there are no universally agreed definitions for 'bed' and 'border' and some attempts provide only a vague dividing line between the two. The definitions given below do give a clear-cut distinction between bed and border and are the meaning of the two terms used in this book.

BORDER

A planted area which is designed to be viewed from two or three sides. Any shape, but usually rectangular.

BED

A planted area which is designed to be viewed from all sides. Any shape, but usually square, round or oval.

This chapter describes numerous areas in the garden where evergreens have an important part to play. Specimen conifers in the lawn, leafy green hedges along the boundary, year-round ground cover under shrubs and so on, but it is in beds and borders that most evergreens are found. Beds and borders are occasionally devoted solely to evergreens (see single-group shrub bed or border on page 119) but it is much more usual to have these plants mixed with deciduous shrubs, perennials and bulbs.

SHRUB BORDER

A shrub border is planted entirely with shrubs, trees and/or conifers and was once a very popular garden feature. It reached the height of its popularity in Victorian times when a shrubbery graced every villa. This 6-10 ft (1.8-3 m) wide strip of land stretched along the boundary and was filled with evergreens. Conifers such as yew and spruce grew next to privet, laurel and box to provide an all-green, leaf-filled feature.

Some of these Victorian-style shrubberies remain, but a shrub border should be a much more attractive feature. First of all it should be a mixture of evergreens and deciduous woody plants — evergreens to provide a stable framework of stems and year-round foliage within which the leaf-losing shrubs and trees present a changing picture of opening leaf buds, fresh green or variegated foliage and then leaf fall with the promise of autumn colours.

When planning your border you should aim for a tiered effect — tall shrubs with perhaps some trees at the back, medium-sized shrubs in the middle and then short, dwarf and ground-covering shrubs at the front. This should not be taken too literally — you should avoid a regular and consistent slope from back to front right along the border. You can break up the line by planting a medium-sized columnar plant close to the front. Aim to achieve variety — when you look at the border at any time of the year there should be an attractive mixture of shapes, sizes and leaf colour. Ideally there should also be something in bloom in every season. Never plant in straight rows and remember that planting distances are determined by the size the plants will achieve when they are mature — see page 102.

Mixed border

Heather/conifer border

Woodland garden

MIXED BORDER

A mixed border is planted with trees and/or shrubs and also other plants such as border perennials, roses and bulbs. It has become more popular than both the shrub border and the herbaceous border because it is easier to create year-round colour and interest than with the other two border types.

This mixed border is essentially a shrub border in which pockets and bays are left for non-woody plants. It is therefore necessary to create a permanent framework of trees, shrubs and conifers, and care should be taken over their selection. You must aim for a year-round effect, and this calls for some leaves and colour during every month of the year. To ensure leaves in winter there will have to be some evergreens among the deciduous shrubs. To ensure colour you will need flowering types, and here evergreens such as Rhododendron, Berberis, Mahonia and Viburnum have an important part to play. Remember you can also get colour from foliage — the A-Z guide has a liberal sprinkling of plants with yellow, bronze, purple, red or variegated foliage.

Year-round leaf and flower colour from shrubs, trees and conifers are important and so is a variety of shapes — a border filled with rounded shrubs can be dull, so remember to consider weeping, columnar and ground cover types.

Within this framework other plants are grown. Make sure the pockets and bays are large enough to give a bold effect. Bulbs, roses and annuals are important, but evergreens have little or no contribution to make here. A few evergreen border perennials such as pinks and carnations can be used to provide winter colour and so can the evergreen ferns.

SINGLE-GROUP SHRUB BED OR BORDER

This special type of shrub border contains one sort of woody plant which is usually one genus. The spectacular one is the rhododendron border which is a blaze of colour in May. If the border is large enough you can have heights ranging from 1-10 ft (30 cm-3 m) and flowers from February to August. The heather border is another popular single-group example. Here the aim is to have something in flower all year round from plants with a wide range of leaf colours and stem heights. A variation is the heather/conifer bed or border. This double-group approach is a distinct improvement on the heather-alone type. The conifers provide a variety of heights, colours and shapes.

HERBACEOUS BORDER

A herbaceous border is a long and narrow strip of land with a backcloth of a wall, screen or hedge and with border perennials planted in tiers, the tallest at the back and clumps of low-growing plants at the front. The herbaceous border has two serious problems. It is labour intensive, requiring regular feeding, staking, dead-heading and replanting. It is also bare and unattractive in winter when all the plants have died down and the use of evergreen border perennials can do little to improve the overall appearance between late autumn and spring.

WOODLAND GARDEN

A woodland garden is a special form of mixed border designed for walking through rather than being admired from outside. Here trees rather than shrubs are dominant. The usual starting point is an overgrown wooded area. The dense shade trees are removed leaving the ones which cast dappled shade — additional suitable trees are planted if required. Below the trees shade-tolerant types are planted — shrubs, ferns, bulbs etc. Evergreen examples include Rhododendron, Camellia, Mahonia and Hypericum.

WALL & TRELLIS PLANTING

A wall and trellis plant is a species which will grow against a solid or open structure to door height or above and provide a decorative effect. Many plants can be used for this purpose, but not many are evergreens.

First of all there are the true climbers, which are defined on page 4 as plants capable of attaching themselves to or twining around an upright structure. If you want the minimum amount of trouble and the wall is in good condition you can grow a self-clinging climber as no supporting wires or frame will be needed. Unfortunately Parthenocissus (Virginia Creeper) and Hydrangea petiolaris both lose their leaves in winter so you will have to grow one of the many varieties of Hedera (ivy) or Hydrangea seemannii.

Other climbers use tendrils or a twining growth habit to attach themselves to a support. Once again the range is limited — examples include the evergreen varieties of Lonicera and Clematis. The third group of wall and trellis plants are shrubs with lax stems which are attached to wires, poles or trellis by means of ties — popular ones include Cotoneaster salicifolius, Solanum crispum and Ceanothus 'Autumnal Blue'. Support can be provided by straining wire fixed about 6 in. (15 cm) from the wall, a trellis made of wood treated with a preservative or a framework of plastic-coated wire netting. Climbers should be planted about 1¹/₂ ft (45 cm) from the house wall and kept well-watered during the first season.

The final group of wall and trellis plants are neither climbers nor varieties with lax stems. They are bushy plants which adopt an upright wall-hugging habit when grown against a wall. Pyracantha is the best known example. Wall planting is usually purely decorative but sometimes the problem is an unsightly object. The procedure then is to grow a climber over it or on wires stretched across it. The deciduous Russian Vine is often used for this purpose — among the evergreens one of the quick-growing varieties of Hedera is the best choice.

TOPIARY PLANTING

Topiary involves the clipping of trees or shrubs into geometrical shapes and dates back to the Roman Empire. It can be used to create birds or animals on top of a hedge or yew figures on the lawn, but it is mostly used to produce green balls or cones in containers to flank a doorway.

There are two types of topiary. The major one uses evergreen shrubs which are densely clothed with leaves and can withstand regular clipping. The big three here are Buxus sempervirens (box), Taxus baccata (yew) and Laurus nobilis (bay). Others include Ilex, Juniperus, Ligustrum and Lonicera nitida. Simple shapes like cones can be cut freehand, but it is better to attach a framework of canes or wire to create the basic shape on to which the stems are tied. For complex shapes it is necessary to use a more complete frame made of stout wire and wire netting. In both cases trim back stem tips as they grow beyond the framework.

Once established the topiary tree or bush will need to be trimmed regularly. For a simple shape using yew an annual cut may be sufficient — at the other end of the scale a complex box topiary may need trimming every month during the growing season to maintain a manicured finish.

The second type of topiary uses leafy climbers. In warm regions several plants including Creeping Fig can be used, but in frost-prone countries Hedera (ivy) is the basic plant material. A frame of wire and wire netting is made to the desired shape and fixed firmly to the ground. Hedera is planted at intervals at the base of the frame and the stems are trained into the netting as they grow. Trim as necessary.

CHAPTER 5
EVERGREEN GROWER'S DICTIONARY

A

ACID SOIL A soil which contains no free lime and has a pH of less than 6.5.

ADULT FOLIAGE Leaves on a mature branch which differ in shape and size from the juvenile foliage.

ALKALINE SOIL A soil which has a pH of more than 7.3. Other terms are chalky soil and limy soil.

ALPINE A rather vague term used to describe low-growing rockery perennials.

ALTERNATE Leaves or buds which arise first on one side of the stem and then on the other. Compare opposite.

ANTHER The part of the flower which produces pollen. It is the upper section of the stamen.

ARMED Bearing strong thorns.

AURICLE An ear-shaped projection.

AWL-SHAPED A narrow leaf which tapers to a stiff point.

AXIL The angle between the upper surface of the leaf stalk and the stem that carries it.

B

BARE-ROOTED A plant dug up at the nursery and sold with no soil around its roots.

BASAL SHOOT A shoot arising from the neck or crown of the plant.

BEARDED Possessing long or stiff hairs.

BERRY A pulpy fruit bearing several or many seeds.

BISEXUAL A flower bearing both male and female reproductive organs — compare dioecious and monoecious.

BLEEDING The loss of sap from plant tissues.

BLOOM A fine powdery or waxy coating.

BOLE An alternative name for the trunk of a tree.

BOSS The ring of stamens when it is prominent and decorative.

BRACT A modified leaf at the base of a flower.

BREAKING BUD A bud which has started to open.

BUD A flower bud is the unopened bloom. A growth bud or eye is a condensed shoot.

C

CALCAREOUS Chalky or limy soil.

CALCIFUGE A plant which will not thrive in alkaline soil.

CALLUS The scar tissue which forms over a pruning cut or at the base of a cutting.

CALYX The whorl of sepals which protect the unopened flower bud.

CAMBIUM A thin layer of living cells between the bark and the wood.

CANKER A diseased and discoloured area on the stem.

CATKIN A chain of tiny male or female flowers which lack coloured petals.

CHELATE An organic chemical which can supply nutrients to plants in a soil which would normally lock up the plant-feeding element or elements in question.

CHLOROSIS An abnormal yellowing or blanching of the leaves due to lack of chlorophyll.

COMPOST Two meanings — either decomposed vegetable or animal matter for incorporation in the soil or a potting/cutting mixture made from peat ('soilless compost') or sterilized soil ('loam compost') plus other materials such as sand, lime and fertilizer.

COMPOUND A type of leaf which is composed of several leaflets.

CRESTED Plant parts (usually a petal) bearing ridged or bristle-like outgrowths.

CRISTATE A plant part such as a leaf, petal or stem with a pronounced crest, which is usually convoluted or finely divided.

CROCK A piece of broken flower pot used at the bottom of a container to improve drainage.

CROSS The offspring arising from cross-pollination.

CULTIVAR Short for 'cultivated variety' — it is a variety which originated in cultivation and not in the wild. Strictly speaking, all modern varieties are cultivars, but the more familiar term 'variety' is used in this book.

CUTTING A piece of stem cut from a plant and used for propagation.

D

DEAD-HEADING The removal of faded flowers.

DECIDUOUS A plant which loses its leaves at the end of the growing season.

DIOECIOUS A plant which bears either male or female flowers. Compare monoecious.

DORMANT PERIOD The time when the plant has naturally stopped growing due to low temperature and short day-length.

DOUBLE A flower with more than a single whorl of petals.

DOWNY Covered with soft hairs.

E

ENTIRE An undivided and unserrated leaf.

EVERGREEN A plant which retains its leaves in a living state during the winter.

EYE Two unrelated meanings — a dormant growth bud or the centre of a single or semi-double bloom where the colour is distinctly different from the rest of the flower.

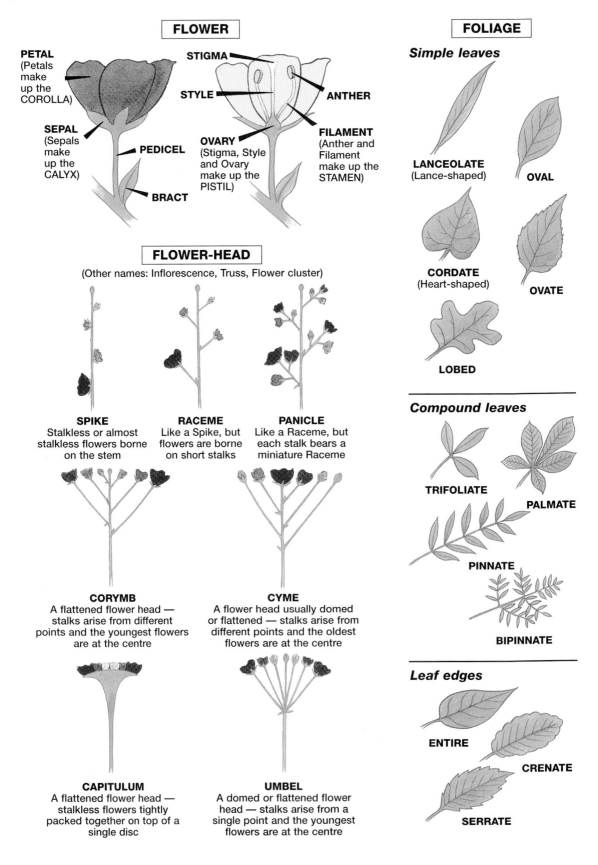

FLOWER

PETAL
(Petals make up the COROLLA)

SEPAL
(Sepals make up the CALYX)

PEDICEL

BRACT

STIGMA

STYLE

ANTHER

OVARY
(Stigma, Style and Ovary make up the PISTIL)

FILAMENT
(Anther and Filament make up the STAMEN)

FLOWER-HEAD

(Other names: Inflorescence, Truss, Flower cluster)

SPIKE
Stalkless or almost stalkless flowers borne on the stem

RACEME
Like a Spike, but flowers are borne on short stalks

PANICLE
Like a Raceme, but each stalk bears a miniature Raceme

CORYMB
A flattened flower head — stalks arise from different points and the youngest flowers are at the centre

CYME
A flower head usually domed or flattened — stalks arise from different points and the oldest flowers are at the centre

CAPITULUM
A flattened flower head — stalkless flowers tightly packed together on top of a single disc

UMBEL
A domed or flattened flower head — stalks arise from a single point and the youngest flowers are at the centre

FOLIAGE

Simple leaves

LANCEOLATE
(Lance-shaped)

OVAL

CORDATE
(Heart-shaped)

OVATE

LOBED

Compound leaves

TRIFOLIATE

PALMATE

PINNATE

BIPINNATE

Leaf edges

ENTIRE

CRENATE

SERRATE

F

FASTIGIATE A plant with erect branches set closely together.

FERTILIZATION The application of pollen to the stigma to induce the production of seed. An essential step in hybridisation.

FIBROUS A root system which contains many thin roots rather than a single tap root.

FIMBRIATE Frilly-edged.

FLORET The small individual bloom borne by a large, flower-like inflorescence.

FLOWER The reproductive organ of the plant.

FOLIAR FEED A fertilizer capable of being sprayed on and absorbed by the leaves.

FOOTSTALK The pedicel or flower stalk.

FRIABLE Term applied to crumbly soil.

FROND The leaf-like part of a fern.

FROST POCKET An area where cold air is trapped during winter and in which tender plants are in much greater danger.

FRUIT The seed together with the structure which bears or contains it.

FUNGICIDE A chemical used to control diseases caused by fungi.

FUNGUS A primitive form of plant life which is the most common cause of infectious disease — mildew and rust are examples.

G

GENUS A group of closely-related plants containing one or more species.

GLABROUS Smooth, hairless.

GLAUCOUS Covered with a bloom.

GRAFTING The process of joining a stem or bud of one plant on to the stem of another.

GROUND COVER An ornamental plant which requires little attention and is used to provide a low-growing carpet between other plants.

H

HALF HARDY A plant which will only grow outdoors in Britain when the temperature is above freezing point. The term is not precise — some half hardy plants can be left outdoors in winter in mild regions of the country.

HARD PRUNING A system of pruning where much of the old growth is removed.

HARDENING-OFF The process of gradually acclimatising a plant raised under warm conditions to the environment it will have to withstand outdoors.

HARDY A plant which will withstand overwintering without any protection.

HEAD The framework of stems borne at the top of the stem of a standard.

HEELING-IN The temporary planting of a new tree or shrub pending suitable weather conditions for permanent planting.

HERBACEOUS A plant which does not form permanent woody stems.

HIRSUTE Covered with coarse or stiff hairs.

HONEYDEW Sticky, sugar secretion deposited on the leaves and stems by such insects as aphid and whitefly.

HUMUS Term popularly (but not correctly) applied to partly decomposed organic matter in the soil. Actually humus is the jelly-like end-product which coats the soil particles.

HYBRID Plants with parents which are genetically distinct. The parent plants may be different cultivars, varieties or species.

I

INFLORESCENCE The part of the plant bearing the flowers; the flower head.

INORGANIC A chemical or fertilizer which is not obtained from a source which is or has been alive.

INSECTICIDE A chemical used to control insect pests.

INTERNODE The part of the stem between one node and another.

INVOLUCRE A whorl of bracts surrounding a flower or cluster of flowers.

J

JUVENILE FOLIAGE Young leaves which differ in shape and size from the adult foliage.

K

KEY A winged seed, technically referred to as a samara.

L

LANKY Spindly growth — a stem with a gaunt and sparse appearance.

LATERAL BRANCH A side branch which arises from a main stem.

LEACHING The drawing away of chemicals from the soil, caused by rain or watering.

LEADER The dominant central shoot.

LEAFLET One of the parts of a compound leaf.

LEAF MOULD Peat-like material composed of partially-rotted leaves.

LINEAR Very narrow with parallel sides.

LOAM Friable soil which is not obviously clayey nor sandy.

M

MONOECIOUS A plant which bears both male and female flowers. Compare dioecious.

MULCH A layer of bulky organic material placed around the stems.

MUTATION A sudden change in the genetic make-up of a plant, leading to a new feature. This new feature can be inherited.

N

NATIVE A species which grows wild in this country and was not introduced by man.

NECTAR Sweet substance secreted by some flowers to attract insects.

NEUTRAL Neither acid nor alkaline — pH 6.5-7.3.

NEW WOOD Stem growth which has been produced during the current season.

NODE The point on the stem at which a leaf or bud is attached.

NUT A one-seeded hard fruit which does not split when ripe.

O

OFFSET Young plant which arises naturally on the parent plant and is easily separated.

OLD WOOD Stem growth which was produced before the current season.

OPPOSITE Leaves or buds which are borne in pairs along the stem. Compare alternate.

ORGANIC A chemical or fertilizer which is obtained from a source which is or has been alive.

OVARY The part of the female organ of the flower which contains the ovules.

OVULE The part of the female organ of the flower which turns into a seed after fertilization.

P

PEAT Plant matter in an arrested state of decay obtained from bogs or heathland.

PEDUNCLE The stalk of an inflorescence.

PERGOLA An arched structure used to support climbing plants.

PETAL One of the divisions of the corolla — generally the showy part of the flower.

PETIOLE The leaf stalk.

pH A measure of acidity and alkalinity. Below pH 6.5 is acid, above pH 7.3 is alkaline.

PITH The spongy material at the centre of the stem.

POLLARD A tree which has had its branches repeatedly cut back to the trunk.

POLLEN The yellow dust produced by the anthers. It is the male element which fertilizes the ovule.

POLLINATION The application of pollen to the stigma of the flower.

PROPAGATION The multiplication of plants.

PROSTRATE Growing flat on the soil surface.

PRUNING The removal of parts of the plant in order to improve its performance and/or appearance.

PUBESCENT Covered with short, downy hairs.

R

RETICULATE Marked with a branched network of veins or fibres.

REVERSION Either a sport which goes back to the colour or growth habit of its parent or a grafted plant which is outgrown by suckers arising from the rootstock.

RHIZOME A horizontally-creeping underground stem which produces shoots and roots.

ROOTSTOCK The host plant on to which a cultivated variety is budded.

ROSETTE Term applied to a whorl of leaves arising at the base of a plant.

RUGOSE Rough and wrinkled.

RUNNER A shoot which grows along the soil surface, rooting at intervals.

S

SCABROUS Rough to the touch.

SCION The technical term for the bud which is grafted on to the rootstock.

SEMI-EVERGREEN A plant which keeps its leaves in a mild winter but loses some or all of its foliage in a hard one.

SESSILE Stalkless.

SIDE SHOOT Same as lateral branch.

SIMPLE A leaf that is not compound.

SINGLE A flower with a single ring of petals.

SNAG A section of stem left above a bud when pruning.

SPECIES Plants which are genetically similar and which reproduce exactly when self-fertilized.

SPIT The depth of the spade blade — usually about 9 in. (22.5 cm).

SPORT A plant which shows a marked and inheritable change from its parent; a mutation.

SPUR Two meanings — a tube-like projection from a flower or a short leaf-bearing shoot which does not increase in size.

STAMEN The male organ of a flower, consisting of the anther and filament.

STANDARD A tree or trained shrub with a single straight stem which is clear of branches for 5-6 ft (1.5-1.8 m) from the ground. This stem length is 4-5 ft (1.2-1.5 m) on a half standard and 3-4 ft (90 cm-1.2 m) on a short standard.

STELLATE Star-shaped.

STIGMA The part of the female organ of the flower which catches the pollen.

STIPULE The small outgrowth at the base of the leaf stalk.

STOLON A shoot at or below the soil surface which produces a new plant at its tip.

STRAIN A selection of a variety, cultivar or species which is raised from seed.

STRIKE The successful outcome of taking cuttings — cuttings 'strike' whereas grafts 'take'.

SUB-SHRUB A perennial with stems which are woody at the base and soft and herbaceous above. This upper growth dies down in winter. This term is sometimes loosely used to describe a low-growing shrub such as Vinca.

SUBSOIL Soil below the fertile top layer.

SUCCULENT A plant with fleshy leaves and/or stems adapted to growing under dry conditions.

SUCKER A shoot growing from the rootstock.

SYNONYM An alternative plant name.

SYSTEMIC A pesticide which goes inside the plant and travels in the sap stream.

T

TAKE The successful outcome of budding — grafts 'take' whereas cuttings 'strike'.

TENDRIL A modified stem or leaf which can wind around a support.

TERMINAL Term applied to organs borne at the tip of a stem.

THICKET Dense growth of upright stems.

TILTH The crumbly structure of soil at the surface.

TOMENTOSE Densely covered with fine hairs.

TOPIARY The cutting and training of shrubs or trees into decorative shapes.

TRANSPLANTING Movement of a plant from one site to another.

TRUSS A cluster of fruit or flowers.

U

UNDERPLANTING Growing low-growing plants below taller shrubs or trees.

V

VARIEGATED Leaves which are spotted, blotched or edged with a different colour to the basic one.

VARIETY Strictly speaking, a naturally occurring variation of a species (see cultivar).

VIRUS An organism which is too small to be seen through a microscope and which is capable of causing malformation or discoloration of a plant.

W

WEED A plant growing in the wrong place.

WHORL Several leaves, branches or petals which are arranged in a ring.

CHAPTER 6

PLANT INDEX

Acknowledgements

The author wishes to acknowledge the painstaking work of Gill Jackson, Paul Norris and Angelina Gibbs. Grateful acknowledgement is also made for the help received from Joan Hessayon, Colin Bailey and Barry Highland (Spot On Repro Ltd), and for the photographs and artworks received from Harry Smith Horticultural Photographic Collection, Pat Brindley, Norman Barber, the late John Woodbridge, Deborah Mansfield, John Dye, David Guthrie/Bluebridge Farm Studio, David Baylis, Friedrich Strauss/The Garden Picture Library, John Glover/The Garden Picture Library, J S Sira/The Garden Picture Library, Joanne Pavia/The Garden Picture Library, Clive Nichols/The Garden Picture Library and Howard Rice/The Garden Picture Library.